D0754536

Residential Care of Children

RESIDENTIAL CARE OF CHILDREN

Comparative Perspectives

Edited by

Mark E. Courtney
Dorota Iwaniec

UNIVERSITY PRESS
2009

OXFORD
UNIVERSITY PRESS

Oxford University Press, Inc., publishes works that further
Oxford University's objective of excellence
in research, scholarship, and education.

Oxford   New York
Auckland   Cape Town   Dar es Salaam   Hong Kong   Karachi
Kuala Lumpur   Madrid   Melbourne   Mexico City   Nairobi
New Delhi   Shanghai   Taipei   Toronto

With offices in
Argentina   Austria   Brazil   Chile   Czech Republic   France   Greece
Guatemala   Hungary   Italy   Japan   Poland   Portugal   Singapore
South Korea   Switzerland   Thailand   Turkey   Ukraine   Vietnam

Copyright © 2009 by Oxford University Press, Inc.

Published by Oxford University Press, Inc.
198 Madison Avenue, New York, New York 10016
www.oup.com

Oxford is a registered trademark of Oxford University Press

All rights reserved. No part of this publication may be reproduced,
stored in a retrieval system, or transmitted, in any form or by any means,
electronic, mechanical, photocopying, recording, or otherwise,
without the prior permission of Oxford University Press.

Library of Congress Cataloging-in-Publication Data

Residential care of children : comparative perspectives / edited by Mark E. Courtney and Dorota Iwaniec.
p. cm.
Includes bibliographical references and index.
ISBN 978-0-19-530918-8
1. Children--Institutional care--Case studies. 2. Children--Institutional care--Cross-cultural studies.
I. Courtney, Mark E. II. Iwaniec, Dorota.
HV862.R469 2009
362.73'2--dc22

2008027000

9 8 7 6 5 4 3 2 1

Printed in the United States of America
on acid-free paper

ACKNOWLEDGMENTS

The editors would like to express their thanks to the Chapin Hall Center for Children at the University of Chicago for all of its help in making this volume possible. Chapin Hall provided the financial support to bring the authors together for the meetings that laid the groundwork for the volume and hosted one of the meetings.

Thanks also to Anne Clary of Chapin Hall for her editing assistance.

We would also like to thank the staff of the Institute of Child Care Research at Queens University, Belfast, Northern Ireland, for hosting the authors conference at which our ideas were first hashed out.

Lastly, we thank the staff of Oxford University Press, including Mallory Jensen, Maura Roessner, and Lynda Crawford, for their patience and support along the way.

Mark E. Courtney and Dorota Iwaniec

CONTENTS

CONTRIBUTORS

FRANK AINSWORTH
James Cook University
Townsville, Australia

DALIA BEN RABI
Brookdale Institute
Jerusalem, Israel

ROGER BULLOCK
Dartington Social Research Unit
Totnes, United Kingdom

MARK E. COURTNEY
University of Washington
Seattle, Washington, United States

TALAL DOLEV
Brookdale Institute
Jerusalem, Israel

OVIDIU GAVRILOVICI
University Alexandru Ioan Cuza
Iasi, Romania

ROBBIE GILLIGAN
Trinity College Dublin
Dublin, Ireland

PATRICIA HANSEN
Australian Catholic University
Sydney, Australia

DARCY HUGHES-HEURING
Northwestern University
Evanston, Illinois

DOROTA IWANIEC
Queen's University
Belfast, Northern Ireland

BONG JOO LEE
Seoul National University
Seoul, Republic of Korea

TAPOLOGO MAUNDENI
University of Botswana
Gaborone, Botswana

DOMINIC MCSHERRY
Queens University
Belfast, Northern Ireland

IRENE RIZZINI
Pontificia Universidade Catolica do Rio de Janeiro
Rio de Janeiro, Brazil

IRMA RIZZINI
Federal University of Rio de Janeiro
Rio de Janeiro, Brazil

MARIE SALLNÄS
Stockholm University
Stockholm, Sweden

BRIAN STOUT
De Montfort University
Leicester, United Kingdom

TAMAR ZEMACH-MAROM
Brookdale Institute
Jerusalem, Israel

INTRODUCTION

MARK E. COURTNEY AND DOROTA IWANIEC

In May 2003, more than 600 individuals representing government, civil society, and the research community in 80 countries attended the second international conference entitled Children and Residential Care in Stockholm, Sweden. The result of the conference was the "Stockholm Declaration on Children and Residential Care," to which the participants had committed themselves. The declaration suggests principles to follow and actions to take for government, civil society, researchers, and the philanthropic community to reduce or even eliminate the use of residential care for children. It begins with the following statement:

> There is indisputable evidence that institutional care has negative consequences for both individual children and for society at large. These negative consequences could be prevented through the adaptation of national strategies to support families and children, by exploring the benefits of various types of community based care, by reducing the use of institutions, by setting standards for public care and monitoring of the remaining institutions.

A reader of the Stockholm Declaration might easily conclude that there is universal agreement that residential care should be eliminated and that it is only a matter of time until responsible individuals and institutions make that happen. In fact, however, the situation is much more complex. Countries' reliance on residential care varies widely. Postindustrial democracies that for decades have had official policies discouraging the use of institutions for children nevertheless continue to use them. Why is this so? What lessons do their experiences have for other countries considering when and for whom to use residential care? Some countries consciously make extensive use of residential care for children, in some cases exceeding the use of family-based out-of-home care. What are their reasons for doing so and are those reasons likely to lead other countries to increase their use of residential care in the future? How does the use of residential care differ from place to place around the world and can this variation tell us anything about how child welfare practice might be improved?

Current international interest makes timely a critical examination of the history and current use of residential care around the world. Only an international comparative perspective on the development and current status of residential care can answer the kinds of questions raised above. *Residential Care of Children: Comparative Perspectives* is intended to fill important gaps in knowledge about residential care of children and in the process inform debates within and between nations about the appropriate use of such institutions. The volume grew out of a series of meetings convened by the Residential Childcare Working Group of the International Network of Children's Policy Research Centers. This network is staffed and supported by the Chapin Hall Center for Children at the University of Chicago and includes centers in Brazil, England, the Republic of Ireland, India, Israel, Korea, Northern Ireland, Norway, South Africa, and the United States. At the time this volume was conceived, the Residential Childcare Working Group consisted of researchers from Brazil, Ireland, Israel, Northern Ireland, Norway, and the United States.

The Residential Childcare Working Group decided to invite interested scholars from member centers to prepare papers for an edited volume on residential care around the world. In addition, to obtain a broader representation of countries, papers were solicited from colleagues in South Korea and Romania. In September 2003 a meeting was held at Queens University, Belfast, to discuss early drafts of papers from Brazil, Ireland, Israel, South Korea, Romania, the UK, and the United States. Based on discussions at that meeting, additional papers were invited from colleagues in Australia, Botswana, Sweden, and South Africa. The country case studies were discussed at meetings of the working group to identify common themes that emerge from the case studies. The papers that emerged from these meetings benefit from the shared wisdom of scholars from eleven countries in Africa, Asia, the Middle East, Eastern and Western Europe, North and South America, and Australia.

Residential Care of Children: Comparative Perspectives is intended to provide the reader with a better understanding of residential care for children around the world. Case study chapters provide a rich description of the development, current status, and future of residential care in eleven countries. The volume focuses on settings where *(1)* children sleep at night (i.e., not day treatment) and *(2)* children are not routinely locked up or denied their freedom (i.e., "open" facilities). Authors were free to note examples of residential care that may be important in their countries that are outside this definition (e.g., juvenile corrections facilities), but for comparative purposes we focus on residential care that meets this loose definition.

This is a broad definition and the case studies show that residential care takes a wide range of forms around the world. Each chapter also describes how residential care has evolved over time, including its history, trends over time, and any landmark events in the evolution of residential care. Authors examine factors (e.g., historical, political, economic, ideological, cultural) that have contributed to the observed pattern of development of residential care and provide a description of the current state of residential care (i.e., number of children in care, ages, average length of stay, reasons that children/youth are placed in residential care, etc.). Last, each case study describes expected future directions for residential care and potential concerns. The case studies are clustered geographically, starting in Europe and moving around the globe to the Middle East, Africa, Asia, Australia, and finally the Americas. Although they were expected to address the topics described above, authors were given wide latitude in deciding how to focus their attention. This decision reflected the varied interests and expertise of the authors and the fact that the nature and availability of historical and empirical literature on residential care varies considerably from country to country. A concluding chapter identifies common and disparate themes in the historical development of residential care to provide an explanation of the underlying factors that drive its use; it also examines similarities and differences across countries in the current status of residential care so as to speculate about the future of residential care around the globe.

Residential Care of Children: Comparative Perspectives was not put together with the intention of providing a summary judgment regarding the proper role(s) of residential care in the provision of services for children. Widely varying opinions regarding the merits of residential care are found within this volume. Indeed, early in the discussions of the Residential Childcare Working Group it became clear to us that trying to come to a consensus regarding the merits of residential care would be premature given the wide heterogeneity in the development and current use of residential care around the world and the poor availability of sound data on the populations served and outcomes achieved. Our hope is that our volume helps illuminate the wide range of individual, family, and social problems that residential care has been used to address around the world, the factors that influence its use, and under what circumstances and in what forms residential care is likely to persevere, if not thrive, in the future.

Residential Care of Children

Residential Care in Ireland

ROBBIE GILLIGAN

Residential care is in decline in Ireland[1] in numbers served and in morale, although expenditure on residential care is considerable and rising because of new investment in expensive specialist provision. Residential care appears to be used, especially, to serve challenging or marginal populations within or on the edge of the child welfare system. A key function appears to be to absorb any slack left by foster care or family placement provision, which is the preferred mode of care in the Irish system. Overall, it might be argued that the Irish residential child care system is at risk of becoming more "child preoccupied" and less "child-centered."

Evolution of the Residential Child Care System in Ireland

The evolution of residential child care in Ireland has three phases: institutionalization and seclusion (1850s to 1970s); professionalization and deinstitutionalization (1970s to 1990s); and secularization, specialization, and accountability (1990s onward). It can be argued that each of these phases reflected developments in wider Irish society and in the world more generally.

Institutionalization and Seclusion (1850s to 1970s)

Developments in residential child care in Ireland seem closely intertwined with the growth in Catholic female (and also new male) religious congregations (residential communities) in the nineteenth century—there was an eightfold increase in the number of nuns in the period 1841–1901 (Clear, 1987, p. 37). Most of these congregations began to pursue their mission through providing institution-based care to different groups seen as needy, including children with particular needs. An emerging legal framework for the formation and operation of reformatories and industrial schools (and later children's homes) allowed these Catholic religious congregations to gain approval (and from 1868 financial support) for their children's institutions. The ensuing developments might be said to represent the "foundation layer" of the subsequent Irish system of residential child care. Gradually these Catholic-managed institutions came to dominate—possibly accounting for 90 percent of provision for children in care for more than a century, with the remainder sponsored mainly by organizations within the Protestant tradition (see Clear, 1987; Raftery and O'Sullivan, 1999). In general, these institutions tended to be large, austere, isolated, unimaginative, and subjected to little effective scrutiny or control by the state. Factors accounting for the origin of these institutions might include the following:

- The availability, in that early period, of large numbers of Catholic women willing to dedicate their lives to this socially valued work by religious congregations (Clear 1987)
- The tradition in Catholic countries, suggested by Hazel and colleagues (1983), of removing the vulnerable from danger into the safekeeping of the institution or monastery[2,3]
- The religious and political tensions between the Catholic and Protestant traditions in Ireland at that time that led to considerable competition—and duplication—in the provision of welfare activity (Luddy, 2005)
- The passivity of the state (the British state that ran Ireland until 1921, and the Irish state that emerged after that date following independence) in matters to do with welfare provision. The state played a limited role in regulating and funding such provision, but almost none at any level in direct delivery of services
- The political power of the Catholic church, meaning that government had little appetite to challenge how religious institutions ran their affairs[4]
- The low status of institutions serving children (presumably because they generally served people of low status); it has been suggested, in the Catholic tradition at least, that these did not necessarily attract the most able members of sponsoring congregations to manage or staff them (Dunne, 2004, p. 42).[5]

Overall, residential child care in this period might be said to mirror a broader and related tendency at that time in Ireland to rely on institutions to hide society's "outsiders" or to "bury" social problems.

Professionalization and Deinstitutionalization (1970s to 1990s)

Gradually a process of deinstitutionalization evident in other spheres (for example, in the fields of disability and mental health) also began to assert itself in the field of residential child care from the 1970s onward. This change, in the case of child care, had multiple roots in addition to the social change of the 1960s that impacted Ireland as elsewhere. The Second Vatican Council of the Roman Catholic Church (1962–1965) was of genuinely historic importance and had quite an impact in Ireland (Whyte, 1980). It urged, among other things, a much more outward-looking attitude and practice among religious congregations, in which they were to engage wholeheartedly with the wider community.

An additional factor was an emerging trend toward the professionalization of child care (child welfare) practice. Some elements in religious bodies saw this professionalization as a necessary step for the benefit of the children but also because the shrinking availability of religious personnel (due to falling recruitment and redeployment) led to greater reliance on lay staff, who increasingly sought and were expected to have training.

A government committee reported in 1970 on residential child care (Kennedy, 1970) and made a series of recommendations that broadly lent momentum to the deinstitutionalization of provision and the professionalization of practice. In this context, the term *deinstitutionalization* generally meant a move to smaller, new units purposely built for child care and often dispersed in local neighborhoods; the recruitment of at least some professional staff; and the greater integration of the lives of residents into the local community (e.g., attendance of the residents at local schools rather than in the institution's own school, participation in clubs, and similar activities).

Additionally, the Health Act 1970, which led to major reforms in the scope, structure, and delivery of health services, led also to the gradual emergence of a state-provided social work service that largely focused on children's issues (Skehill, 1999). One priority was implementing preexisting but neglected official policy that favored foster family care as the placement of choice for children in care. These efforts certainly had an impact; for example, recent official figures suggest that the absolute numbers of children in foster care doubled to around 4,000 from 1989 to 2003.

Broadly, in this period, residential child care was characterized by an optimism about the capacity of reform, training, and investment to transform radically the nature of care in the direction of a more child-centered provision.

Secularization, Specialization, and Accountability (1990s Onward)

Closely linked to the trend of professionalization has been a move toward bureaucratization in which there are modest but ever increasing attempts to define, measure, standardize, and generally "regulate" child care practices. This is evident in provisions in the Child Care Act 1991 and related regulations, in the later Children

Act 2001, in the publication of national standards for residential care (and foster care), in some efforts to gather standardized national data about child care services, and in attempts to promote more standardized practices in relation to child protection and interagency cooperation (Department of Health and Children, 1999). In the residential child care field, the clearest sign of a new official resolve to hold the field to some accountability (and to deflect criticism of past—or current—neglect) is in the emergence, in 1999, of the Social Services Inspectorate (SSI). While its title implies a broad authority across various client groups, the immediate trigger for its establishment and the focal priority for its early work was the residential child care field.

Perhaps the most remarkable trend in residential child care in the past decade or so has been the almost complete and largely unnoticed withdrawal of religious bodies as direct providers of residential child care, virtually completed in late 2003 with the final withdrawal from this work of the (Catholic) Mercy congregation (Social Services Inspectorate, 2005a), which in recent times had been the largest single provider of residential child care places. A series of factors accounts for this historic withdrawal from the work:

- The aging profile and rapidly shrinking membership of the congregations involved
- The precipitate drop in morale among those involved in this work as a result of the avalanche of allegations of past wrongdoing (physical and/or sexual abuse) or mismanagement directed against members of many congregations (Raftery and O'Sullivan, 1999)
- The logistical and other challenges posed by bureaucratic demands for compliance with higher professional standards
- The behavior of what seemed like ever more troubled children, who demanded a paradigm of care far different from the one traditionally embraced by religious service providers of rearing or minding (largely compliant) children who needed care

Interestingly, in the late twentieth century, as Irish society opened up to self-questioning and acknowledged more fully its own social problems, the proportionate importance of residential care declined. One of the social problems increasingly acknowledged was the degree of physical and sexual abuse suffered by children who had been placed in residential centers, mostly those run by at least some Roman Catholic congregations. This phenomenon has triggered a remarkable outpouring of public testimony from former victims and a very strong public response. A range of victim accounts has appeared in various media. A significant review of available evidence (and one that is critical of implicated Church providers and of state reactions) has been undertaken by Mary Raftery and Eoin O'Sullivan. In response, the government established a Commission of Inquiry into Child Abuse, whose work is ongoing at the time of writing (April 2008). It has worked on two levels: receiving testimony from victims, and investigating the circumstances in which the alleged abuses occurred and what might have contributed to or inhibited such occurrences.

While much current public debate about residential child care has focused on past failures, it is important to acknowledge that there is important progress in seeking to secure a better quality service to children being cared for today:

- The Social Services Inspectorate (SSI) will undoubtedly come to be seen as having played a critical role in anchoring and promoting high standards of practice at a critical period of change and uncertainty in the residential child care field. While the title of "Inspectorate" might carry connotations of policing and control, the Inspectorate has operated more on the basis of constructive cooperation with the management and staff of centers. It also is careful to model good practice in how it conducts inspection visits. It is careful to draw on the views of all stakeholders, especially children. It also publishes all its reports—not an intrinsic, nor common, feature of Irish administrative or political practice. This level of public transparency (including the availability of reports or appropriate summaries on the Inspectorate's Web site) seems to be a powerful incentive for providers to comply with the Inspectorate's broad agenda and specific messages in individual locations. The Inspectorate also plays a further developmental role in the system through a series of guidance notes.
- The United Nations Convention on the Rights of the Child (UNCRoC) has had an impact on the National Standards for Residential Care (against which SSI inspects), in particular concerning children in the area of consultation, complaints, and information. Special separate versions for children and young people in residential (and foster) care have been produced and circulated. In addition, the National Children's Strategy highlights the needs of children in state care.[6]

There has been progress but also recurring failures—for example, in the absence of systematic evidence about outcomes for children in residential care whether based on consumer or other studies. Also, data are not systematically gathered about the extent of abuse reported among children currently living in residential care.

Overall, this most recent period seems to be characterized by a growing disillusionment because of revelations about earlier failings in the care system and about more current limitations that have been exposed. The period has also witnessed efforts to regulate/standardize provision of care, and despite the influence of UNCRoC it is possible to discern a drift from a system that strives to be child-centered toward one that very often finds itself "child preoccupied" in relation to hard-to-serve children and young people. Rather than serving (or aspiring to serve) the needs of children in a proactive, holistic child-centered way, the residential care system finds itself increasingly trapped in responding *reactively* and possibly suboptimally to the needs of young people who present challenging behavior that many residential centers have proven unable to accommodate (this, of course, reflects at least as much on the nature of the center as on the children's behavior).

Chronology of Recent Key Legal /Policy Developments in Residential Child
Care Field

1970	Kennedy Report—major review of residential care system and related provision that provided important impetus for the first wave of reform
1971	First professional training course established for residential child care workers
1984	Responsibility for industrial schools transferred to Department of Health from Department of Education
1991	Child Care Act 1991 (first comprehensive child welfare legislation since foundation of the Irish state in 1921; implemented in stages until 1996)
1995	Child Care (Placement of Children in Residential Care) Regulations, 1995, Statutory Instrument No. 259 of 1995
1996	Report of Madonna House Inquiry published (with certain chapters censored but published in 1999 by States of Fear TV program) Enactment of Child Care (Standards in Children's Residential Centres) Regulations, 1996, Statutory Instrument No. 397 of 1996
1997	Freedom of Information Act 1997 passed (entitles any person to access to any records held about him or her)
1999	Irish Social Service Inspectorate established Commission to Inquire into Child Abuse appointed to investigate historical child abuse in children's institutions *Child First* published—national child protection guidelines (see especially Section 10.5—10.10.5)
2000	Expert group recommends that child care workers be accorded professional status (with implication that untrained staff in residential care be eventually phased out)[7] *National Children's Strategy* published
2001	Special Residential Services Board appointed Children Act 2001 is passed, providing for wholesale reform of the juvenile justice system *National Standards for Children's Residential Centres* published by Department of Health and Children. These standards are used for inspections of residential centers by the Social Services Inspectorate
2002	Residential institutions reviewed under auspices of Department of Education and Science http://www.education.ie/servlet/blobservlet/sped_education_review.doc Residential Institutions Redress Act, 2002 passed
2003	Special Residential Services Board placed on statutory basis with responsibility for advising minister on policy relating to children placed in Special Care Units (November) Last institution run by Mercy congregation closes; Mercy had been the largest religious provider of residential child care in the country and this closing virtually ended the role of Catholic religious in the direct provision of residential child care Administrative and legal responsibility for the four children detention schools (located in Finglas and Lusk) transferred from the Department of Education and Science to the Irish Youth Justice Service, an executive office of the Department of Justice, Equality and Law Reform (March 1)[8] Children Acts Advisory Board replaces Special Residential Services Board and is to play a stronger advisory and promotional role, especially in coordinating provision for children in detention schools and special care units Health Information and Quality Authority established; its remit includes the work of the Social Services Inspectorate (which retains its own identity)

How Residential Child Care Is Defined in Ireland Today

Residential child care in Ireland currently embraces a number of models for different groups of children and young people and operates under the auspices of a number of different sectors and legal arrangements. In this paper, the focus is primarily on the child welfare system.

At the end of 2004 (latest year for which data are available for the numbers of children in care at a point in time), there were 5,060 children in the care of the child welfare system in Ireland. Residential care provided for a small minority of these children. Nine percent (442) were in residential care, with 84 percent placed with families (with nonrelatives and with relatives) and 7 percent in other arrangements (Health Information and Quality Authority Social Services Inspectorate, 2007, p. 4). Approximately 105 additional young people are placed in residential settings under the juvenile justice system at any one time (derived from Special Residential Services Board, 2005, p. 18).

In terms of admission to care, figures for 2002 indicate that of 2,054 admissions to care (child welfare system), 209 (10.2%) were to residential care settings; of these, 59 children were younger than 12 years old (or 4.1% of children under 12 admitted to care).[9]

In the past 20 years, the following patterns have been evident in provision for children in the Irish care system:

- There has been a steady growth in absolute and relative terms in the numbers of children in care (from 3,724 in 1980–1981 to 4,508 in 2001) (Department of Health, 1983; Department of Health and Children, 2003).
- Foster care has become the dominant mode of care (more than doubling its absolute number of placements at any one time since 1989).
- There has been a corresponding dramatic decline in the number of children cared for in residential (nonfamily) placements.
- Kinship care (placement with relatives) has become an important mode of care and has recently eclipsed residential care in its share of care places provided.

The current state of residential care provision for children and young people presents a mixed picture. Most children are cared for in the child welfare system and, to some extent, in the juvenile justice system. There is also a residue of relevant provision that does not fall neatly into either of these two sectors. This chapter does not cover boarding schools or institutions serving children with disabilities.[10]

This range of legal categories of current residential facilities embraces the following:

- Children's residential centers serving children in the child welfare system and made up of four categories

  Mainstream units
  High support provision
  Special arrangements serving a single child
  Special care units
- Young offenders
  Children's detention centers
- Other provision for the following:
  Children and adolescents requiring in-patient psychiatric care
  Separated asylum-seeking children
  Homeless children and young people

Children in Care in Children's Residential Centers

A children's residential center is any home or other institution providing residential care for children in the care of health boards, or other children who are not receiving adequate care and protection (Child Care Act 1991, S. 59). According to the Social Services Inspectorate (2005b) there were 148 such centers in October 2004. Individual children's residential centers in the child welfare system typically cater to an average of four to five children and are generally located in ordinary domestic houses in local neighborhoods. (Note that this average size of residential unit is somewhat distorted by the number of single child placements—see below). As of October 2005, there were 146 centers, 87 operated by public bodies and 59 by nonstatutory groups (including 15 centers privately run for profit) (Chief Inspector, Social Services Inspectorate, personal communication, March 16, 2006).

In a sample of such units inspected by the SSI in 2004 (equivalent figures for 2003 in parentheses), 36 percent (22%) of care staff had recognized qualifications, 46 percent (44%) had another related qualification (degrees in social science, psychology, and education; diplomas and certificates in counseling, addiction studies, child protection and welfare, youth and community studies, supervisory management; and nursing qualifications in general, mental handicap, and psychiatric nursing), and 18 percent (34%) held no qualification (SSI, 2005a, pp. 48–49; 2005b, p. 41). A separate national survey whose methodology or response rate was not clearly set out reports that "14% of all social care staff in the child care area [including apparently 71 in nonresidential settings] had no professional qualification" compared with 44 percent who did and a further 33 percent who had a related qualification (Joint Committee on Social Care Professionals, undated [2003?]).

Provision for staff development and support in individual units can be found, but coverage seems to be patchy. In only nine of 31 centers for which information was available in 2003 did staff have access to regular formal supervision. In just over half of the centers (17), staff teams had regular (or recent) access to a staff facilitator/consultant (SSI, 2005a, p. 50). Half the staff in the sample reviewed here had a permanent contract; the balance were on temporary contracts, including 10 percent who were agency staff—that is, employed on a short-term contract by an agency (SSI, 2005a, p. 48).

Regular Formal Supervision (individual level)	7
Regular Formal Supervision (individual and group level)	2
Irregular (or not covering all staff) Formal supervision	14
No formal supervision	8
Missing case	1

Source: Derived from SSI, 2005, 50

Figure 1.1. Availability of Professional Supervision for Staff in Centers (n = 32)

"Specialist" Children's Residential Centers

In the latter half of the 1990s, health boards (at that time the responsible child welfare authority, now superseded by the Health Service Executive) had experienced sustained pressure from a series of child welfare crisis cases brought before the High Court under the newly enforced Child Care Act 1991 (see Whyte, 2002). In these cases, health boards had failed to provide care for children whose challenging circumstances clearly and legally required such care. The health boards' handling of these cases was reviewed harshly by the courts and in the media; and in response the health board system began to develop a set of resources, drawing in part on proposals of a consultant, Mike Laxton (1998), brought in from Scotland. He recommended provisions to serve high need children and young people based on High Support Units and Special Care Units. According to the Minister of State for Health and Children, the number of high support and special care places had increased from 17 in 1996 to over 120 in 2003.[11]

HIGH SUPPORT UNITS   High support is an evolving methodology in the Irish child welfare system that may be used in either residential or community contexts (Social Information Systems, 2003). While there are different models and approaches, the following features tend to typify high support:

- Short- to medium-term intensive care
- Nonsecure environment aimed at stabilizing an extreme situation
- A high staff-to-child ratio, usually 3:1
- Through-care and after care
- Access to education
- Access to therapy (Social Information System, 2003, p. 67)

In a recent study of high support in dedicated (high support) residential settings, it was found that 74 children and young people had been admitted to such care in a 12-month period, although the authors caution that special factors (including planned changes in provision) limit the generalizability of the findings across other time periods (Social Information Systems, 2003). In October 2004, 13 high support units were operational, with a capacity for 83 children but an actual occupancy of 47 (Social Services Inspectorate, 2005b, p. 25).

SPECIAL ARRANGEMENTS   Special arrangements—ad hoc wraparound residential arrangements mostly for one child or sometimes a specific small group of challenging cases—emerged in the late 1990s as health boards struggled to meet the needs of children who could not be served within existing facilities. In October 2004, the number of such special arrangements was 11, 14 in 2003, and 26 in 2002 (SSI, 2005a, p. 26; 2005b, p. 25).

SPECIAL CARE   A Special Care Order (for not less than three months and not more than six) may be made under the Children Act 2001 when

(a) the behaviour of the child is such that it poses a real and substantial risk to his or her health, safety, development or welfare, and

(b) the child requires special care or protection which he or she is unlikely to receive unless the court makes such an order.

(2) A special care order shall commit the child to the care of the health board concerned for so long as the order remains in force and shall authorise it to provide appropriate care, education and treatment for the child and, for that purpose, to place and detain the child in a special care unit . . .

(3) Where a child is detained in a special care unit pursuant to a special care order, the health board may take such steps as are reasonably necessary to prevent the child from—

(a) causing injury to himself or herself or to other persons in the unit, or (b) absconding from the unit.

(Children Act, 2001)

There are two Special Care Units in Ireland offering 25 places (Special Residential Services Board, 2005). These units "offer a short-term programme of detention, care and intervention for children and young people whose behaviour puts them at serious risk of harm or injury to themselves. . . . They should only be admitted if they are a serious risk to themselves and are not willing or able to benefit from assistance in an open setting" (SSI, 2003, p. 54). Youngsters on being found guilty of an offense may not be detained in a special care unit.

Units for Young Offenders in the Juvenile Justice System

Children Detention Schools (for under 16s)/Centres (for ages 16–18)
Children Act 2001 states in part:

158.—It shall be the principal object of children detention schools to provide appropriate educational and training programmes and facilities for children referred to them by a court and, by—

(a) having regard to their health, safety, welfare and interests, including their physical, psychological and emotional wellbeing,

(b) providing proper care, guidance and supervision for them,

(c) preserving and developing satisfactory relationships between them and their families,

(d) exercising proper moral and disciplinary influences on them, and

(e) recognising the personal, cultural and linguistic identity of each of them, to promote their reintegration into society and prepare them to take their place in the community as persons who observe the law and are capable of making a positive and productive contribution to society (Section 158, Children Act 2001).

There are five units offering approximately 114 places (including 27 secure places) aimed mainly at young offenders; but one or two of these units also accept "child welfare" referrals. In 2004, 146 males (average age 15 years of age) and 24 females were admitted to these units (by court order or Health Service Executive referral) (Special Residential Services Board, 2005, p. 18). The proportion of qualified staff in these units ranges from 17 percent to 62 percent. According to heads of units consulted in a recent review, a significant proportion of children (33% to 50%) were "misplaced" in these units (Department of Education and Science, 2002).

Other Categories

CHILDREN AND ADOLESCENTS REQUIRING IN-PATIENT PSYCHIATRIC CARE Three units serve the under-16 age group in four health board areas. There are no facilities for this age group in the remaining six health board areas and none for the 16–18 age group in any area (Working Group on Child and Adolescent Psychiatric Services 2003). Young people over 16 must rely on access to adult services although this anomaly is being addressed following passage of the Mental Health Act 2001, which defines a child as being under 18 years of age. In 2001, the three centers serving under-16s dealt with 47 new admissions and 14 readmissions.

SEPARATED ASYLUM-SEEKING CHILDREN Children who arrive in the Ireland on their own and seek asylum under international law are known as *separated asylum-seeking children*. There is usually a long delay while their claim is investigated and, during this period, the issue of interim care and accommodations arises. In the case of such children (under 17 years) in 2004, according to the Social Services Inspectorate, "the vast majority were placed in private unregistered hostels. A minority were placed in fostering and five were placed in a registered children's residential centre" (Social Services Inspectorate, 2005b, p. 28).

HOMELESS CHILDREN AND YOUNG PEOPLE A limited amount of places is provided in hostels for homeless young people (under 18), most of whom are not formally in the care of the child welfare system.

Past and Future

Looking back over the past 30 years or more, there are now fewer residential places in the care system and they make up a shrinking proportion of all placements.

On the other hand, it is clear that residential care will continue to have a place in two key roles. First, it will be used for challenging children who must be in special facilities. Second, it will be used as a fallback when foster care or relative (kinship) care is unavailable. It is likely that pressure on both these fronts may lead to some resurgence in the relative proportion and absolute number of residential care places in the Irish care system.

Looking to the future, the residential child care system faces a number of challenges:

- Recruiting and retaining a stable and well-qualified workforce, particularly to serve young people with "high end" needs. There problems in the recruitment and retention of staff especially in units providing for harder to serve children[12] and more generally despite improved pay and long-term commitment to phasing out untrained staff. There is also additional evidence that the proportion of qualified staff in the heavier end and more costly provision is comparatively low (Department of Education and Science, 2002). These problems may be due to various factors including the challenging nature of work with troubled young people, the unsocial demands of 24-hour duty, and the increasing competition from community-based employment options with daytime shifts.
- Achieving a greater gender balance within this workforce. A recent study suggests a major decline in the numbers of male workers, who may actually be outnumbered by two to one (Kennedy, 2000; also summarized in Buckley, 2002, pp. 218–220). This may prove difficult given the general difficulty in recruiting men to front-line work in fields such as teaching and social work with the additional difficulty of the stigma for men in this field due to associations with past abuse.
- Adapting existing models of training to the actual demands of the work role, especially in terms of attracting older applicants with life experience, and equipping younger entrants to deal with the behavior and demands of troubled adolescents.
- Providing front-line care staff with sufficient opportunity for developmental or reflective professional supervision that might help them to find meaning and purpose in working with young people's difficult behavior and their own responses (see Figure 1.1).
- Restoring a positive perception of residential child care despite the stigma arising from episodes of historical abuse that have emerged.
- Securing sufficient scale, capacity, diversity, and commitment to child-centered approaches in the providers of residential child care in the future. While there are likely to be statutory and private-for-profit providers, it seems especially important to retain a strong child-focused nongovernmental organization presence in the field that places particular emphasis on values, ethos, and innovation.

- Integrating residential care provision in innovative ways with foster care, community-based programs and after-care services, building on limited initiatives of this kind to date (Murphy and Gilligan, 2002).

Generating knowledge about the experiences of children and adults in the world of Irish residential child care and about the practices and processes that can enhance those experiences is an important next step. There is still remarkably little such research, although one exception is the work of Emond (2002), which is an example of what can emerge from detailed research; in this case, Emond generated important insights about the school experiences of children in residential care: about the home–school–family relationships in their lives and how adults can productively support the children's educational and social progress at school. Another example is the work of Fagan (1997). His study of administrative records in a residential unit found that patterns of trouble and disorder tended to occur in shifts when the rostered staff were on short-term contracts whereas rosters dominated by more securely employed long-term staff were associated with more stable environments.

Conclusion

Overall it seems that residential care is in decline in Ireland if one considers its proportionate share as a form of care provision. This share has fallen considerably over recent decades. It is also in decline if one considers its status or reputation as a form of care. But if one looks at the level of public spending on residential care and the heavy investment in recent years in a small number of specialist residential places (roughly 140 in a care system of over 5,000 places), then a simple picture of decline becomes a great deal more complex.

Looking back to the origins of our current system of residential child care, it is evident that the system did function to provide care. But it also served to advance the interests of providers. In addition, it played a part in shielding society from "social problems." It continues to play a part in dealing with what are seen as marginal groups. But most of all, it seems that its current function can be argued as serving as a "fall-back" to foster care.

Residential child care may be in decline, but this decline does not seem terminal. Residential child care plays too many important functions for wider society in Ireland and the care system more specifically to be allowed die. But increasingly, its role seems to be defined in terms of serving children regarded as extreme or on the margins in some way. In this sense, residential care risks becoming more "child preoccupied" than child centered, that is, focusing to a significant degree on the needs and capacity of the *system* in planning responses to individual children whose behavior has proven challenging for the services.

The lack of real competition from other modes of care suggests that residential care in this segment of the system remains virtually a monopoly provider. There seems the prospect of an unhealthy combination: a monopoly status for residential provision (at the "hard-end") and a reliance on an under-trained or under-provided workforce, given the difficulty in recruiting and retaining qualified staff. In such circumstances, the caliber of senior management staff would seem to become critical, as will the role of external monitoring systems.

Clearly any reasonable appraisal of the present state of Irish residential care would have to acknowledge certain strengths. The Health Information and Quality Authority Social Services Inspectorate, whose own existence is a key strength of the current system, recognizes positives in its annual reports, notably in the area of education. While smaller units may be harder to manage collectively, it seems likely that they are less prone to the remarkably stubborn institutionalizing pressures of larger settings. The emergence of the Special Residential Services Board (now succeeded by the Children Acts Advisory Board, with its brief to rationalize and strengthen provision for hard-to-serve young people) may also prove to be an important development in securing greater coordination and coherence in planning and providing for young people at the hard-to-serve end of the spectrum of care.

NOTES

1. Ireland as used here refers to what is known as the Republic of Ireland—that part of the island that has had independent government since 1922.
2. Hazel et al. (1983) contend that in Protestant countries, foster care in families provides an alternative to the institutional tradition.
3. It should be noted, however, that not all Catholic theology or adherents necessarily support such an institutional model of response. For example, Margaret Aylward, who went on to found a Roman Catholic female congregation, invested a lot of energy in the running of St. Brigid's Orphanage, which operated a scheme of foster family care for children admitted (an approach that was not without its critics at the time) (Prunty, 1999).
4. There is some evidence that individual officials may have sought to do this ultimately with little support from superiors.
5. Dunne, who claims this, is a former member of the Christian Brothers, one of the more famous congregations involved in providing residential child care in Ireland.
6. The National Children's Strategy was developed by a cross-government team of officials based in the National Children's Office (now subsumed in the Office of the Minister for Children and Youth Affairs), following consultation with all stakeholders, including children, and in response to vigorous criticism by the UN Committee on the Rights of the Child that was aimed at Ireland's policy performance in relation to vulnerable children.
7. Dail Eireann Parliamentary Debates, Vol. 566, Written Answer No. 96, May 7, 2003.
8. http://www.education.ie/robots/view.jsp?pcategory=17216&language=EN&ecategory=34313.
9. A recent national report has sought to examine the circumstances of 93 children aged 12 and under placed in residential care (despite long-standing custom in the Irish system that this should be avoided) (Health Information and Quality Authority Social Services Inspectorate, 2007).

10. Children with disabilities: There are dedicated facilities providing ongoing care for a certain proportion of children with physical, sensory, or intellectual disabilities. Some of these may have education on site; others may not. Facilities serving children with disabilities were excluded from residential child care regulations, apparently due to lobbying from service providers in this sector, but this anomaly has now been rectified by a provision in the Children's Act 2001. There are likely, of course, also to be children with disabilities receiving care within public care facilities but there are no data available on this group. Relevant sources in relation to this provision are National Intellectual Disability Database established in 1995; National Physical and Sensory Disability Database, under development.

11. Dail Eireann Parliamentary Debates, Vol. 567, Written Answer No. 286, May 20, 2003.

12. Dail Eireann Parliamentary Debates, Vol. 566, Written Answer No. 96, May 7, 2003; Dail Eireann Parliamentary Debates, Vol. 567, Written Answer No. 286, May 20, 2003.

REFERENCES

Buckley, H. (2002). *Child protection and welfare—innovations and interventions.* Dublin: Institute of Public Administration.

Clear, C. (1987). *Nuns in nineteenth-century Ireland.* Dublin: Gill and Macmillan.

Department of Education and Science. (2002). *Residential provision for children under the auspices of the Department of Education and Science—a preliminary review.* Dublin: Author.

Department of Health. (1983). *Survey of Children in the Care of Health Boards* Dublin: Author.

Department of Health and Children. (1999). *Children first: National guidelines for the protection and welfare of children.* Dublin: Author.

Department of Health and Children. (2001a). *National standards for children's residential centres.* Dublin: Author.

Department of Health and Children. (2001b). *National youth homelessness strategy.* Dublin: Author.

Department of Health and Children. (2003). *Survey of Children in the Care of Health Boards* Dublin: Author

Department of Health and Children. (no date). *National standards for special care units.* Dublin: Author.

Dunne, T. (2004). *Rebellions—memoir, memory and 1798.* Dublin: Lilliput Press.

Emond, R. (2002). *Learning from their lessons: A study of young people in residential care and their experiences of education.* Dublin: Children's Research Centre.

Fagan, A. (1997). Young people and violence in residential care—a case study. *Irish Journal of Social Work Research, 1*(1), 9–22.

Hazel, N., Schmedes, C., and Korshin, P. (1983). A case study in international cooperation. *British Journal of Social Work, 13*(6), 671–678.

Health Information and Quality Authority Social Services Inspectorate. (2007). *The placement of children aged 12 and under in residential care in Ireland.* Cork: Author.

Joint Committee on Social Care Professionals. (undated [2003?]). *Report of Joint Committee on Social Care Professionals.* Dublin(?): Author.

Kennedy Committee—Committee on Reformatory and Industrial Schools. (1970). *Report on the reformatory and industrial schools system.* (Kennedy Report). Dublin: Stationery Office.

Kennedy, M. (2000). *An exploration of the role of male staff working in residential child care.* Doctoral dissertation, Trinity College, Dublin.

Laxton, M. (1998). *On the requirement and necessity for special care and high support residential child care provision in Ireland.* Report to Department of Health and Children.

Luddy, M. (2005). *Women, philanthropy and the emergence of social work in Ireland.* Dublin: School of Social Work and Social Policy, Trinity College.

Murphy, C., and Gilligan, R. (2002). *Building family placements. An evaluation of the Lisdeel Family Placement Initiative.* Dublin: Daughters of Charity & Northern Area Health Board.

National Children's Office (2000) *Our Children – Their Lives* Dublin: The Stationery Office.

Prunty, J. (1999). *Margaret Aylward 1810—1889: Lady of charity, sister of faith.* Dublin: Four Courts Press.

Raftery, M., and O'Sullivan, E. (1999). *Suffer the little children—the inside story of Ireland's industrial schools.* Dublin: New Island Books.

Skehill, C. (1999). *The nature of social work in Ireland, a historical perspective.* Lampeter: Edwin Mellen Press.

Social Information Systems. (2003). *Definition and usage of high support in Ireland—report to the Special Residential Services Board.* Dublin: Special Residential Services Board.

Social Services Inspectorate. (2002). *Annual report Social Services Inspectorate 2001.* Dublin: Author.

Social Services Inspectorate. (2003a). *Annual report Social Services Inspectorate 2002.* Dublin: Author.

Social Services Inspectorate. (2003c). *National guidelines on the use of single separation in special care units.* Dublin: Author. http://www.issi.ie/doc/National%20Guidelines%20on% 20the%20use%20of%20Single%20Separation.doc.

Social Services Inspectorate. (2005a). *Annual report Social Services Inspectorate 2003.* Dublin: Author.

Social Services Inspectorate. (2005b). *Annual report Social Services Inspectorate 2004.* Dublin: Author.

Special Residential Services Board. (2005). *Annual report 2004.* Dublin: Author.

Whyte, G. (2002). *Social inclusion and the legal system: Public interest law in Ireland.* Dublin: Institute of Public Administration.

Whyte, J. (1980). *Church and state in modern Ireland 1923–1979.* (2nd ed.). Dublin: Gill and Macmillan.

Working Group on Child and Adolescent Psychiatric Services. (2003). *Second report.* Dublin: Department of Health and Children.

WEB SITES

Child Care Act, 1991. http://193.120.124.98/ZZA17Y1991.html.

Children Act, 2001. http://www.ucc.ie/law/irlii/statutes/2001_24.htm#z2.

Children Acts Advisory Board. http://www.caab.ie/.

Commission to Inquire into Child Abuse. http://www.childabusecommission.ie/.

Health Information and Quality Authority Social Services Inspectorate. http://www.hiqa.ie/ functions_ssi.asp.

Health Statistics Children in Care and Child Abuse, 2002. http://www.doh.ie/statistics/
    health_statistics/2002/secte.pdf.
Residential Institutions Redress Board. http://www.rirb.ie/.
Social Services Inspectorate—see Health Information and Quality Authority.
Special Residential Services Board—see Children Acts Advisory Board.
Youth Homelessness Strategy. http://www.doh.ie/publications/ythhmlss.html.

2

Residential Care in Great Britain and Northern Ireland

Perspectives from the United Kingdom

ROGER BULLOCK AND DOMINIC McSHERRY

Great Britain and Northern Ireland are known collectively as the United Kingdom. Great Britain itself is comprised of England, Scotland, and Wales. England (population 50 million) shows similarities with Wales (population 3 million) and Northern Ireland (population 1.5 million), but Scotland (population 5 million) is noticeably different.* This makes it difficult to talk generally about child welfare across the different regions of the United Kingdom.

Historical Legacy

The history of residential homes and schools in the United Kingdom is marked by a close link with extremes of wealth and poverty (Parker, 1988). In England, especially, the upper classes have long sent their children to prestigious boarding schools whose development was bound up with the growth of empire and religious division. It meant that many top administrators and politicians were favorably disposed to residential solutions to social problems. At the same time, the Poor Law, which governed provision for destitute and abandoned children following the dissolution of the Roman Catholic monasteries in the sixteenth century, established procedures that can be now seen as a forerunner of much modern residential child care. These two strands have been especially important in England, Wales, and Ireland but less

---

*We wish to thank Professors Roy Parker and Andrew Kendrick for their help in providing information on Scotland.

so in Scotland and some parts of central Wales where the influential historical and economic factors are different.

In Scotland, there was no mandatory local tax to support the poor, and over-seers did not have the power to borrow capital. Thus, relatively few workhouses were built and there were few workhouse schools. Outdoor relief was also banned at various times, which posed difficulties for the care of needy children. Complementing this situation was an extensive rural economy based on self-suffi-ciency in which children were generally welcomed as extra hands. Thus, there was always limited use of residential care.

When children's homes were provided in Scotland, they often reflected reli-gious affiliation—Scotland had a relatively high Roman Catholic population—and tended to be funded by local groups. As a result, homes opened and closed with some regularity. The relatively small size of the Scottish upper class also meant that fewer of those holding high office had been socialized into thinking of residential provision. The development of industrial and reform schools in the nineteenth and twentieth centuries, in contrast, was more similar to the rest of the United Kingdom, largely because they were funded centrally.

Previous Legislation

Although the economic and social circumstances were different in each part of the United Kingdom, there are general patterns. The Poor Law arrangements clearly influenced the type of care provided for destitute children and the funding available for new buildings. In the nineteenth century, the problems of industrialization and the growing number of poor and homeless children roaming around the cities led to the provision of expanded residential care. The new buildings ranged from large orphanages, often built by local industrialist-philanthropists, to small homes, usually run by small, local charities. It was not until the end of the century that organizations with a national reach, such as Dr. Barnardo's (now called Barnardo's), were established.

Every decade since the industrial revolution has been marked by child care legislation. For example, in 1889 powers were granted to charities to enter private houses if child abuse or neglect was suspected, and the 1908 Children's Charter gave an ear to children's wishes. Legislation often followed scandal or war, and particu-larly important was the 1946 *Report of the Care of Children Committee* (the Curtis Committee; His Majesty's Stationery Office, 1946), which was influenced by the high-profile death of a foster child. It castigated the whole child care system, includ-ing residential provision, and criticized many facilities, especially residential nurs-eries. Its recommendations informed the Children Act 1948, which set up a specialist children's department in every local authority. Voluntary residential provision tended to decline thereafter, not only because of the increasing power of the state but also because of the poor condition of buildings requisitioned in the Second World War and the diminishing pool of unmarried females who staffed them.

Further legislation in 1969 brought young offenders into the care system, only for them to be separated out again in the 1990s.

Current Legislation

In England, the current legislation governing the use of residential care is the Children Act 1989 and accompanying regulations. The act also applies in Wales, and there is similar legislation in Northern Ireland, the Children (Northern Ireland) Order 1995. The legislation allows for children to be looked after under voluntary arrangements—that is, by agreement between social services, the child, and his or her family. In the absence of consensus, a care order can be obtained from a court of law to enable professionals to act in what they consider to be the child's best interests. To qualify for a care order, a child must have suffered or be at risk of significant harm, and this must be attributable to the care the child is receiving or may receive.

The act is underpinned by a number of principles, including that the child's welfare should be paramount, that attention should be paid to the wishes and feelings of the child, and that no legal order should be made unnecessarily. There is also guidance specifying how children's homes should be run and what constitutes good practice with children and families.

Under the Children's Homes Regulations of 1991, all children's homes are required to have a written "statement of purpose and function," laying out the reason for which the home has been established, the objectives to be attained in relation to the children accommodated therein, the agency responsible for running the home, the types of children served, and the organizational arrangements. But despite these good intentions, Berridge and Brodie (1998) found that the majority of the homes they studied had no written statement of purpose and function three years after this was required by legislation.

Currently, all children's homes in Northern Ireland are also required to have a written statement of purpose that describes what the residential unit should provide for the children and young people it accommodates. This includes details of the person or organization with overall responsibility for the unit; the unit's status and constitution; its organizational structure; its aims and objectives; the philosophy of care; safeguards for the children and young people; the accommodation, services, and facilities in the unit; numbers of children and rationale for setting those numbers; the planned age range and gender of children and young people, and reasons for these plans; and any other selection criteria (Department of Health, Social Services, and Public Safety, 2004). However, although these statements have been formalized in principle, research has suggested that at times placement can occur on the basis of what is available at the time rather than any matching of statement of purpose with the specific needs of the child (Campbell and McLaughlin, 2005).

The relevant legislation in Scotland is the Children Act (Scotland) 1995; an element that distinguishes it from the rest of the United Kingdom is the Children's Hearings, established in 1971. A Reporter in each area, who is usually a law specialist, scrutinizes all referrals to the system and allocates some to voluntary supervision by the local social work department. The rest, who are likely to be child protection cases, school refusers, or young offenders, are referred to a panel of three lay volunteers who decide the intervention and direct the local authority accordingly, provided all parties accept the reason for the referral. If there is disagreement, the case goes to the Sheriff Court for proof and then is returned to the hearing for a decision.

Reviews of Residential Care

There have been several national reviews of residential child care in the United Kingdom, usually carried out following high-profile cases of abuse in children's homes. In the 1980s, there were several such scandals, and residential care seemed doomed. However, a subsequent government report (Department of Health, 1991) concluded that residential care is an essential service and is most appropriate for adolescents presenting challenging behaviors, for those children whom foster care has failed or may be inappropriate, for sibling groups, and for seriously damaged young people who require specialist help. The report also made a number of recommendations that emphasized the welfare of children, competent management, adequate resources, and staff qualifications and pay.

Subsequent reports (Department of Health, 1992; Scottish Office, 1992) examined the selection and recruitment methods and criteria for staff in children's homes. They made more than 80 recommendations concerning recruitment procedures, application forms, advertising, references, police checking, interviews, appraisal, training, and support. Utting's later review of the safeguards for children living away from home (Department of Health, 1997; Scottish Office, 1997) commented that the recommendations concerning the recruitment and selection of staff made in the 1992 reports had been satisfactorily implemented by most local authorities.

Standardization and Inspection

Partly in response to these reviews, the Care Standards Act (2000) introduced a new regulatory system for care services in England and Wales starting in 2002. It created the National Care Standards Commission, which is an independent, nondepartmental public body. It took over the regulation of social and health care services that had been formerly regulated by local councils and health authorities. Its role is to assess whether a children's home should be registered and to check whether achievable outcomes for children and young people are attained.

Types of Residential Care

A UK government publication has defined a residential placement as "a place where children live and sleep, for at least one night. As a rule the adults who look after the children will be employed for that purpose" (Department of Health, 1998, p. 7). This definition covers many different forms of residential provision, and only a portion of these are for the purposes of "residential care." Other placements are associated with adolescent behavior or parental choice over their children's education. Table 2.1 shows the range of residential placements, the number of residents, and the main reasons for admission in England. It can be seen that for every 100 children aged 0–18 living in some kind of residential setting, six will be in places designed primarily for children in need who are looked after by Social Services Departments.

There are approximately 320 such children in Northern Ireland, 550 in Wales, 960 in Scotland (the Scottish figure includes some young offenders), and 7,000 children in England. The total for the whole United Kingdom is just under 9,000 living in children's homes for welfare reasons. This represents 68 per 100,000 children aged 0–17 and 201 per 100,000 for those aged 12–17.

Later figures (March 31, 2002) show that 11 percent of the 59,700 children in out-of-home care in England lived in a children's home or hostel. The remainder were in foster care (68 percent), living with relatives (10 percent), or living independently or in some other situation (11 percent). Very low numbers of children under 10 (2.5 percent) were in residential homes, but the figure rises to 16.7 percent for those aged 10–15 and to 23.2 percent for those over 15 years of age. Moreover, another 10 percent currently living in out-of-home care are likely to have had a previous residential experience. Figures provided by the Social Services Inspectorate in Northern Ireland (Department of Health, Social Services, and Public Safety, 2007) indicate that percentage (12 percent) of looked-after children in residential care has remained relatively static since 2001. The current figure ($n = 283$) fills the system to capacity and is 117 places short of the 400 statutory places recommended within the *Children Matter* review (Department of Health and Social

Table 2.1. Range of Residential Placements in England

Range of Residential Placements	Number of Residents	Reason for Admission
Children's homes	7,000	Care and accommodation
Boarding special schools	21,000	Disability/special educational need/ emotional and behavioral disorder
Provision for disabled children	2,000	Disability
Young offenders institutions	2,000	Offending
Boarding schools (not special)	84,000	Parent choice
Hospitals	12,000	Health
TOTAL	128,000	

Services, 1998), suggesting that a fresh impetus may be needed to meet these objectives.

Level of Provision of Residential Care

In March 1996, there were 836 local authority homes in England spread across 132 social services departments. There were also 202 private and 64 voluntary children's homes (Utting, 1997). In Northern Ireland in March 2005 there were 52 homes (42 statutory, nine voluntary, and one private) providing 386 beds, and at present in Wales there are 127 homes with 563 beds. Scotland in March 2002 had 139 local authority homes and a few voluntary or private establishments (and many more schools) providing for 960 and 1,196 children, respectively. These figures show that in the United Kingdom as a whole there are approximately 1,400 establishments that meet the criteria for inclusion in this book. A number of studies have found the average number of children and young people in children's homes in England and Wales to be seven (Berridge and Brodie, 1998; Whitaker, Archer, Hicks, et al., 1998).

There has been a dramatic decrease in the number of children and young people entering children's homes over the last 20 years, perhaps by as much as 50 percent (Berridge and Brodie, 1998). However, there has been no corresponding fall in the level of foster care, with the numbers of placements remaining relatively stable (approximately 35,000) and rising in percentage terms as the number of children in out-of-home care has fallen (Hayden et al., 1999). Some authorities have reduced their quota of children's homes to very few or even none, with a number of residential placements being purchased in voluntary and private facilities (Cliffe and Berridge, 1991). However, these can be expensive and may involve placing the child or young person a considerable distance away from the family home.

It has been argued that factors such as policy and practice shifts toward preventive services, a change in awareness and attitudes about children's needs, and financial considerations have all contributed to this decline (Gooch, 1996; Hayden, et al. 1999; Utting, 1997). Also, many persistent offenders are now the responsibility of a separate agency, the Youth Justice Board. As a result, many of the children who now enter children's homes are older and have more complex problems than the children previously cared for (Sinclair and Gibbs, 1998; Frost, Mills, and Stein, 1999).

Because of a combination of family-centered ideology and fiscal considerations that stressed the benefits of foster care over residential care, the 1980s and 1990s saw a major retraction of the residential sector in Northern Ireland, a decline similar to but greater than that in England and Wales (McSherry and Larkin, 2006). Between 1986 and 1996, the number of places in both statutory and voluntary children's homes fell by almost 50 percent, from 688 places to 358. This declined by a further 33 percent between March 1996 and September 1997. In November 1997 there were 240 places in children's homes, and 42 of these were phased out by the middle of 1998. Consequently, from 1986 to 1998 there was a 70 percent drop in the number of residential places available within Northern Ireland (Department of Health and Social Services 1998). Essentially, Northern Ireland had shifted to the precarious position of placing all its eggs in one foster care basket (Kelly and Coulter, 1999).

One of the main consequences of this major retraction in residential services, as in England and Wales, was that it left space only for children with the most serious problems, making the residential care task much more difficult and demanding. Whether such low numbers of available places are sustainable is a matter of debate, and in Northern Ireland there has recently been a review of residential care, known as *Children Matter* (Department of Health and Social Services 1998), which set forward an action plan to reverse this trend and increase the number of beds available by almost 50 percent (an extra 155 places). Since the review was completed, seven new homes have opened.

Recent Changes in the Provision of Residential Care

At least a dozen separate trends within children's homes can be identified (Gooch, 1996):

- The replacement of single-sex establishments by ones that are coeducational but, in practice, are dominated by boys
- The increasing age of residents at entry
- More young people with apparent health problems, behavior disorders, and disabilities
- Greater racial and ethnic mix
- Larger catchment areas, raising problems for educational continuity and contact with home
- More provision by private agencies
- Less specialization by sector with a resulting mix of needs in each establishment
- Assessment by need criteria rather than social role categories, such as disabled or special educational needs
- A more generalist service
- Shorter stays
- Rising cost
- More concerns about rights and protection
- Further reductions in the size of units and in the numbers accommodated by the system but, paradoxically, a larger proportion of the total places in secure accommodation or other specialist centers such as therapeutic communities

Naturally, the factors that explain changes in the use of private boarding schools, establishments for children with special educational needs, or penal institutions may be different from those that affect children's homes, but in all sectors viable alternatives have been created. Even in those primarily concerned with delinquent and disruptive adolescents, the emergence of a coherent juvenile justice service has been important, although there is still considerable reliance on custody as a last resort.

Characteristics of Children and Young People in Residential Care

The children placed in residential homes are mixed in terms of their needs, but most present difficult behavior or reject offers of foster care. Many "troublesome" children will also be "troubled," having suffered harm, deprivation, and failure. There will be a mixture of those on care orders (a legal order that transfers some parental rights to the local authority) and those accommodated voluntarily. The majority of young people in children's homes are male teenagers (Sinclair and Gibbs, 1998; Whitaker, et al. 1998).

Difficult behavior at home, at school, or in the community is most common among the young people. However, Berridge and Brodie (1998) also noted the prevalence of problems associated with poor self-esteem and educational failure. Similarly, Dartington's *Matching Needs and Services* studies (1999) have revealed high levels of mental health and relationship problems in the children's families. Sinclair and Gibbs (1998) aggregated the data for the children in their study of 48 homes, and Table 2.2 shows the extent of children's problems in seven selected areas, based on a high-score, low-score comparison.

Length of Placement

The average length of time spent in a children's home has halved since 1985 (Berridge and Brodie, 1998), and many young people leave within a month (Bullock, Gooch, and Little, 1998). However, Brown et al. (1998) pointed out that it is not unusual for children to enter residential care on a short-term basis but remain there for months or even years.

Table 2.2. The Extent of Children's Problems Among Residents in 48 Homes

The Proportion of Children Scoring High and Low	*High %*	*Low %*
Health (growth and development)	96	4
Identity (self-esteem)	23	77
Presentation (communication skills)	58	42
Emotional development (problems)	70	30
Self-care (ability to care for oneself)	76	24
Education and employment (attainments)	34	66
Family and friends (emotional ties)	63	37

Staff

Staff-to-child ratios have greatly improved over the last 20 years, but there have been only modest improvements in the proportion of staff holding relevant qualifications. Staff members continue to be viewed as professionally inferior to their fieldwork counterparts (Berridge and Brodie, 1998; Sinclair and Gibbs, 1998). The Department of Health (1998) reported that although 60 percent of children and young people in residential placements are male, 60 percent of the staff are female. It was also noted that the average age of staff is 40, with 20 percent under 30 and 15 percent over 50. Most have at least two years' experience. Berridge and Brodie (1998) found that, on the whole, relationships between staff and young people in the homes they studied were good. They found that when asked to comment on the staff in the children's homes, young people were "overwhelmingly positive" (p. 159). Recent research conducted in Northern Ireland illustrates a close link between the clarity and relevance of the statement of purpose for residential units and staff morale (Campbell and McLaughlin, 2005). Residential staff commented that inappropriate admissions had an enormously negative impact on staff morale, leaving them feeling deflated and deskilled at having to deal with children presenting extremely challenging behavioral problems.

Staff Training

Training for residential work with children has long posed difficulties in the United Kingdom. Few staff members have relevant qualifications for residential practice, although in Northern Ireland the proportion reaches one-third. Staff turnover is also high. Sinclair and Gibbs (1998) could find no evidence that either more qualified staff or a higher ratio of staff to children predicted better outcomes for children.

Yet it is equally clear from the numerous studies discussed in the 1998 Department of Health overview and in subsequent research (Hicks et al., 2007) that the staff world is a very important factor in successful residential work. It may be that a certain level of training is essential for good outcomes or that some other staff factors, such as confidence, morale, culture, or leadership, are more influential. In addition, it may be that training courses have not been appropriate to the residential task or that staff have not been able to put their training into effect.

The recognized professional qualification for working in residential child care is a Diploma in Social Work or one of its predecessors. The UK is the only European country that sees social work as the core professional discipline for residential work with children, but many trainers have argued that this does not adequately prepare people for the work and is not a satisfactory professional base for effective practice. Some training arrangements offer a "residential pathway" for staff, such as that provided by Strathclyde University in association with the Scottish Institute for Residential Child Care.

Who Pays for and Provides Residential Care?

Local authorities run most children's homes. Fewer than 10 percent of the homes are private or voluntary (House of Commons Health Committee, 1998). Carr-Hill et al. (1997) estimate that the average annual cost of a place in a children's home in England and Wales is more than seven times as much, currently around £80,000 per annum, as foster care.

It is important to note, however, that these amounts are average and are not marginal costs. There are few savings to be made in reducing the numbers of residents in a home; homes have to be closed to release money for alternative services (Cliffe and Berridge, 1991). There is also a tendency for difficult cases with poor prognoses for long-term outcomes to cost more, producing a correlation between high expenditure and limited success.

Issues in Residential Care

Recent child care policies in the United Kingdom have sought to address several of the issues that confound effective residential care, including abuse and neglect, poor educational achievement, relations with families and home communities, physical and mental health, and leaving care.

Abuse and Neglect

A number of high-profile inquiries have revealed instances of physical and sexual abuse by staff working in children's homes, such as in Northern Ireland (Department of Health and Social Services, 1986, 1993), England (Kirkwood, 1993), and Wales (Waterhouse Report, 2000). As a result of these, measures have been introduced to improve recruitment, create conditions that make aggression less likely, make care more visible, and encourage children and young people to assert their rights.

Abuse can also emanate from peer cultures (Sinclair and Gibbs, 1998), and one of the main criticisms of residential approaches has been the risks of generating delinquent and violent subcultures by putting troubled and troublesome teenagers together. Efforts have been made to divide the residential population into small groups, work with children individually, and make sure that adults and outside visitors are available to the children.

Poor Educational Achievement

Numerous studies have shown that a sizable proportion of children and young people in children's homes are not attending school because of suspension, exclusion, or difficulty gaining entry to a new school (Hayden et al., 1999; Sinclair and Gibbs, 1998; Utting, 1997). Carlens (1992) argued that stigmatizing and humiliating treatment by teachers and bullying by peers exacerbate the difficulties already suffered by children in out-of-home care, as do practical problems such as transport. As a result, the children may come to be perceived as unreliable and unpunctual, fueling their feelings of helplessness and alienation. Jackson and Sachdev (2001) add to this list several issues, including the low priority and poor planning given to the education of the young people, failure to set and monitor educational targets by education authorities and social services, and the lack of support given to children and young people to help them succeed at school. Social workers consistently underestimate the difficulties. Social workers are increasingly expected to exercise sensitivity in the placement of young people by ensuring proximity to their present school or postponing moves until exams have been completed (Bullock, Little, and Millham, 1994).

Parker (1988) gives another reason, namely that in the UK "care" has traditionally been divorced from "education." The two were administered by different government departments until 2003 (both are now the responsibility of the Department for Children, Schools and Families) and were thus considered to be distinct. He points out that in the pedagogic system found in some other European countries, care is an integral part of the education system and consequently is less stigmatizing.

Relations with Families and Home Communities

The Children Act 1989 and the Children (Northern Ireland) Order 1995 state that the interests of most looked-after young people are best served by maintaining or creating links with their natural families and working in partnership with parents. This aspect of the act was influenced by studies carried out in the 1980s suggesting that maintaining parental contact has a strong positive effect on the child's sense of well-being and increases the chances of returning to parental care. It also enables the child to understand the reason he or she is being looked after, hence avoiding self-blame and promoting positive self-image. Kosonen (1996) argued that maintaining sibling relationships is especially important because siblings provide a sense of identity, highlighted earlier as a problem area.

A number of studies have shown that contact with family is now generally encouraged and facilitated and that staff understand its importance (Berridge and Brodie, 1998; Cleaver, 2000; Sinclair and Gibbs, 1998). But the involvement of children's families in care plans and the provision of services to them by field social workers are less common and remain a weakness of many interventions.

Physical and Mental Health

Several studies have addressed aspects of children's physical and mental health. Bundle (2001), for example, found serious gaps between the assessment process and accurate recording of children's health, with significant medical conditions unknown to caregivers. Studies of children's mental health have also shown a high incidence of psychological problems. McCann et al. (1996) reported that 96 percent of adolescents in residential care in an English county showed some form of psychiatric disorder, a significant number of which had gone undetected; 23 percent, for example, were assessed as having a major depressive illness. Nicol et al. (2000) found that three-quarters of the young people living in all residential establishments in a geographical region of England had significant problems, which included hyperactivity, conduct disorders, substance abuse, and depression. This situation makes observers such as Rushton and Minnis (2002) doubtful about the alleged benefits of residential care.

Leaving Care

The Children Act 1989 and the Children (Leaving Care) Act (2000) in England established the duty of local authorities to prepare young people for leaving care and set an obligation on local authorities to advise and befriend young people up to the age of 21 in instances when they left care after their 16th birthday. Local authorities also have discretionary powers to provide financial assistance to young people in the areas of education, training, employment, and housing.

In the United Kingdom, 3,000 adolescents aged 16–17 leave residential care every year to live independently. For those who do not return home, the services provided are variable (Broad, 1998; Pinkerton, 2002; Pinkerton and McCrea, 1999). Broad argued that the gains from the Children Act 1989 in England have been modest and inconsistent as the legislation is too discretionary. Local authorities can avoid investing in services for those who leave care.

Several of the studies cited in this chapter have highlighted just how poorly prepared young people leaving care are for independent living. Generally accepted figures are that 75 percent of children leave care with no academic qualifications; more than 50 percent of those older than 15 are unemployed, and 17 percent of young women quickly become pregnant. In addition, 10 percent of all 16- to 17-year-olds claiming welfare payments have previously been in care, as have 23 percent of adult prisoners, 38 percent of young prisoners, and 30 percent of those who are young, single, and homeless.

Long-Term Outcomes

Traditionally, residential approaches have been seen as offering several benefits: to provide stability and a stimulating environment, to widen cultural and educational horizons, to create a framework for emotionally secure relationships with adults, and to provide a setting for intensive therapeutic work. These have to be set against difficulties of providing unconditional love, constraints on children's emotional development, poor staff continuity, and the marginalization of children's families and other welfare services (Bullock, Little, and Millham, 1993; Clough, Bullock, and Ward, 2006).

But such global statements cannot be true, as what applies in a prestigious boarding school is unlikely to be relevant to a small residential home, and vice versa. The evidence to support these claims is also suspect. But what is clear from numerous studies is that residential settings do have a marked effect on young people while they are there. Academic achievement and displays of difficult behavior, such as running away or violence, differ widely across residential establishments, and these differences are not explained by the characteristics of the intake. However, the long-term effects on children's development, behavior, and social relationships are less clear (Little, Kohm, and Thompson, 2005).

This uncertainty is exacerbated by the methodological difficulties of establishing discrete long-term effects. For example, the resident young people are likely to have faced considerable difficulties in the past and are poor candidates for success on global outcomes measures such as educational qualifications or stable relationships. Nevertheless, progress often occurs, and a qualitative assessment of individual children over time yields more encouraging results (Department of Health, 1998; Hill, et al. 1996; Little and Kelly, 1995). Additional evaluation problems arise from fluctuations in the stability of young people's living situations, antisocial behavior, and social situations, making the follow-up period selected a variable influencing the results. There is also the possibility of a "placebo" effect, unrelated to any residential intervention, producing the observed changes.

Residential care is, of course, only one experience among many for young people. It comes at certain points in their lives and is used to resolve difficulties that arise in particular areas and times. It is not an "'all or nothing" input, and its effects will be influenced by what preceded and follows it.

Whitaker and colleagues (1998) are the most optimistic about the effects of residential care. They conclude that although there is no list of circumstances under which residential care should be a preferred option, there are occasions when residential care could be helpful: when there was a deficit in attachment-forming capacity and a young person could benefit from having available a range of caregivers; when a young person had a history of having abused other children; when a young person felt threatened by the prospect of living in a family or needed respite from it; when multiple potential adult attachment figures might forestall a young person from emotionally abandoning his or her own parents; when the emotional load of caring for a very disturbed or chaotic young person was best distributed among a number of caregivers; and when the young person preferred residential care to any form of family care and would sabotage family care if it were provided.

In a more recent review of research into residential and foster care, however, Rushton and Minnis (2002) are less convinced. They express concern that staff in residential homes have no training or contact with specialist child mental health services to help them deal with the problems they face. They suggest, as do Sinclair and Gibbs, that all of the treatments offered to troubled and troublesome teenagers can be delivered in foster care where there is less likelihood of bullying, sexual harassment, and delinquent cultures. In contrast to Whitaker, they argue that when children have attachment difficulties, therapeutic foster care seems preferable. But, given the control difficulties that some young people present, there is probably a need for a small number of high-quality residential establishments for children who cannot be accommodated any other way or for whom there is a policy to keep them out of prison.

How Can Residential Care Be Improved?

The following characteristics of good homes have been identified by UK child care research: establishments are child-oriented in the sense that children want to talk to staff and that staff are warm and caring; there is appropriate contact with family members; children and, as appropriate, parents are properly involved in decisions about their lives; children are treated with respect; children have the same access to education, health, and leisure as their peers; children have access to the special services they may need; the aspects of behavior that are known to be poor indicators for a child's future adaptation are minimized; children are helped in mainstream education and employment; and children are supported on leaving the home both in practical skills and in managing the potentially lonely experience of being on their own.

Such good homes are achieved by the following: harmony between the goals of different systems and of professionals; the structure of the home influencing the staff culture, which in turn influences the child culture; clear and coherent leadership; well-articulated objectives that are consistent through the organization; local authorities who understand the nature and responsibilities of being a "corporate parent"; and staff who feel that they have significant responsibility for life within the home.

The ingredients of high-quality residential care extend to appointment procedures and support mechanisms for heads of homes. Replacement managers with a track record of turning around failing homes are a particularly valuable asset. Residential staff have broad responsibilities, and it is important to have mechanisms that encourage them to keep sight of their principal responsibilities, the priorities for the child and the home, and cooperation with other professionals.

There have been several government-led initiatives to improve the situation of children in out-of-home care in all four UK countries. In England, Quality Protects and Choice Protects set clear expectations about the issues highlighted—for example, by specifying how many children should move or pass examinations. This approach is mirrored by Children First in Wales and Children Matter in Northern Ireland. Similarly, the requirements on local authorities to produce service plans and child care strategies should produce a broader range of services provision sensitive to the needs of children and families.

The Future of Residential Care in the United Kingdom

The future direction in children's services in the United Kingdom is likely to be on prevention and early intervention. A series of initiatives is being introduced by which service providers will identify children at risk and act accordingly, preferably by providing help in family and home community settings. For children in out-of-home care, there is likely to be a move to speedier permanency. This most certainly means quicker family reunions for some and more adoptions for younger children unable to return home.

The trends described earlier are likely to continue. In this context, residential care is likely to continue to play a small but significant role in children's services, but because of expense, alleged ineffectiveness, and difficulties of staffing, it will continually be replaced by foster care that shelters children who are difficult to place (Sinclair, 2006). However, there will be a limit to what is possible, as the evidence from Northern Ireland suggests, and difficult cases will be off-loaded more readily to the criminal justice system. There may be some growth in private provision as local authorities find it difficult to cope. Similarly, some specialist fostering arrangements may become more quasi-residential settings than traditional family settings.

The main criterion for entry to residential care will remain difficult behavior, especially dangers to self and others. There is no reason to believe that this population will fall, as psychological disturbances among juveniles seem to be growing, so the major struggle with new services provision may be to maintain the status quo. But financial constraints will mean little growth in psychotherapeutic facilities despite the fact that the cognitive-behavioral approaches introduced widely in the 1990s appear to be producing disappointing results for some groups of children. If there are to be regime changes, they are likely to emphasize flexibility with other living arrangements, education, social skills, and employment.

Neither should the pragmatic difficulties be underestimated. The numbers of unaccompanied asylum seekers requiring emergency accommodation will grow if wars and revolutions continue. Similarly, it may prove just as difficult to recruit specialist foster caregivers as it is residential workers.

In summary, the future of residential care over the next 20 years is likely to be consolidation rather than major change. The value of a residential approach will be what it can offer the care process. There are some areas of "added value," and two that are especially important are predictability (in that much of the young person's life is enacted in the same value framework) and the creative use of groups to develop good relations with a range of adults and peers.

There is a danger of interpreting the absence of clear research findings on beneficial effects as indicating that "nothing works." It is true that findings using global outcomes measures are generally disappointing, but there are several ways forward. The first is to look more closely at the link between specific residential interventions and specific groups of adolescents. To do this, the taxonomies of young people need to be developed and linked to a careful scrutiny of interventions (Sinclair and Little, 2002). If this is done, more encouraging results should emerge. A second is to view treatment in the wider context of the young person's needs and the services that best meet them. Young people in residential care will almost certainly be complex cases, and a variety of approaches may be needed.

The starting point for this is the needs of the young person and what is deemed necessary to meet them. The first question to be asked, therefore, is what does the young person and his or her family need? Does he or she need residential care, and if so for what, of what type, for how long, and with what else? For those selected, the next question is what regime and treatment approaches are shown by research to be the most effective for meeting those needs? To answer this properly, we again need to develop a validated taxonomy of young offenders and to consider the evidence on intervention and outcomes for groups of children with different needs. In doing so, the criteria employed to assess the effects of treatment have to be clearly specified.

This sequence of questions should focus attention on the aims of residential care and highlight gaps between desired and actual outcomes. The experience is thus related to an individual's needs and seeks an auspicious setting with the application of specific therapies.

These perspectives inform answers to questions about the place of residential care in a comprehensive service for children in need. It is clear that approaches need to be multifaceted and that prevention and diversion can make important contributions, as can residential care (Little and Mount, 1999). A needs perspective has the advantage of avoiding a "for" and "against" stance. Considerable effort may be needed to develop these suggestions, but the benefits of a comprehensive service should be apparent in improved outcomes for children and enhanced job satisfaction among staff.

REFERENCES

Berridge, D., and Brodie, I. (1998). *Children's homes revisited.* London: Jessica Kingsley.

Broad, B. (1998). *Young people leaving care: Life after the Children Act 1989.* London: Jessica Kingsley.

Brown, E., Bullock, R., Hobson, C., and Little, M. (1998). *Making residential care work: Structure and culture in children's homes.* Aldershot: Ashgate.

Bullock, R., Gooch, D., and Little, M. (1998). *Children going home: The reunification of families.* Aldershot: Ashgate.

Bullock, R., Little, M., and Millham, S. (1993). *Residential care for children: A review of the research.* London: Her Majesty's Stationery Office.

Bullock, R., Little, M., and Millham, S. (1994). Children's return from state care to school. *Oxford Review of Education, 20*(3): 307–316.

Bundle, A. (2001). Health of teenagers in residential care: Comparison of data held by care staff with data in community health records. *Archives of Diseases in Childhood, 84*, 10–14.

Campbell, A., and McLaughlin. A. (2005). *Views that matter: Staff morale, qualifications, and retention in residential childcare in Northern Ireland.* London: National Children's Bureau.

Carlens, P. (1992). Pindown, truancy and the interrogation of discipline: A paper about theory, policy, social-worker bashing . . . and hypocrisy. *Journal of Law and& Society, 19*(2): 251–270.

Carr-Hill, R., et al. (1997). *A model of the determinants of expenditure on children's personal social services.* York, UK: Centre for Health Economics, University of York.

Cleaver, H. (2000). *Fostering family contact: A study of children, parents and foster carers.* London: Her Majesty's Stationery Office.

Cliffe, D., and Berridge, D. (1991). *Closing residential homes: An end to residential childcare?* London: National Children's Bureau.

Clough, R., Bullock, R., and Ward, A. (2006). *What works in residential care: A review of research evidence and the practice implications.* London: National Children's Bureau.

Dartington Social Research Unit. (1999). *Matching needs and services.* Dartington: Warren House Press.

Department of Health. (1991). *Children in the public care: A review of residential care.* London: Her Majesty's Stationery Office.

Department of Health. (1992). *Choosing with care: The report of the committee of inquiry into the selection, development and management of staff in children's homes.* London: Her Majesty's Stationery Office.

Department of Health. (1997). *People like us.* London: Her Majesty's Stationery Office.

Department of Health. (1998). *Caring for children away from home: Messages from research.* Chichester: Wiley.

Department of Health and Social Services. (1986). *Report of the committee of inquiry into children's homes and hostels.* Belfast: Her Majesty's Stationery Office.

Department of Health and Social Services. (1993). *An abuse of trust: The report of the social services inspectorate investigation into the case of Martin Huston.* Belfast: DHSS.

Department of Health and Social Services. (1998). *Children matter: A review of residential child care services in Northern Ireland.* Belfast: DHSS.

Department of Health, Social Services, and Public Safety. (2004). *Children's homes: Registration and inspection standards. A consultation document.* Belfast: DHSSPS. An Roinn Sláinte, Seirbhísí Sóisialta agus Sábháilteachta Poiblí.

Department of Health, Social Services, and Public Safety. (2005). *Children order statistical bulletin 2007.* Belfast: DHSSPS An Roinn Sláinte, Seirbhísí Sóisialta agus Sábháilteachta Poiblí.

Frost, N., Mills, S., and Stein, M. (1999). *Understanding residential child care.* Aldershot: Ashgate.

Gooch, D. (1996). Home and away: The residential care, education and control of children in historical and political context. *Child and Family Social Work, 1,* 19–32.

Hayden, C., Goddard, J., Gorin, S., and Van Der Spek, N. (1999). *State child care: Looking after children?* London: Jessica Kingsley.

Hicks, L., Gibbs, I., Weatherly, H. and Boyd, S. (2007). *Managing children's homes: Developing effective leadership in small organizations.* London: Jessica Kingsley.

Hill, M., Triseliotis, J., Borland, M., and Lambert, L. (1996). Outcomes of social work intervention with young people. In M. Hill and J. Aldgate (Eds.), *Child welfare services.* London: Jessica Kingsley.

His Majesty's Stationery Office. (1946). *Report of the care of children committee,* Cmnd. 6922. London: Author.

House of Commons Health Committee. (1998). *Children in out of home care by local authorities.* London: Her Majesty's Stationery Office.

Jackson, S., and Sachdev, D. (2001). *Better education, better futures: Research, practice and the views of young people in public care.* Essex: Barnardo's.

Kelly, G., and Coulter, J. (1998). The Children (Northern Ireland) Order (1995): A new era for fostering and adoption services. *Adoption and Fostering, 21*(3), 5–13.

Kirkwood, A. (1993). *The Leicestershire inquiry.* Leicestershire, UK: Leicestershire County Council.

Kosonen, M. (1996). Maintaining sibling relationships: Neglected dimension in child care practice. *British Journal of Social Work, 26,* 809–822.

Little, M., Kohm, A., and Thompson, R. (2005). The impact of residential placement on child development: Research and policy implications. *International Journal of Social Welfare, 14,* 200–209.

Little, M., and Kelly, S. (1995) *A life without problems: The achievements of a therapeutic community.* Aldershot: Arena.

Little, M., and Mount. K. (1999). *Prevention and early intervention with children in need.* Aldershot: Ashgate.

McCann, J., James, A., Wilson, S., and Dunn, D. (1996). Prevalence of psychiatric disorders in young people in the care system. *British Medical Journal, 313,* 1529–1530.

McSherry, D. & Larkin, E. (2006). Developments in residential care in Northern Ireland. In: D. Iwaniec (Ed.), *The child's journey through care: Placement stability, care-planning, and achieving permanency* (pp.133-146). Chichester: Wiley.

Nicol, R., et al. (2000). Mental health needs and services for severely troubled and troubling young people including young offenders in an NHS Region. *Journal of Adolescence, 23,* 243–261.

Parker, R. (1988). Children. In I. Sinclair (Ed.), *Residential care: The research reviewed* (pp. 57–124). National Institute for Social Work. London: Her Majesty's Stationery Office.

Pinkerton, J. (2002). Developing an international perspective on leaving care. In A. Wheal (Ed.), *The RHP companion to leaving care* (pp. 34–44). Dorset: Russell House.

Pinkerton, J., and McCrea, R. (1999). *Meeting the challenge? Young people leaving care in Northern Ireland.* Aldershot : Ashgate

Rushton, A., and Minnis, H. (2002). Residential and family foster care. In M. Rutter and E. Taylor (Eds.), *Child and adolescent psychiatry* (pp. 359–372). Oxford: Blackwell Science.

Scottish Office. (1992). *Another kind of home: A review of residential child care.* Edinburgh: Author.

Scottish Office. (1997). *Children's safeguards review.* Edinburgh: Author.

Sinclair, I. (2006). *Fostering now: Messages from research.* London: Jessica Kingsley

Sinclair, I., and Gibbs, I. (1998). *Children's homes: A study in diversity.* Chichester, UK: Wiley.

Sinclair, R., and Little, M. (2002). Developing a taxonomy for children in need. In H. Ward and W. Rose (Eds.), *Approaches to needs assessments in children's services* (pp. 127–145). London: Jessica Kingsley.

Utting, W. (1997). *People like us : The report of the review of the safeguards for children living away from home.* London : The Stationery Office.

Waterhouse Report. (2000). *Lost in care.* London: Her Majesty's Stationery Office.

Whitaker, D., Archer, L., and Hicks, L. (1998). *Working in children's homes: Challenges and complexities.* Chichester: Wiley.

3

Swedish Residential Care in the Landscape of Out-of-Home Care

MARIE SALLNÄS

Swedish out-of-home care has been subject to major changes in recent times. A long trend of stable or decreasing entry into care was broken at the beginning of the 1990s. Foster care is the most common form of out-of-home care—and the principally preferred option—but lately the number of placements in privately run residential homes has risen. In fact, in initiated placements, residential care has taken over territory from foster care. It is not possible in the Swedish context to discuss the current situation and trends in residential care without taking foster care into consideration. Changes in the field of foster care affect residential care and vice versa, because both decisions are made by local authorities. The aim of this chapter, then, is to give an overview of the "landscape" of out-of-home care and to discuss the changing role of Swedish residential care in that landscape, along with the possible explanations for the most important alterations that have taken place.

Family Service

The Social Services Act (SFS 2001:453) states that all Swedish children have the right to grow up under favorable and secure conditions. If this is not fulfilled, child welfare is both authorized and obliged to intervene. This should, as far as possible, be done in partnership with the biological parents and should take into consideration the views of the child. When children are placed in out-of-home care, both the regulations and the official ideology emphasize voluntary measures and regular contact between children and parents. Placements should principally be temporary and must be evaluated and reconsidered every six months. Children are supposed to return to their biological parents (custodians) as soon as circumstances allow. According to Gilbert (1997), compared with other countries such as the United States, Canada, or Great Britain, Swedish (and Nordic) child welfare can be described as oriented to family service, in contrast to child protection. This long tradition of family service orientation is not uncontroversial. It has repeatedly been debated and questioned with the argument put forward that a trend toward more protective elements can be identified (Wiklund, 2006).

Swedish child welfare is characterized by far-reaching decentralization; because this is the province of local municipal authorities—nearly 300 in number and sometimes very small—there are differences in the organizational settings (Bergmark & Lundström, 2005) as well as in the use of out-of-home care (Sallnäs, 2005a; Wiklund, 2006). Regulations in law also make relatively general but heavy demands (Palme et al., 2002). On a macro level, Sweden can be characterized as a welfare state with a universal approach. This means that most benefits are directed to all citizens, not just to those in need, although some parts of the welfare state, such as care of the elderly and child day care, have historically been linked to the few. Today these areas are part of a universal, nonstigmatizing service system (Hessle & Vinnerljung, 1999; Sunesson, 1990; see also Palme et al., 2002). Child welfare is, however, still closely connected to the residual components of the welfare state, that sector to which people turn, or are forced into, when the universal welfare system is not enough. Child welfare, in other words, is a system that by nature individualizes social problems and where the measures taken are organized and applied according to that principle (Lundström, 2000).

Historical Background

Residential homes for children have existed in Sweden for several hundred years. They were established to a greater extent in the second half of the nineteenth century. This period can be considered a starting point when society began to take responsibility for the welfare of children and youth besides education—in other words a "modern child welfare" (Lundström, 1993). The ongoing urbanization led to increasing numbers of children in cities. Certain influential persons and organizations discovered that some children and youth were living under severe conditions, more or less abandoned by adults, suffering in their homes, or drifting around in the streets. Infants of poor mothers were often placed in foster homes but were sometimes so badly treated that they died. If older children were taken care of at all, they were placed together with adults in institutions for criminals, mental hospitals, or poverty asylums (Ödman, 1991). The "child welfare issue" was publicly debated, and separating children from adults became an important societal task. This led to the introduction of special child protection legislation and to the establishment of special residential homes for children. The reasons for establishing residential care were not only idealistic, however. The prevailing belief was that badly behaved, poor, or amoral children and youth should be kept away from well-behaved children so that the well behaved were not negatively affected. It is a recurrent theme in the history of Swedish residential care to differentiate between the "good" children who have to be protected and the "bad" ones who have to be kept away from society and from their peers. Different types of residential care were created for the two categories, a separation that still exists.

Initially, the central state played only a minor role. Voluntary organizations or foundations ran the majority of residential homes, and the legislation to exercise control was weak. However, the state gradually began to intervene, and in the 1940s the central state became responsible for the supply and number of institutions. Increasingly, public authorities also became owners of residential homes. By the time the current legislation, the Social Services Act, came in to effect in 1982, public ownership dominated, with fewer than 10 percent of homes in the hands of voluntary organizations or foundations.

The first decades of the twentieth century were characterized by construction and expansion, with a steady increase in the number of both residential care units and beds to a peak in the late 1930s and early 1940s. This was followed by a gradual decline up to the beginning of the 1980s. In sum, the number of homes decreased from 400 to approximately 200 during this period, and the reduction in the number of beds was even greater—from 8,500 to fewer than 2,000. At the beginning of the 1980s, Sweden had—in a historical perspective—extremely few residential homes in the landscape of out-of-home care (Sallnäs, 2000).

Why Deinstitutionalization?

How could the expansion in residential care during the first half of the twentieth century turn into deinstitutionalization from the 1940s and the following decades? Clearly, the decrease was not related to changes in demographics. The number of children has been almost constant (around 2.2 million) in the postwar period. Neither was residential care quantitatively replaced by foster care. The statistics are uncertain, but it is estimated that during the 1950–1980 period the total number of children served in out-of-home care in a given year dropped from approximately 33,000 to 23,000 (Vinnerljung & Sallnäs, 2006) and that the group counted by the authorities as "foster children" decreased dramatically from approximately 28,000 children in the 1950s to approximately 10,000 in 1990 (Vinnerljung, 1996). In other words, the decreases in residential care and foster care following World War II were parallel phenomena.

It has been argued that important factors behind the deinstitutionalization of child welfare were expansive Swedish social policies in combination with severe criticism of residential care during the 1960s and 1970s, when living conditions for people placed in institutions were in glaring contrast to general societal standards. Moreover, the construction of the welfare state made it possible for more individuals to cope outside the institutions, which meant that the need for residential (and foster) care diminished. An obvious example was the material improvement in the living conditions of single mothers and their children, a group that historically has populated residential care units. With the rise of the welfare state—especially the establishment of general day care for children—homes for single mothers without social problems faded out of the landscape.

During the period of deinstitutionalization in the 1960s and the 1970s, public ownership of residential homes gradually came to dominate, with fewer then 10 percent of homes still run by voluntary (nonprofit) organizations. County and municipal authorities were the main owners of residential homes. This situation changed dramatically in the decades after the implementation of the Social Services Act, something that we discuss below.

The Idea of Treatment

The kinds of problems resulting in placement in residential care in Sweden have varied over time, as have the ways in which the practice of care has been carried out. During the demolishment of the old institutional structures in the 1960s and 1970s, a "new therapeutic" context was formulated. Small-scale dimensions and treatment concepts such as environmental therapy and psychodynamics became cornerstones in the "new" residential care. The principle of working with entire families rather than with the child alone grew in importance, as well as ideas of integrating residential care into the neighborhood and the society as a whole.

Placements in institutions today are in principle motivated by "social problems," such as antisocial behavior in teenagers, substance abuse by parents, or severe conflict between children and parents, and residential care is generally supposed to involve some kind of treatment. This is in contrast to foster care, which is supposed only to offer the chance of living in an "ordinary" family. The idea of treatment in a residential setting was articulated early on but has become stronger over time and can be seen as a historically rooted, fundamental premise of residential care today. "Modern" Swedish residential homes are often presented as centers for treatment and are described in that manner in the official discourse. The methods of treatment are, however, often unspecified.

Residential care is generally seen as an option for use when foster care is not possible—for instance, when the children's problems are so grave as to need some kind of treatment, when children cannot be mastered because of their deviant behavior, or when the authorities want to place siblings together. Some residential homes have the limited function of giving children somewhere to stay in acute situations or as an intermediate station while another placement is being arranged.

The Social Services Act: A Wide Definition of Residential Care

For more than two decades now, child welfare work has been carried out within the legal framework set out by the Social Services Act of 1982. This has been described as "an ambitious piece of legislation" emphasizing citizens' social rights, including children in care and their parents (Olsson Hort, 1997, p. 109). Here, the principle of deinstitutionalization is still valid on a rhetorical and ideological level. Residential care is intended as a last resort, used only in acute situations or to handle very severe cases. In other words, the proclaimed ambition is to minimize residential care for young people and to regard foster care as a superior solution whenever a child must be placed outside his or her own family. One crucial point in the legislation is the very wide definition of residential care. All establishments used by child welfare that accept children "for care and living" on a professional basis are defined as residential homes. This means that large foster homes, with more than three foster children, are also considered residential homes if the adults make a living out of taking care of children. Another important aspect of the legislation—with major consequences—is the opening of the door to private individuals to establish residential homes, something not possible under the old legislation.

Homes for Care and Living

In the decades since the Social Services Act was introduced, several new, privately operated residential homes have been established whereas public homes to a great extent have been closed down. Today, there are approximately 400 to 500 residential homes for children and youth (including specially approved homes) in operation, with roughly 3,500 to 4,000 beds (the Swedish population is about 9 million) (Sallnäs, 2000; SOU Reports of the Government Commissions, 2005). The major type of residential home is the so-called HVB home (the Swedish acronym for Homes for Care and Living). The HVB home label is applied to a variety of care facilities with very different modes of operation and serving a very wide range of children. Some HVB homes may seem to an outsider more like foster homes than residential homes, and a number of them have indeed been foster homes in the past but have been transformed into small residential homes now labeled "like a family" or "like a foster home" (Sallnäs, 2003). The Swedish landscape of out-of-home care visibly illustrates a wider trend apparent in several countries: the dissolution of the distinction between foster care and residential care. Some of the new private Swedish residential units would probably be viewed as "special foster care" or "treatment foster care" in other countries (Chamberlain, 1994, 1996; Hessle & Vinnerljung, 1999). So it is no longer relevant to talk about the two forms of care as a simple dichotomy. Berridge (1985) and Colton (1988) have suggested that foster and residential care should be viewed as intervals on a continuous scale. This is applicable to Swedish out-of-home care.

Homes for "the Worst Offenders"

At the very beginning, when the residential care system for children and youth was first established, special homes for "the worst" cases of antisocial behavior were set up; today, a small part of residential care still consists of specially approved homes for severely antisocial youth. A youth judiciary is part of the Swedish child welfare system, and young people exhibiting severe antisocial behavior (substance abuse, criminal acts, violence) constitute a substantial part of teenagers in care (Vinnerljung et al., 2001). Specially approved homes can be operated only by the state and have the legal authority of incarceration. They make up approximately 10 percent of ongoing compulsory placements (National Board of Health and Welfare, 2007).

Small-Size Care

The deinstitutionalization project concerned not only closing down homes. The issue of the size of the remaining residential homes was also important. Generally, residential homes in Sweden are small-scale. According to the latest known figures, three-quarters of all homes have fewer than 10 beds (Sallnäs, 2000). In fact, approximately one-fifth of homes have four or fewer beds, and nearly all of the smaller units are privately operated. A pattern can be identified, then, of very small, privately operated homes on the one hand, some of them former foster homes, and publicly run, bigger establishments on the other. Specially approved homes are generally relatively large-scale establishments but are often subdivided into smaller units.

Weak Methodology

Despite the overall treatment mandate, Swedish residential care is weak in expertise and has an unclear relationship between methods and goals. Theories and models to govern work are often unspecified or nonexistent. According to a national study, only half of the managers were able to specify a "known" theory or model (for example, psychodynamics or environmental therapy) by which work at the residential home should be carried out (Sallnäs, 2000). A connection emerged between the use of theory and professional qualifications. Staff in homes using theories or models had a higher educational level. Generally, the role of education for personnel working with young people is viewed with ambivalence; personality and private experiences are often seen as having at least as much importance as training. Consequently, the educational level among staff in Swedish residential care is low compared with the training of social workers in municipal social service units (where the placement decisions are made). As little as 25 percent of staff in residential care are qualified social workers or psychologists, and one-third of the homes totally lack personnel with such formal qualification. However, publicly run homes tend to have a higher level of education among staff than do private units.

Residential and Foster Care: Trends and Developments

For slightly over a decade—since the beginning of the 1990s—there has been some growth in the number of children placed in foster and residential care in Sweden (Lundström & Vinnerljung, 2001; Sallnäs, 2000). In the period 1999–2004, the

Table 3.1. Number of Children in Care on a Given Day in 2006, by Age Group, per Thousand of the Population

Age Group	Number of Children in Care per Thousand
0–6	2.6
7–12	5.2
13–17	11.2
18–20	6.2
0–20	6.2

Source: National Board of Health and Welfare (2007), p. 54.

increase was between 17 and 22 percent, depending on how it was counted (SOU Reports of the Government Commissions 2005). This rising number of placements is an anomaly in a long trend of stable or decreasing entry into care.

On average, just under 15,000 Swedish children and youth were placed in some form of out-of-home care on a given day in 2006 (National Board of Health and Welfare, 2007). Put another way, that is 6.2 children per thousand aged 0–20 years.

As shown in Table 3.1, age is an important factor in prevalence of placement in out-of-home care. The highest risk of being in care was found in the age group 13–17, whereas younger children are far less likely to live in out-of-home care. These figures reflect Swedish child welfare as a whole. For example, teenagers constitute approximately 50 percent of new cases (Lundström & Vinnerljung, 2001). In other words, child welfare in the Swedish context to a large extent is occupied with caring for problematic teenagers.

A Significant and Expanding Role for Residential Care

As shown in Table 3.2, foster care is the dominant kind of care in ongoing placements, residential care constituting 23 percent, with boys experiencing more frequent placement.

When initiated placements are measured, residential care grows in importance and a change over time becomes apparent. Residential care constituted 29 percent of initiated placements at the beginning of the 1980s but as much as 45 percent by

Table 3.2. Number of Children in Care on a Given Day in 2006

Type of Care	Boys	Girls	All
HVB homes	1,570	1,253	2,823
Specially approved homes	380	219	599
Total in residential care	1,950	1,472	3,422
Foster care	5,594	5,381	10,975
Other	286	197	483
Total in out-of-home care	7,830	7050	14,880
Percentage of children in residential care	25	21	23

Source: National Board of Health and Welfare (2007), p. 63.

the mid-1990s (Sallnäs, 2000); that is, residential care has taken "territory" from foster care. In the period 1999–2004, the number of residential placements begun each year increased by about 600 boys and girls (SOU Reports of the Government Commissions, 2005). There has also been a small increase in new placements for girls in specially approved homes. The overall picture is that residential care has a significant and growing role in the landscape of out-of-home care, which is at least partly a development at the expense of foster care.

In a closer analysis it becomes obvious that the expansion in residential placements primarily can be explained by a rise in teenage placements (13–17 years). This is in line with the fact that a majority of homes in operation today accept primarily teenagers, and that problems *among* teenagers and problems *with* teenagers (their behavior and life situations) to a growing extent are handled by placement in residential care. Thus, the traditional predominance of teenagers in Swedish residential care, and in child welfare in general, has become even stronger.

Some small children are still placed in institutional care. Of those in the age group 0–12 in ongoing out-of-home care, 21 percent were in privately operated residential homes and 13 percent in public homes (Swedish National Audit Office, 2002). There is a lack of systematic knowledge about background factors, but it is reasonable to assume that when small children are placed in residential care it is either a matter of short-term placements (a few days) or joint placements with a parent or other relative. Formerly traditional children's homes have been transformed into establishments taking on small children accompanied by parents and sometimes siblings. The basic idea is to avoid separating small children from their known caregivers and to use a short spell of residential care (about one month) to evaluate the status of the child and how parents cope with their parental role (assessment homes). Nine out of 10 residential homes for children up to 12 years of age also accept parents and offer these kinds of assessments (Sallnäs, 2000). The small numbers, by Swedish standards, of young children placed in long-term residential care are most probably cared for in some of the above mentioned privately run homes labeled "like a foster home" (Sallnäs, 2003). The ideology is strong—backed by known praxis—that small children should not be placed in traditional residential homes with staff coming and going on a rotation schedule. If young children must be placed in residential care, there are in principle two ways of addressing the situation: one is to provide care for both the child and his or her parents, and another is to make placements in small residential units replicating a family.

There are substantial differences in how municipalities use out-of-home care. Shares of young people in care vary as well. Use of residential care can differ from none at all to roughly 80 percent of the total number of days in care (foster and residential care taken together) (Sallnäs, 2005a). Some municipalities are "frequent users" of residential care and others are "infrequent users," the latter often small, nonurban communities. A placement in a residential home is on average far more expensive per day (SEK 3500 ≈ 376 euros) than placement in a foster home (SEK 870 ≈ 94 euros) (SOU Reports of the Government Commissions, 2005). A national study shows that economic considerations are a contributing factor in the use of residential care in contrast to foster care when other factors are controlled for (Sallnäs, 2005a). On the other hand, child and youth care and placements in out-of-home care have been a protected zone and given high priority even in economically difficult times (Palme et al., 2002; Sallnäs, 2000). It is noteworthy that despite the high costs of residential care, the noted rise in placements took place during the 1990s, a notoriously difficult economic period for Sweden.

Lengths of Care and Background to Placements

The overall picture is that most placements in out-of-home care in Sweden are short term. This is in line with the basic principles that placements should be temporary solutions and that children should return to their biological families as soon as circumstances allow. There are, however, significant differences between age groups. National statistics show that the median length of a placement is seven months. In optional care it is four months whereas in compulsory care it is 18 months. When children are placed in both optional and compulsory care the median length of placement is 42 months (National Board of Health and Welfare, 2007). Detailed analysis of terminated placements during one year (special approved homes excluded) has shown that about half of the placements of children in the age group 13–20 years lasted more than one year. For children aged 0–12 years, placements lasted that long in only 23 percent of the cases (National Board of Health and Welfare 2006a). It should be noted, however, that even if every single placement is of short duration, some children experience multiple placements. A relatively small group consists of children who repeatedly move back and forth from birth home into care or between placements within the care system, perhaps because of a breakdown in care (see Hessle & Vinnerljung, 1999). In Sweden, as in many other countries, breakdown in both foster and residential care is a problem (Sallnäs et al., 2004; Vinnerljung et al., 2001) as is recidivism (Vinnerljung et al., 2004). There are also children who spend more or less their entire childhood and adolescence in out-of-home care. These children are almost exclusively in foster care but might also have experienced short periods in temporary residential care (Vinnerljung et al., 2005).

Statistics on the length of placements unfortunately do not differentiate between foster and residential care, so it is impossible to give details about how different groups of children move in and out of residential homes or how long they stay. According to available figures, the mean time in privately operated residential homes (constituting the great majority of beds) was 8.3 months (SOU Reports of the Government Commissions, 2005). Although placements in homes taking children in acute situations or for assessment are meant to last only for weeks or maybe a few months, another type of residential home working with older children in a clearer treatment context operates with treatment programs of one or two years' duration.

The specific backgrounds motivating placement of children in care are nevertheless poorly studied in Sweden. Official statistics give no information that can be used to analyze the detailed circumstances that lead to out-of-home care or tell what factors determine the choice between residential and foster care, a central aspect of the process shaping the landscape of out-of-home care.

Yet some things we do know. Swedish child welfare is characterized by an emphasis on voluntary measures and on partnership with parents, reflected in the statistic that 70 percent of children in ongoing care are placed with the formal consent of their parents. Only 30 percent are in compulsory care (National Board of Health and Welfare, 2007). Approximately the same magnitude, three out of four (in compulsory care), are placed because of the conditions in their homes and one in four because of their own behavior. A general pattern is that placements of older children are more often motivated by their own behavior (National Board of Health and Welfare, 2003), and boys are overrepresented among these (Vinnerljung et al., 2001). Children of 0–12 years of age are placed mainly because of deficiencies in the home environment (National Board of Health and Welfare, 2003). Children of immigrant background (at least one parent born outside Sweden) are strongly overrepresented in the out-of-home care population, especially teenagers. The risk of ending up in out-of-home care is 2–2.5 times higher for a teenager with one parent born outside of Sweden than for teenagers with both parents born in Sweden, and 3–3.5 times higher if both parents were born outside the country (Lundström & Vinnerljung, 2001). The overrepresentation of young people of immigrant background is especially strong in specially approved homes—that is, the "hardest" and most restrictive type of care. However, a recent study has shown that the overrepresentation of young people with immigrant background in out-of-home care will be significantly altered when adjustments are made for socioeconomic background. In such an analysis it is even a protective factor to have a mother born outside Europe (National Board of Health and Welfare, 2006b).

Why the Increase in Residential Care?

How can we explain the change toward more frequent use of residential placements (using the broad Swedish definition that includes some former foster homes)? This is not an easy question to answer, but some possible explanations can be identified. First, it is probable that increasing difficulties in recruiting foster parents have more or less forced social service caseworkers to use residential homes. Several reports have pointed out the difficulty of finding good foster homes, especially for teenagers, the group dominating out-of-home care. Quite a few of the young persons placed in care have problems of a kind that "ordinary" foster parents can hardly master. Second, caseworkers may have become less resistant to residential care as a "solution" when children have to be placed out of their homes. Residential care has been heavily criticized, but it is obvious that the alternative, foster care, can also be problematic. Quite a few placements in foster homes recruited by authorities (in contrast to kinship homes) end in breakdown. Among teenagers with both antisocial behavior and psychiatric problems, the frequency of breakdown in foster homes recruited by authorities is as high as roughly 80 percent (Sallnäs et al., 2004;

Vinnerljung et al., 2001). Third, residential care has increasingly become a "market" in which the supply of care alternatives may have an impact on demand. The private actors dominating residential care work with active marketing. During some periods, the expansion in this field has been extreme. The conditions for starting new homes have been favorable, and authorities have put up few discriminatory restrictions. Small residential homes like those in Sweden can be seen as "simple organizations," relatively easy to open as well as to shut down (Sallnäs, 2000, 2005b). A fourth possible explanation is that the share of residential care has increased because problems among youth have escalated. There are, however, no substantial facts to support this idea (Lundström & Vinnerljung, 2001). A fifth possible explanation might be a hardening attitude in society at large. There has been a shift in the way teenagers with "problems" are viewed, and changes in the legislation now put emphasis on "young offenders" rather than "children in need" (see Goldson, 2000). This change might have influenced child welfare to be more "activist" and to direct more young people to institutions.

What Followed in the Footsteps of Privatization?

Privatization in the field of residential care has been fast and far-reaching compared with such areas of the welfare state as health care, education, and child day care (Trydegård, 2001). One motive for allowing private actors into a field that for decades had been operated mainly by public authorities was the idea of promoting diversity and new and innovative ways of working with children and youth in need of care (Prop. 1979/80, 1; see also Støkken, 2004, on a similar situation in Norway); and indeed, new types of homes have emerged, entailing a great variety of methods and treatment programs. There is, however, an almost total lack of evaluation and follow-up of consumer experiences, so it is unknown whether the changes taking place have been in favor of the children placed in care. The entrance of private actors into the field has taken place over time and is roughly parallel with the increase in placements in residential care. However, we have no evidence to support this as a causal relation; so far we can state only the contemporaneousness of the changes occurring.

All in all, the field of residential care has undergone a major restructuring, leaving its mark on the wider landscape of out-of-home care. Part of foster care has been included in the residential sector, professional foster homes having turned into residential homes, and some tendencies toward the professionalization of "regular" foster care have also been indicated (Sallnäs, 2003). Moreover, costs have been affected. There is now a broader spectrum of charges reflected in residential homes: more expensive care with a higher density of personnel on the one hand, and less expensive homes with fewer personnel on the other (Lindqvist, 2007; Sallnäs, 2005b). A major problem is that it is almost impossible to relate the cost of placements in residential homes to the content and quality of care in any other sense than density of personnel, an important factor but hardly sufficient to measure quality of care. The large number of private institutions has also meant a growing deprofessionalization because private homes in general have a lower level of education among staff than publicly run homes. Levels of education are unevenly distributed, but it is among the privately run homes that staff with a total lack of education are found. The far-reaching and rapid privatization of the field has also raised the issue of control and supervision. No sufficient system of control was set up when the great number of private actors began to enter the field, and little attention was paid to international research results pointing to the risk for children in care to be subjected to peer group or staff abuse (Barter et al., 2004; Colton, 2002; Levy and Kahan, 1991). Despite a massive entrance of new actors and other major changes, the field of residential care has been permitted to operate on its own terms and without an effective system of control and restrictions. It is striking that despite the Swedish tradition of strict state control of the welfare system, no official register exists of the privately run residential homes in operation.

Future Directions and Potential Concerns

There is an obvious duality in how residential care has been understood. Historically, residential institutions have been regarded as both the problem and the solution for certain groups of children. A strong belief in what can be achieved through residential care has been present, but there is also criticism of the more unfortunate sides of the institutional environment and its damaging effects, especially on young children. Historical descriptions of residential institutions in the past reveal a dreadful interior. In the official ideology, children in residential care (as well as in foster care) should be brought into "a good home," but the reality has often been something quite different.

This duality is still apparent today. Major criticisms have been formulated, more or less constantly, against residential care. Even if Swedish residential care has been spared such crises as the Pindown scandal in Great Britain (Levy & Kahan, 1991), it has been the subject of a very critical professional and media discussion. Repeatedly, government control and supervision have been pointed out as far too weak. Authorities have too little and too random knowledge about what is actually going on in residential homes and about the consequences of care and its long-term results, and there does not appear to be enough concern for the potential harm that peer groups or staff can do to children in residential settings. The criticism, however—as has been shown— has not affected the volume of this kind of service. The development is rather in the opposite direction.

Moreover, the discussion about knowledge- and evidence-based social work is high on the agenda in residential care. An international influence is becoming apparent, and programs and ways of working from other countries are now being implemented in at least some residential homes in Sweden. We do not know exactly where this is going to lead but certainly there will be more emphasis on professional skills and methods to be used in the work and an increased optimism about what can be achieved even in the residential setting.

Swedish residential care of today is poorly evaluated. Despite the overall treatment mandate there are basically no effect studies and few attempts to make systematic follow-ups of children in residential homes or to compare their "care carriers" and trajectories to those of children in foster care. However, research has been done on the prevalence of breakdown, indicating major problems in "service outcome" for residential care as well as for some types of foster care (Sallnäs et al., 2004; Vinnerljung et al., 2001. Prevalence of breakdown has been used as a global measure of how well care is functioning for children and youth and how satisfied they are with their placements (Redding et al., 2000).

Further, several cohort studies show that persons who have been in care (foster or residential home) during childhood generally have a difficult situation in several areas of life as adults compared to the normal population: low level of education, frequent psychiatric problems, suicide attempts, teenage parenthood, and a high prevalence of deceased mother and/or father in early adulthood (for an overview, see National Board of Health and Welfare, 2006b). Results from a national, representative follow-up study of young people placed in care during their teens shows that if "doing well" in adult life is defined as absence of seriously negative outcomes (being alive at age 25, not having been to prison or received a probation sentence at age 20–24, not having been hospitalized for a mental-health problem at age 20–24, and not having become a teenage parent), then approximately 35 percent of boys who were placed in HVB homes because of behavioral problems did well. Among girls the corresponding figure was 50–55 percent. Having been placed in special approved homes was even more strongly associated with negative outcome; only 14 percent of the boys and one-third of the girls did well. Young people who were originally placed in care for other reasons than behavioral problems did better but still far worse in comparison with peers who had not been in such care. The overall picture is a dismal long-term outcome for adolescents placed in care for behavioral problems, and especially for those placed in special approved homes. Outcomes in early adulthood for the other group (young people placed for reasons other than behavioral problems) was considerably better in all types of care (Sallnäs and Vinnerljung, forthcoming; see also Vinnerljung and Sallnäs, 2008).

Despite obvious problems of specifying content of care, weakness of detailed knowledge about consequences of care, and the largely negative substance of what is known, social services will most probably, maybe even to a growing extent, continue to place children in residential homes. Nothing indicates that community care has the ability to offer enough services or that foster care can reverse the trend of decrease in this type of provision and recover lost territory. Several proclamations about more use of noninstitutional measures have been made by national and local authorities; however, they seem to have very limited practical impact. It will probably not get easier to recruit good foster homes, and programs for support and supervision in the home environment are still few and not very well worked out. In addition, residential care has become a market with potential for high profits and few impediments to starting up business. Gate-keeping has been weak, both externally and by professionals. There will undoubtedly be a position for residential care in the future, whether proclaimed by authorities or not. The development and formatting of the landscape of out-of-home care has taken place in the last decades without strong intervention from authorities. The growing territory of residential care, the major privatization, the increase in placements, the low level of education among staff, and the lack of evaluations and knowledge of content of care are not in line with official rhetoric. When comparing official texts and legislation with what is known about actual developments, it becomes apparent that there is a wide discrepancy between the rhetorical level—what is said about residential care and how it should be—and how it functions on the level of praxis, and there is nothing to indicate any incipient change in this.

REFERENCES

Barter, C., Renolds, E., Berridge, D., & Cawson, P. (2004). *Peer violence in children's residential homes*. London: Palgrave MacMillan.

Bergmark, Å., & Lundström, T. (2005). En sak i taget? Om specialisering inom socialtjänstens individ- och familjeomsorg [Piece by piece? On specialization within personnel social service]. *Socialvetenskaplig tidskrift, 12*, 125–148.

Berridge, D. (1985). *Children's homes*. Oxford: Basil Blackwell.

Chamberlain, P. (1994). *Family connections: A treatment foster care model for adolescents with delinquency*. Eugene: Castalia.

Chamberlain, P. (1996). Intensified foster care: Multi-level treatment for adolescents with conduct disorders in out-of-home care. In E. Hibbs and P. Jensen (Eds.), *Psychological treatments for child and adolescent disorders*. Washington: American Psychological Association.

Colton, M. (1988). *Dimensions of substitute child care: A comparative study of foster and residential care practice*. Avebury: Aldershot.

Colton, M. (2002).Factors associated with abuse in residential child care institutions. *Children and Society, 16*, 33–44.

Gilbert, N. (1997). Introduction. In N. Gilbert (Ed.), *Combating child abuse. International perspectives and trends*. Oxford: Oxford University Press.

Goldson, B. (2000). "Children in need" or "young offenders"? Hardening ideology, organizational change and new challenges for social work with children in trouble. *Child and Family Social Work, 5*(3)255–265.

Hessle, S., & Vinnerljung, B. (1999). *Child welfare in Sweden—an overview*. Stockholm: Department of Social Work, Stockholm University.

Levy, A., and Kahan, B. (1991). *The Pindown experience and the protection of children: The report of the Staffordshire Child Care Inquiry, 1990*. Stafford: Staffordshire County Council.

Lindqvist, E. (2007). *Essays on privatizations, identity and political polarization*. Stockholm: School of Economics.

Lundström, T. (1993). *Tvångsomhändertagande av barn: en studie av lagarna, professionerna och praktiken under 1900-talet* [Compulsory care of children: A study of legislation, professions and practice in the 20th century]. Stockholm: Department of Social Work, Stockholm University.

Lundström, T. (2000). Om kommunernas sociala barnavård [Child welfare in the municipal social services]. In M. Szebehely (Ed.), *Välfärd, vård och omsorg* [Welfare and care] SOU *2000,38*. Stockholm: Reports of the Government Commissions.

Lundström, T., & Vinnerljung, B. (2001). Omhändertagande av barn under 1990-talet [Out-of-home care for children in the 1990s]. In *Välfärdstjänster i omvandling SOU 2001,52* [Welfare services in transition Reports of the Government Commissions *2001,52]* Stockholm.

National Board of Health and Welfare. (2003). *Socialtjänsten i Sverige: en översikt* [Social services in Sweden: An overview 2003]. Stockholm: Author

National Board of Health and Welfare. (2006a). *Individ- och familjeomsorg, Lägesrapport 2005* [Social welfare services. A report on the situation 2005]. Stockholm: Author.

National Board of Health and Welfare. (2006b). *Social rapport* [A social report]. Stockholm: Author.

National Board of Health and Welfare. (2007). *Statistik socialtjänst, barn och unga - insatser år 2006* [Statistics social welfare, children and young persons subjected to measures 2006]. Stockholm: Author.

Ödman, P-J. (1991). Liv och pedagogik vid Stora Barnhuset på 1760-talet. Idyll eller inferno? [Life and pedagogy at the children´s home in the 1760s. Idyllic spot or inferno?] In K. Ohrlander (Ed.), *Barnhus: om rättningsanstalter, barnhem, idiotanstalter, uppfostrings-sanstalter i Norden från 1700-talet till våra dagar* [Children´s homes in the Nordic countries from the 1760s until today]. Stockholm: Allmänna Barnhuset.

Olsson Hort, S. E. (1997). Toward a deresidualization of Swedish child welfare policy and practice. In N. Gilbert (Ed.), *Combating child abuse. International perspectives and trends.* Oxford: Oxford University Press.

Palme, J., et al. (2002). *Welfare in Sweden: The balance sheet for the 1990s.* Translation of Part 1 of the final report of the Welfare Commission, Reports of the Government Commissions 2001,79. Stockholm.

Proposition 1979/80:1. *Om socialtjänstlagen* [Proposition on Social Services Act]. Stockholm.

Redding, R., Fried, C., and Britner, P. (2000). Predictors of placement outcomes in treatment foster care: Implications for foster parent selection and service delivery. *Journal of Child and Family Studies, 9*(4), 425–447.

Sallnäs, M. (2000). *Barnavårdens institutioner: framväxt, ideologi och struktur* [Residential care in child welfare—development, ideology and structure]. Stockholm: Department of Social Work, Stockholm University.

Sallnäs, M. (2003). *Som en familj? Om små privata institutioner för barn och ungdomar* [As a family? On small privately run residential homes for children and youth]. *Socionomens forskningssupplement, 15,* 2–16.

Sallnäs, M. (2005a). *Institution eller familjehem? Om kommunal variation och vad den hänger samman med.* [Residential care or family foster care? On municipal variation and what it is related to]. *Socionomens forskningssupplement, 18,* 15–28.

Sallnäs, M. (2005b). *Vårdmarknad med svårigheter—om privata aktörer inom institutions-vården för barn och ungdomar* [A care market with problems. On private entrepreneurs in residential care for children and youth]. *Socialvetenskaplig Tidskrift, 12*(2–3), 226–245.

Sallnäs, M., and Vinnerljung, B. (forthcoming). Samhällsvårdade tonåringar som vuxna—en uppföljande registerstudie [Young adults who have been in out-of home care during their teens—a follow-up study]. *Socionomen.*

Sallnäs, M., Vinnerljung, B., and Kyhle Westermark, P. (2004). Breakdown of teenage placements in Swedish foster and residential care. *Child and Family Social Work, 9,* 141–152.

SFS 2001:453 *Socialtjänstlagen* [The Social Services Act]. Stockholm.

SOU Reports of the Government Commissions 2005,81. *Källan till en chans: Nationell handlingsplan för den sociala barn- och ungdomsvården* [A source for prospects. A national plan for action for child welfare services]. Stockholm: Author.

Støkken, A. M. (2004). En velferdshybrid i endring: Private barneverninstitusjoners samspill med det offentlige. [A welfare hybrid in change. The interplay between privately operated residential homes and the public sector]. *Tidsskrift for Velferdsforskning, 7*(3), 118–130.

Sunesson, S. (1990). Familjehemsvården, en del av individ- och familjeomsorgen i socialtjänsten [Foster family care, a part of the social services administration]. I Socialstyrelsen *Sju perspektiv på barns och ungdomars levnadsförhållanden* [Seven perspectives on the living conditions of children and youth]. Stockholm: National Board of Health and Welfare.

Swedish National Audit Office [Riksrevisonsverket]. (2002). *Tillsyn av behandlingshem för barn och ungdomar* [Supervision of residential homes for children and youth]. Author.

Trydegård, G-B. (2001). *Välfärdstjänster till salu – privatisering och alternativa driftformer under 1990-talet* [Welfare services for sale—privatization and nonprofit organizations during the 1990s]. In SOU Reports of the Government Commissions 2001, 52. Stockholm.

Vinnerljung, B. (1996). *Fosterbarn som vuxna* [Foster children as adults]. Lund: Arkiv.

Vinnerljung, B., Öman, M., and Gunnarsson, T. (2004). Återplacering av barn i dygnsvård(I): - hur vanligt är det? [Replacement of children in out-of-home care (I)]: How common is it?] *Socialvetenskaplig Tidskrift, 11,* 54–75.

Vinnerljung, B., Öman, M., and Gunnarsson, T. (2005). Educational attainments of former child welfare clients—a Swedish national cohort study. *International Journal of Social Work, 14,* 265–276.

Vinnerljung, B., & Sallnäs, M. (2006). *Estimation of the number of children in residential care 1950–1980.* Working paper.

Vinnerljung, B., & Sallnäs, M. (2008). Into adulthood: A follow-up study of 718 young people who were placed in out-of-home care during their teens. *Child and Family Social Work, 13*(2) 144–155.

Vinnerljung, B., Sallnäs, M., and Kyhle Westermark, P. (2001). *Sammanbrott vid placeringar av tonåringar i dygsnvård* [Breakdown in teenage placements in out-of-home care]. Stockholm: CUS/National Board of Health and Welfare.

Wiklund, S. (2006). *Den kommunala barnavården—om anmälningar, organisation och utfall* [Municipal child welfare in Sweden. On referrals, organization and outcome]. Stockholm: Department of Social Work, Stockholm University.

4

Residential Care for Children in Romania

A Model for Child Protection Reform in Central and Eastern Europe

OVIDIU GAVRILOVICI

Traditionally, Romania's child welfare policies were based on residential care. A kingdom until 1945 at the end of the Second World War and a component of the communist block (member of Warsaw Pact) for over 40 years, Romania regained its democratic status in December 1989. In Romania, as in other countries of Central and Eastern Europe and former Soviet Union countries, a legacy of the command economies and of communist social control was "the reliance on residential institutions for the care of children, the elderly, and people with disabilities. As a result, there are almost no community-based alternatives to care for large and growing numbers of vulnerable individuals" (Tobis, 2000, p. vii). Recently, a coherent and inclusive system of child protection began to develop.

Changes in the child protection system were slow in the first 10 years following the regime change after December 1989. Even though the United Nations Convention on the Rights of the Child was ratified in 1990, the reforms advocated by this convention did not appear in Romania until seven years later. Some of the factors that led to this long delay are intuitive, coming from the legacy of communism; to name only a few: claims of over 100,000 children in institutions, a highly centralized residential care system with authority divided among four ministries, the lack of specialized human resources, and no community social work.

From a child's perspective, the changes have come painfully slow. From a policy perspective, the changes can be seen as an exponential expansion within a very short period of actual history. The magnitude of the burden of residential care—the sole protective policy in existence at the beginning of the new democratic Romania—and the waves of systematic restructuring may make it difficult to compare and contrast Romania with other countries in terms of residential care systems. To do so, it is important to weigh carefully the historical and cultural dimensions of Romania's situation and bring into perspective the interaction between the size of the problem and the time span for changes.

A Statistical Description of Child Protective Services in Romania (as of June 30, 2005)

Romania's child protection system reforms were enacted in two waves: June 1997 and January 2005. The next paragraphs describe the situation of child protection six months after the second and most important reform.

At the end of June 2005, child protective services cared for 2.2 percent of over 5 million children and youth under the age of 18 in Romania. A total of 18,560 children were in protective services while they were maintained in their biological families; of those, more than 88 percent received family preservation services, and almost 12 percent of the beneficiaries received prenatal care services (prevention of child abandonment) (NAPCR, 2008b).

Table 4.1 shows the distribution of children in child protective services in Romania in June 2005. At that time, there were 80,287 children residing in substitutive families (more than 60 percent) or institutions (almost 40 percent).

The average cost per child per month in professional foster care or professional maternal assistance during the second trimester of 2005 was approximately $243U.S.[1] The cost per child per month in placement centers was $287U.S. in June 2005. The average cost per child per month in day centers was $170U.S., and the cost per beneficiary per month in mother and baby centers was $392U.S. Even if these real expenditures are more conservative than previous estimates, it is significantly cheaper to care for children in alternative services than to institutionalize them.

Table 4.1. Children Protected in Substitute Families or in Institutions (June 30, 2005)

Children Protected in Substitute Families (61.26%)	*49,180*
• professional foster caregiver (public) (20.63%)	16,563
• professional foster caregiver (private) (0.38%)	305
• extended family (32.24%)	25,888
• other persons / families (7.31%)	5,865
• entrusted for adoption (0.70%)	559
Children Protected in Residential Care (38.74%)	*31,107*
• public placement centers (32.14%)	25,808
• private placement centers (6.60%)	5,299

Source: NAPCR 2008b.

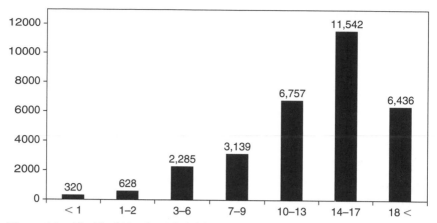

Figure 4.1.   The Total Number of Children by Age Group in Placement Centers (June 2005)

Of the 1,108 children and youth deinstitutionalized from public and private institutions in June 2005, 41 percent were reintegrated into their biological families, one child (0.09 percent) was adopted internationally, 44 percent reached the age limit of 18 (or 26 years, for those who are in schools or universities until that age), and 15.25 percent exited the institutions for other causes. There were 104 children adopted nationwide in June 2005 (NAPCR, 2008b).

Almost 80 percent of all institutionalized children are 10 years of age or older. These statistics indicate that with the development of a more responsive monitoring system and of new alternative services to institutionalization, child protection in Romania has started to curb the presence of babies and small children in placement centers (see Table 4.1). With the implementation of the new Children's Law in January 2005, there should be no more children under 2 years of age in these centers since babies under 2 years should be placed in emergency foster care.

The total number of staff in the child protection field in Romania in June 2005 was 40,851 persons: specialized public service for child protection staff (n = 5,311, 13%), placement centers staff (16,863; 41.28%), professional caregivers/foster carers (13,213; 32.34%), and other services staff (5,464, 13.38%). Within the public placement centers, the ratio of children to adults was 1.5 whereas the ratio of children to foster parents or professional maternal assistants was 1.2.

At the end of June 2005, there were 572 public services options aside from institutionalization, almost a linear increase between 2000 and 2003, and reaching a plateau since 2003 (see Fig. 4.2). More than a third of the services represent day care centers or services for children from families in difficulty and for handicapped children (NAPCR, 2008b).

There were 1,407 residential centers for children as of June 30, 2005. More than 73 percent of these centers were public: 888 residential centers were transferred from a central administration entity to the National Authority for Child Protection and Adoption (NACPA) during 1997–1998 and another 108 centers were transferred

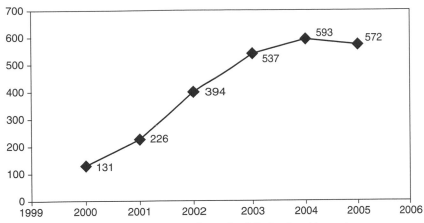

Figure 4.2. The Evolution of the Number of Public Services Alternatives to Institutionalization

from the Ministry of Education, 19 were transferred from the Ministry of Health, and 12 were transferred from the Secretariat of State for Handicapped Persons. The public residential system included 375 apartments, 303 family-type homes, 123 modulated or restructured large institutions, and 226 classic placement centers. Three-quarters of all residential care centers, public and private, were in urban areas. More than 75 percent of the care centers in urban areas were public, as were 61 percent of the ones in rural areas.

An important component of the child protection system of today's Romania is the system of care for children with disabilities or medical conditions that require long-term medical care. Romanian law classifies four degrees of severity of disabilities. There were 68,805 certified disabled children who were monitored by specialized services for child protection from public and private centers, professional foster caregivers, extended families, and biological families as of December 31, 2004. The law supports a disabled person's right to a personal assistant, employed by the Mayor Houses, for certain degrees of handicap, and in 2004 there were 26,341 such assistants (some of whom are family members). Almost 95 percent of the monitored children have a personalized plan of medical and social services. More than 7,000 children benefit from alternative services (day care services, treatment centers, etc.) from public agencies, and more than 1,300 children receive such services from nongovernmental organizations (NGOs). Table 4.2 shows the distribution of handicapped children in public and private residential care.

Because all children in residential care are offered free access to public education (mass general education and special education), children with disabilities are offered inclusive education according to their various degrees of handicap. A total of 5,344 children certified as having a handicap degree were integrated in mass education, 11,929 were in special education (segregated schools), and 871 were studying at home under a visiting teaching scheme operated by County School Inspectorates under the Ministry of Education in 2005 (NAPCR, 2008b).

Table 4.2. Care Type for Children Certified as Having a Handicap Degree (December 31, 2004)

Children in public placement centers (66.2%)	5,909
Children in private placement centers (6.8%)	604
Children with professional foster caregiver (public) (26.3%)	2,344
Children with professional foster caregiver (private) (0.8%)	67

Another group with special needs was the children and adolescents with HIV/AIDS. There were 3,390 HIV-infected children in Romania's child protection system as of March 31, 2005. Out of this total number, 55 resided with professional foster caregivers, 244 resided in public placement centers, 290 were hosted in private placement centers, 121 were placed or entrusted to other families or to the extended family, and 2,680 were living with their biological families.

Finally, a major "feeder" of the institutional care field was child abandonment in hospital units: 4,614 children were abandoned during 2004: 61 percent in maternity units and 39 percent in pediatric units. A total of 940 children were placed with substitute families, 768 children were placed in public and private placement centers, and the remainder was reintegrated with their families using various support services. This diversity of options for responding to children and families in need was not conceivable until recently; it is outlined later in the chapter.

The distribution of residential centers for children and the number of institutionalized children vary by county. The level of development of the region was a factor, as were the size of the major city (municipality) or the presence of higher education institutions; some counties had only a few hundred children in residential care during 2000, whereas Iasi County, for example, had over 4,000 children in its institutions.

The actual situation of residential care has its roots deep in Romania's history. The church had a major role in setting up the first shelters for the poor, the disabled, and the abandoned. The first historical documents mentioning institutional care for children in need are dated before and during the sixteenth century in Walachia and later in Moldova. At the very beginning of the twentieth century, private initiatives were begun by the aristocracy and were maintained by local administrations. The first half of the twentieth century saw a rapid modernization; occurring during this period were the first reports on child abandonment and on child protective services, the development of the first university-level education in social work (1929), the first set of coherent social work laws, and the first public administration structures that specialized in child welfare issues.

The history of social work education and associated professions in Romania is an important factor. In 1952, the Romanian Communist Party closed the university-level Social Work School, which had been founded in 1929, transforming it into a vocational-level school until 1969 when social work education in Romania completely stopped. No social work training was available until 1990. At the end of the communist regime, there were at most 200 trained social workers in all of central and county social administration, the only types of social work existing until

1990 (Manoiu and Epureanu, 1996). There was no need for social work as communist party cells were developed in every organization at the national, county, and local levels, and there were only public organizations in Romania (with the exception of associations such as the Red Cross, for example). The communist party cells doubled every management structure and were linked in a vertical hierarchy, converging at the top to Nicolae Ceausescu, the Communist Party Secretary General (1965–1989).

The situation was similar with psychologists and special educators, two associated professions. Higher education in psychology and special education was forbidden in Romania for almost 15 years, until 1990. As a result, there were only approximately 1,300 licensed psychologists working in various state institutions at the beginning of 1990 in a climate where there were no professional associations.[2] With such a disastrous human resources policy and disregard—or rather, ideologically distorted regard—for social problems, the communist regime failed to support its citizens. This lack of support became critical during the crisis of the 1980s—a time when hardships of day by day living were coupled with the hopelessness and grim lives lived by most Romanians in a bankrupted economy—and undoubtedly contributed to the December 1989 revolution that toppled the Ceausescu regime.

The Failure of Child Protection During Communism (1947–1989)

During the communist second half of the twentieth century, there was a virtual absence of community social services, and institutionalization was regarded as the simplest and only solution for social problems. As the Anti-Poverty and Social Inclusion Promotion Commission stated in 2002, "the essence of the socialist state policy was in fact to shut off in institutions the offspring of the poorest population categories" (APSICPC, 2002, p. 17). In Romania, as in other communist countries, the majority of the residents in child protection institutions were "social orphans": children whose parents were unable to care for them because of economic or social factors (Tobis, 2000, p. 8).

In order for the birthrate to increase, Law 770/1966 was introduced prohibiting abortions unless the pregnancy endangered the life of the woman. As an immediate result of this law, the birthrate increased, and women were encouraged to bear children. "In 1966–67, Romania experienced the greatest fertility increase [recorded] in a large population. It rose 100 percent in one year (from 1.80 to 3.66)" (Teitelbaum and Winter, 1998, p. 327).

There is an increasing agreement that among the factors that contributed to child abandonment by families before 1989 were the extreme economic crisis of the 1980s, the demographic policies of banning abortion and family planning, and their immediate result, the increased pressure on already poor families with many children (Stephenson et al., 1997). In time, a belief that children were better off in state-run residential care units than in their families justified and explained such behaviors.

The First Seven Years (1990–1997): Building Blocks for Child Protection Reform

The socioeconomic changes during the democratization of Romania after 1990 caused an immediate increase in overall poverty (from 7 percent in 1989 to 22–39 percent in 1994); between 1997 and 1999, a second period of exponential poverty increase doubled the extreme poverty and increased the overall poverty rate to 42 percent (APSIPC, 2002).

Romania was one of the first countries to sign and ratify the United Nations Convention on the Rights of the Child (UNCRC) on November 20, 1989. This convention came into force in Romania in September 1990 with Law 18/1990. The convention attributes primary responsibility to the parents for the upbringing and the development of the child. Even so, in the new general legislative framework, institutionalization of children has been Romania's primary alternative for children not living with their biological families both during the communist regime and under the new democracy in the 1990s. The second alternative to institutionalization was adoption, either national or international. At the beginning of the 1990s, Romania became a major international adoption country.

Starting in 1993, the UNCRC required National Plans of Action from ratifying countries. One of Romania's first coordinating mechanisms at the national level was the 1993 National Committee for Child Protection (CNPC). In October 1995, Government Decision 972/1995 approved the National Plan of Action (NPA), which described a "coherent, efficient and complementary strategy on how the UN Convention of the Rights of the Child should be implemented in Romania" (National Authority for the Protection of Children's Rights [NAPCR], 2000). Despite the quality of the strategy, the child protection system was still far short of fulfilling the needs of children and families.

Until 1997, different national ministries supervised the activity of institutions. Institutions designed to host and care for children 0–3 years old were administered by the Ministry of Health. Most of the institutions for children 7–18 (if children had no special needs, health, or mental health problems) were run by the Ministry of Education. In 1996, the Ministry of Education erased the distinction between children's homes for school-age children and children's homes for preschool children. The Inspectorate of State for the Handicapped supervised the activity of institutions for children with special needs and mental health problems.

Even if child protection policy evolved slowly between 1990 to 1997, children were not facing a change in their lives in institutions. Dumitrana (1998) vividly describes life in residential institutions for children during the last 20 years of communism. Until the 1990s, these institutions were rather "closed" to the outside world; they looked more like self-contained military camps. There were almost no early intervention or socialization programs and no means to maintain parent-child relationships during a child's stay. In a recent study, Stativa (2002) describes in harsh terms the orphanage model that was found well into the 1990s: over-crowded institutions, with babies involved only in common, monotonous programs for all children.

Placements were decided on the basis of openings in institutions and not proximity to family. Placing siblings together was not always possible, especially if there were age differences between them. Age and the level of disability were the most important eligibility criteria in deciding what type of institution would be the first destination for the to-be-institutionalized child. Intake included a psychomedical evaluation, but many evaluations were incomplete. An endemic issue was that reevaluation of a child's situation was seldom performed, and if done, it did not take into account the family situation.

In this environment, another major stressor is exposure to violence from senior residents as well as to abuses and negligence from the untrained and unrewarded staff. During institutionalization, children were exposed to an environment that lacked male role models, especially for children under 7 years of age. As recent studies (Gavrilovici and Groza, 2007; Gavrilovici, 2004; Stativa, 2002) indicate, children's personal and family histories were not preserved: some children permanently lost their origin, their identity, and their ancestry.

Some of the staff had no qualifications but had no other job opportunities in their vicinity. Residential centers for children lacked therapists—except speech therapists and some pediatrician support—especially for those with disabilities. Finally, children reaching the age of 18 (or 26 if they were still in full-time education) suddenly became "ineligible" for residential care services; they were once more "abandoned," this time by the child protection system itself, because no public services were offered to them except some demonstration projects run by different charitable organizations for a very small number of beneficiaries.

Dumitrana (1998) mentions the two major principles of authoritarianism around which residential care in socialist Romania revolved until the December 1989 regime change: authoritarianism in affirming hygiene and in imposing school attendance. The two principles are at the foundation of Law 3/1970, regulating state-run residential care for children and adolescents as a response to the increasing child abandonment rate and the growing dependence on state care of needy families. The hygienist model was pervasive in residential care for children under 3 years of age in institutions administered by the Ministry of Health during communism and for a long time after the revolution, until the 1997 child protection reform.

Within this context, it became evident that the cosmetic changes to children's situations in institutions and the lack of real reform of the system could no longer be accepted. A tumultuous and explosive stage of reform was to start in 1997, at the beginning of a new administration after the 1996 national and local elections.

Child Protection Reform, 1997–2001

Romania's case as a candidate for entry into the European Union (EU) was special: on top of the economic criteria (a functioning market economy and capacity to cope with increased competition) and the political criteria (stability of democratic institutions, the rule of law, human rights, and protection of minorities), a conditional criterion was added "to improve the situation of the 100,000 children in institutionalized care" (Micklewright and Stewart, 2000, p. 2).

UNICEF was instrumental in helping the National Committee for Child Protection (CNPC) transform itself in January 1997 into the Department for Child Protection (DCP). Soon after, in November 1999, the first five-year report (1993–1998) to the Committee on the Rights of the Child was released (NAPCR, 2000). June 12, 1997, is the birth date for the implementation of Child Protection Reform policy under Government Ordinance 26/1997. At that time, there were 39,569 documented children in residential care in Romania in the placement centers administered by DCP.

In August 1997, the national child protection entity overseeing and administering all residential centers for children was given a new name: the National Agency for Child Protection (NACP). Two years later, it transformed into the National Authority for Child Protection and Adoption (NACPA), which coordinates all institutions for children previously under the authority of the Ministry of Education. After the residential institutions were transferred into the new child protection system on December 31, 2000, the system hosted 57,181 children. This started a linear trend of deinstitutionalization, with 49,965 residents on December 31, 2001, and 43,170 children on July 31, 2002.

Among the major supporters of NACPA's reforms was a group of major donors who joined with the Romanian government in the fall of 1998 to initiate the "project to reform the child protection system for the years 1999–2001." The World Bank helped this project with a Learning and Innovation Loan, supporting, among other aims, sustainable and cost-effective alternatives to institutionalized child care. One of the major incentives was to stimulate public-private partnerships, building on previous nongovernmental organization (NGO) expertise.

At the county level, decentralized County Directorates for Children's Rights Protection were initiated in 1997 to supervise the activity of institutions for children under the age of 18. Initially "placement centers" included institutions for abandoned children under 6 and children's homes for those of ages 7–18. Since 2000, all residential institutions have been called "placement centers." The county directorates took over 314 residential institutions for children from different ministries: the Ministry of Education, the Ministry of Health, and the Ministry of Labor and Social Protection (Government Emergency Ordinance, GEO 26/1997). The financing of these institutions came via county or local councils, but they were still dependent on the state budget.

The decentralization of the child protection system in Romania and the development of an entire new system of services at the county and local levels started rather painfully. A clear image is captured in the midterm evaluation of a large Child Welfare and Protection Project (funded by USAID, between 1997 and 2002):

> Child welfare reform is a national goal because without it accession to the European Union is virtually impossible. While the transfer of authority to local government is a critical part of the overall plan, the transfer does mean that responsibility for progress is placed with individual *Judets* [counties, in Romanian] that collectively, but separately must change the utilization of placement centers. Control over the course of reform stemming from the National Agency is now more indirect, more administrative, while the practical tasks of transforming the system fall to local government where the capacity and political will to change is uneven, the problems are in many ways more tangible, and the appeal of the status quo is more irresistible. (Wulczyn et al. 2000, p. 7)

Residential care reform in Romania cannot be fully understood without knowledge of the developments in the alternative services to institutionalization. Adoption legislation, as a component within the larger child welfare reform, was changed in 1997. The Romanian Committee for Adoption (RCA) was reorganized (Government Decision 502/1997), and a (later, much contested) Government Decision (no. 245/1997) regulated NGO authorization for international adoptions. The legal aspects of adoption were detailed in Emergency Ordinance 25/1997 and later approved by Law 87/1998 (NAPCR, 2000).

It is now evident that the decentralization was not followed by adequate funding. A major legislative omission happened with the abrogation of Law 3/1970, which ensured funding for both residential care institutions for children and the special residential care units for the disabled in medical units "for the irrecoverable."

The dependency of Romania on massive external funding became evident during 2000 when, because of dysfunctions in the implementation of local funding legislation, the maintenance of child protective services was in jeopardy. It was the second major media "scandal" over the situation of children in residential care in Romania, after the first media releases on the dramatic situation of children in orphanages at the beginning of the 1990s. The crisis triggered an "inflexion point" in the national strategy for child protection and a push toward a major partnership effort with all levels of internal stakeholders and with strong external funding and technical support.

During 2000, most of the 256 residential institutions for children with disabilities were transferred to the NACP from the Ministry of Education (schools from the special education system), the Ministry of Health (hospitals or health units specialized in dystrophy recovering, neuropsychomotor rehabilitation, and children with HIV/AIDS), and the State Secretary for the Handicapped (Government Decisions GD 61/2000, GD 1137/2000, and GEO 206/2000). Seventeen of these institutions were closed.

The total number of adoptions increased as another opportunity for deinstitutionalization, but almost two-thirds of these were international, based on the figures for 2000, underlining the small changes in national adoption trends.

Until 1997 the international adoptions were not strictly regulated (NAPCR, 2006). NACPA's statistical report (July 2003) indicated a total of 36,543 staff (roughly 10 percent at the county or national public administration level, over 50 percent working in residential centers for children, almost 30 percent maternal assistants or foster care parents, and the remaining staffing other services for children in child protection).

In 1997 the Ombudsman Institution was created in Romania as the only extra-judiciary means of protecting citizens from abuses by the public administration. The first cases administered were cases of child protection. During 1998–2000, of the 490 cases administered, 40 percent were child protection cases (Laudatu, 2000).

The diverse child protection cases reported in the Ombudsman's Report (Laudatu, 2000) show vividly the system's struggle for a new identity and exposed a structure in which children were "lost" out of sight. The report mentions separation of children from their families as characteristic of the only real child protection system still in place during 1998–2000 because there was as yet no systematic national model to prevent this. The system lacked financial supports for single mothers raising their babies, and the new legal provisions were difficult for local authorities to implement. Poverty was the major reason for institutionalization of children in residential care units. Because the legislation had no clear criteria for separation from the family, children's situations were assessed and decided unevenly across Romania by county commissions charged with child protection.

Another critique was directed at the practice of international adoption of children from institutions, maternal assistants, or family placements; sometimes, local administrations favored the legal declaration of child abandonment to enable an international adoption case, despite the interest of a child's relative to raise him or her. The report rightfully observes the pressures on the residential care institutions of maintaining their services in a context of intense inflation and lack of timely indexation of state supports for the institutionalized children or for the provisions for families, situations in which external funds obtained from international adoption were perceived as the only means of institutional survival.

The inefficiency of the first years of real reform is due to the fragmentary approach, characterized by administrative and financial decentralization but superficial action in reducing institutionalization and the development of alternative community-based services for children and families in need; one exception, perhaps, is the development of a maternal assistants' network at the county level.

The situation of children in institutions was not very well known or understood because of the lack of a database or tracking system and of a dearth of studies, especially at the national level; the publication in 2002 of the first national study offered a unique opportunity to examine the child welfare system. The first epidemiologic research on child abuse and neglect in Romania using a representative sample of institutionalized children during October–November 1999 was implemented two years after the initiation of reform in the child protection system. This study showed that in Romania, 53.8 percent of children lived in placement centers for school-age children. It was not possible to find the placement history of 40.7 percent of the school-age residents in placement centers because many of these children had experienced multiple transfers from institutions or had been abandoned in maternity houses with no papers (Stativa, 2002).

The national survey of placement centers sampled showed that their population was 11.8 percent children under 7 years old, 67 percent children 8–15 years old, and 21.3 percent children 16 years and older. The law allowed placement centers to host residents until the age of 18 or, for residents still pursuing their education, up to 26 years old. Despite regulations that children's cases should be reassessed every three months, two years after child protection reform started, more than 72 percent of children had not been reassessed in the past year; the law did not take into account the lack of resources at the county level for this reassessment (Stativa, 2002). Research by Stephenson et al. (1997) showed that 41 percent of children in infants' homes suffered from dystrophy. The HIV/AIDS infection rate was 22 per 1,000 in infants and 6.1 per 1,000 in children.

Most placement centers had been orphanages created after Law 3/1970. After 1990, some institutions were closed whereas others were rehabilitated and their staffs retrained. Some new models of residential living, such as "the family residential model," were promoted as coexisting with "classic" residential homes for children. In 1999 most of the institutionalized children lived in the classic-type residential centers (68.2 percent), almost a quarter of children stayed in mixed institutions, and 7.5 percent lived in family-type institutions.

Most residents have families. In 2000, more than 77 percent of the students in state residential institutions had parents who maintained their parental rights. In 2000, more than 75 percent of institutionalized siblings were housed in the same institution (Stativa, 2002). This is in accord with studies indicating that only 4% of young children in residential institutions have no biological parents living (Browne et al.e, 2006, p. 487). Socioeconomic conditions and a long history and culture of institutionalization coupled with the lack of social work services at the community level created this practice among some parents of entrusting their children to the state.

Length of stay of institutionalized children varies. In a national cross-sectional study on a probabilistic sample of residential care institutions in Romania, Stephenson et al. (1997) found that the average stay in children's homes was 3.6 years (standard deviation = 3.1). The cross-sectional study on Iasi County institutions by Gavrilovici (2004) revealed a much higher self-reported length of stay (more than six years) when subjects were asked to report the total length of their stay in residential care (not only the present institution).

Beyond demographic and institutional situation statistics at the national or county level, studies like Stativa (2002) and Gavrilovici (2004) also indicate a high rate of self-reported exposure to violence. Gavrilovici (2004) underscores the psychological correlates of such high levels of exposure to violence for children 8–17 years old: more than 21 percent of the girls and 15 percent of the boys exposed to high levels of violence report clinical-level posttraumatic symptoms (symptoms of depression, anxiety, anger, posttraumatic stress, and/or dissociation).

Child Protection Reform Accelerating in 2001

At the very beginning of 2001, the government instituted a minimum income for poor families—those most at risk of abandoning their children, the same year the National Authority for Child Protection and Adoption (NACPA) was created. This is when child protection reform became a national priority with respect to the goal of joining the European Union. The purpose of the NACPA was the protection, defense, and guarantee of children's rights, as defined in the UNCRC, in the context of fundamental human rights and liberties and ensuring a partner role for the child in the decision-making process concerning his or her placement in order to improve child welfare (NACPA, 2002a).

Under the revised legislation, children were considered to be "in difficulty" if their physical or moral integrity or development was endangered. The most important target group of children in difficulty in 2001 was children in residential care.

These conceptual transitions from "abandoned children" to "children separated from family," and finally, to "children in difficulty" describe the successive adaptations of Romanian child welfare policies, embracing a more holistic view of the problems of the child and, in recent years, a more comprehensive integration of child and family social welfare.

The Romanian government has funded public services development on a project-based approach since 2000 through a funding stream called National Interest Programs. These funds supplemented the regular budgetary resources for the maintenance of residential care services, depending on the national priorities set each year. Starting with 2002, new practices allowed NGOs to access these funds via public-private partnership projects.

However, the national resources could not support the fast and intense new stage of reform in the absence of international support. There have been several major identifiable funding streams since 2001 including the EU Phare program; the International Bank for Reconstruction and Development (IBRD) loan for the Reform of Child Protection System Project; the 2001–2005 Romanian-USA Partnership in Child Protection; the ChildNet Program; NACPA-USAID-World Learning; and the NAPCA-UNICEF Cooperation Program. Bilateral cooperation programs (with France) and technical assistance to NACPA (from the UK) add to the international support received by Romania.

Another legislative change to support the reforms, Law 705/2001 addressing the national system of social work, was implemented on January 1, 2002. It was an important contribution supporting the development of the social work community networks necessary to the current and future steps of child protection reform in Romania, a second wave of decentralization of family and child protection at the community level.

This was the moment of refining the social policies relative to children, families, and the elderly in Romania: new county-level departments of social work were created, and the county directorates for protecting children's rights became one of the subdivisions of this new public administration entity. In a sense, the reactive phase of almost the sole public policy targeting institutionalized children in Romania ended and a new phase was instituted involving a more comprehensive system of services revolving around the family.

Under heavy international pressure to change the situation of its protected children and with a goal of meeting requirements to enter the European Union, Romania adopted in 2001 a moratorium on international adoptions. The resolve came with the Child Rights Law enacted in January 2005, increasing the responsibility of the natural family to raise its children and the local and regional government to support at-risk families and children by developing a large array of preventive, supportive, and special protection (including residential care) services, all of which drastically limit international adoptions.

In 2002, based on World Health Organization sources, the rate of children under 3 in institutional care in Romania was 33 per 10,000 (Browne et al., 2006, p. 486). The same source shows other European countries with similar or higher rates of institionalization for young children per 10,000: Spain, 23; Lithuania, 46; Hungary, 44; Bulgaria, 60; Belgium, 56; and France, 13.

On August 8, 2002, a working group presented four legislative proposals to the government as a new child protection law package. The legislative proposals were the result of intense consultation with national and international experts for the purpose of creating a comprehensive and integrated approach to child protection in Romania. The whole Children's Law package passed in June 2004 and was enacted January 1, 2005 (Law 272/2004).

The values at the core of the actual child protection reform come from the UNCRC and the new Child Rights Law, which states the principles at the foundation of children's rights protection:

   a) respecting and promoting the best interest of the child;
   b) equality of chances and nondiscrimination;
   c) priority for children being raised within their natural, extended, or substitute family;
   d) multisectorial intervention and public-private partnership;
   e) ensuring individualized and personalized care;
   f) respecting children's dignity and opinion, according to their age and capacity for understanding;
   g) ensuring the stability and continuity of care, raising, and education, taking into account ethnic, religious, cultural, and linguistic specificity when deciding on a protective measure; and
   h) celerity in deciding appropriate protection measures.

An individual permanency plan is one of the major innovations in the new law. Also, the County Commissions for Child Protection, which had the legal authority to decide on measures of protection at the local level, are no longer used in the newly proposed structure; decisions on measures of protection will be made by a judge in a court of law. Another innovation is the interdiction of placement of children under 2 years old in residential care institutions, one of the most important "feeders" or sources of children for the system. A national toll-free hot-line for child protection is operational (0800 8 200 200) as a component of the major deinstitutionalization campaign after 2001.

An intense training program for all professionals working directly in child protection or having professional linkages to child protection was implemented; educators, social workers, psychologists, policemen, judges, and foster carers, as well as parents, were targeted.

The process of placing a child at risk based on Child Rights Law is more complex than before, requesting a higher level of cooperation among social, medical, and legal services at the county level (NACPR, 2006). An initial report of a child "at risk" is followed by preventive measures (if it is not an emergency situation) to support the at-risk individual or family. The centerpiece of this last wave of reform in child protection is the family. If abandonment of the child cannot be prevented or the family cannot be kept together, special protection measures of substitute family placement or, in the last resort, residential institution placement will be decided. If the family does not agree with the decision of the county child protection services, then judicial intervention is granted by the law. The court is also involved in situations of neglect and abuse, removal or restriction of parental rights, or urgent placement decisions (NACPR, 2006, p.18).

Conclusion

Romania's progress in improving child protective services has been remarkable, especially in the past few years, taking into account the long 16 years of little improvement that followed the revolution. The humanitarian aid and the large increase in international adoptions that occurred at the beginning and during the 1990s can be perceived now as a double-edged sword. The aid benefited many of the victims of a malfunctioning system of residential care institutions by improving the conditions in numerous orphanages, and the adoptions offered some abandoned children the chance of a new family. Some claimed that with international aid the institutions offered children better conditions than were available in their families of origin. Also, the international adoptions helped the public sector cut costs for operating the institutions, a disincentive to improve their cost-effectiveness. Both the aid and international adoptions, however, seemed to justify the existence of the institutions in the shape and function inherited from communist Romania, but by perpetuating the already corrupt and inefficient system, they eventually led to real child protection reform.

The trajectory of residential care for children in Romania was and still is tumultuous. From a system based solely on residential care, a major transformation has made residential care the last option as a measure of placement. Deinstitutionalization reform is predicted to end roughly 8–10 years from now. But alternatives to institutionalization such as long-term foster care and excessive use of group homes (especially as orphanages-in-disguise) are mistakes with which the United States has had considerable experience (USDHHS, 2002). Because international adoptions are practically forbidden by the new Children's Law, there is a need to stimulate national adoption.

As a recent report on Romania's child protection system emphasized, what was needed on the verge of the child protection reform of 2004 was technical assistance and training, implementation and enforcement, reporting and measurement of accomplishments, and public education (USDHHS, 2002). Tobis (2000) also strongly suggested making evaluation a central component of a national social safety net to ensure quality services. The inclusion of child protection experts— perhaps from schools of social work or from NGOs—on review teams can add to the quality of the review and at the same time help to sharpen the skills and knowledge of the county and national authority participants (Ambrose, 2002). These recommendations were already implemented in the national policies regarding child protection, including the residential care services for children. As of December 2006 (NAPCR, 2008) the whole child protection system registered 73,976 children in state care (out of 4,770,000 children under age 18), of which 26,105 were in residential care facilities. In December 31, 2007, the decreasing trend of placing children in residential care continues; only 25,114 still live in placement centers while 46,160 are in foster care and placed in families. The total number of children temporarily abandoned in hospital units decreased steadily and sharply after the implementation of 2004 child protection legislation: from 4,614 children in 2004, to 2,580 in year 2005, and 2,216 one year later, in 2006.

There is a need to define clearer roles for universities beyond the initial training of social workers, educators, special educators, and psychologists, and, more recently, managers of social services in the child protection field. Universities are needed to contribute in community-based, service-oriented research. Related to this, adequate funding streams for such studies are needed. Professional and regulatory organizations are still in pioneering development stages, such as the College of Psychologists and the College of Social Workers. Their role in further professionalizing the field is extremely important.

Decentralizing from national to county levels and ensuring and stabilizing funding streams for the changing systems proved to be a painful but nonetheless successful enterprise. The challenge resides now in future decentralization of child protective services from county to local (city, commune) levels. The rediscovery and redevelopment of social safety nets in suburban and rural areas are battles of the present and of the future for some years ahead.

Residential care for children and adolescents in Romania has deep historical roots, a contorted evolution during dramatic regime changes in the last 60 years, a cosmetic and contradictory approach to child welfare in the first seven years after the regime change of 1989, and an explosive development within the last nine years, embracing the UNCRC framework at its core. Entering the EU in January 1, 2007, Romania has reached a high goal, a goal of caring for its own children and families in a profoundly different way from what was traditionally the case. There are already signs that in terms of child protection, Romania is well ahead of other areas in need of modernization and has become a model of child welfare policy for other European countries.

NOTES

1. Currency conversion done at the Romanian National Bank Web site, http:// www.bnr.ro/Ro/Info/Istoric/Curs_l.htm, January 30, 2006. 29,891 RON (Romanian LEU) = $1US on June 30, 2005.
2. As of June 2004, a legislative initiative promoted by the Romanian Psychologists' Association was enacted and created the "College of Psychologists," the professional accrediting and licensing authority in the field. A similar development happened with the "College of Social Workers" later on.

REFERENCES

Ambrose, T. (2002). *Financial incentives and other sources of support for child protection reform in Romania.* Washington, DC: DHHS, NACP, and USAID. Retrieved February 25, 2004 from http://www.acf.dhhs.gov/programs/cb/publications/romaniacwreform2002/ chapone.htm.

Anti-Poverty and Social Inclusion Promotion Commission. (APSIPC). (2002). *The national anti-poverty and social inclusion promotion plan.* Bucharest: Romanian Government. Retrieved October 23, 2002 from http://www.caspis.ro/romanian/pnainc.htm.

Browne, K., Hamilton-Giachritsis, C. Johnson, R., and Ostergren, M. (2006). Overuse of institutional care for children in Europe. *British Medical Journal 332,* 485–487.

Dumitrana, M. (1998). *Copilul institutionalizat.* [The institutionalized child.] Bucuresti, Romania: Editura Didactica si Pedagogica.

Gavrilovici, O. (2004). *Exposure to violence and its psychological correlates in children and adolescents 8 to 17 years old in placement centers in Iasi County, Romania.* Unpublished doctoral dissertation, Case Western Reserve University, Cleveland, OH.

Gavrilovici, O., and Groza, V. (2007). Incidence, prevalence and trauma associated with exposure to violence in Romanian institutionalized children. *International Journal of Child and Family Welfare, 10*(3–4), 125–138.

Laudatu, E., Datcu, E., Deftu, A., and Popa, R. (2000). *Raport special. Protectia drepturilor copilului. Octombrie 1998–August 2000.* [Special report. Children's rights protection. October 1998–August 2000.] Bucharest: MarLink.

Manoiu, F., and Epureanu, V. (1996). *Asistenta sociala in Romania* [Social work in Romania]. Bucharest: ALL.

Micklewright, J., and Stewart, K. (2000). *Child well-being in the EU—and the enlargement to the East.* Florence: UNICEF Innocenti Research Center.

National Authority for the Protection of Children's Rights (NAPCR). (2000, December). *National report on the follow-up to the World Summit for Children.* Bucharest: Author.

National Authority for Child Protection and Adoption. (2001, May). *Buletin statistic.* [Statistical bulletin.] Bucharest: Author.

National Authority for Child Protection and Adoption. (2002a, September 27). *Intalnirea Grupului la Nivel Inalt: Evolutia reformei iulie 2001–septembrie 2002.* [High level group meeting: Evolution of the reform between July 2001 and September 2002.] Bucharest: Author.

National Authority for Child Protection and Adoption. (2002b, September 27). *Intalnirea Grupului la Nivel Inalt: Prezentare pachet legislativ.* [High level group meeting: Presentation of the legislative proposal package.] Bucharest: Author.

National Authority for Child Protection and Adoption. (2002c, September 27). *Intalnirea Grupului la Nivel Inalt: Progresul Grupului la Nivel Inalt.* [High level group meeting: The high level group progress.] Bucharest: Author.

National Authority for the Protection of Child's Rights (NAPCR). (2006). *Child welfare in Romania. The story of a reform process.* Bucharest: Author.

National Authority for the Protection of Child's Rights (NAPCR). (2008a). *Statistical notes.* http://www.copii.ro/content.aspx?id=55 (March 12, 2008).

National Authority for the Protection of Child's Rights (NAPCR). (2008b). *Statistical notes.* http://www.copii.ro/Files/20050630_statistica_20073231633911.xls. (March 12, 2008).

Stativa, E. (Ed.). (2002). *Abuzul asupra copilului in institutiile de protectie sociala din Romania.* [Child abuse in child protection institutions in Romania.] Bucharest: UNICEF, NACPA, IOMC, FICF.

Stephenson, P., Anghelescu, C., Stativa, E., and Pasti, S. (1997). *Cauzele institutionalizarii copiilor din Romania.* [The causes of children institutionalization in Romania.] Bucharest: UNICEF and International Foundation for Children and Families.

Teitelbaum, M., and Winter, J. (1998). *A question of numbers: High migration, low fertility, and politics of national identity.* New York: Hill and Wang.

Tobis, D. (2000). *Moving from residential institutions to community-based social services in Central and Eastern Europe and the former Soviet Union.* Washington, DC World Bank.

Wulczyn, F., Orlebeke, B., Miller, J., and ePoede, G. (2000). *The Child Welfare and Protection Project mid-term evaluation.* Chicago: Chapin Hall Center for Children, University of Chicago.

5

Residential Care for Children "At Risk" in Israel

Current Situation and Future Challenges

TALAL DOLEV, DALIA BEN RABI, AND
TAMAR ZEMACH-MAROM

Out-of-Home Care in Israel—Residential Care in Context

Between 65,000 and 75,000 children and youth (approximately 3 percent of the child population) live outside of their family home. These children and youth may be divided into two major groups:

- Youth (ages 14–17) who are educated and reside in boarding schools, in many cases out of personal preference; this group comprises approximately 60,000 youth.
- Children and youth (ages 0–17) who have been placed out of their homes by social services in different settings, according to their age, needs, and reasons for placement; this group includes 12,473 children and youth, the majority of whom are in residential care (see Table 5.1).

Most children are placed by the Ministry of Social Affairs, the government division responsible for child welfare services. These children are placed as a result of a professional decision that out-of-home care is required to protect and ensure their well-being. Placement decisions are made by local welfare decision committees—interorganizational professional committees coordinated by local child welfare services. However, when parents disagree with the decision, a protection order can

We extend our thanks to Susan Elster for her support in completing the final version of this chapter.

Table 5.1. Out-of-Home Placements by Age, Type of Placement, and Responsible
Ministry

| Age Group | Number of Children* | Services for Children and Youth | | |
		Residential Facilities**	Foster Care**	Youth Protection Authority**
0–5	721	82	639	
6–13	4,585	3,981	595	
14–17	7,167	4,851	416	1,900
Total	12,473	8,214	1,650	1,900

* Includes 709 children placed in facilities financed and supervised by the Ministry of Education (1999).
** Data from Service for Children and Youth, Ministry of Social Affairs (2003).

be requested from the juvenile court; approximately 25 percent of the placements
require a court order.

Most children are placed in residential facilities (8,214) and only a minority in
foster families. A smaller group is placed in facilities operated and financed by the
Ministry of Education according to the same procedures used for children placed
under the responsibility of the Ministry of Social Affairs. The Youth Protection
Authority operates out-of-home facilities,[1] which are geared for juvenile offenders
and youth with severe behavioral problems. In addition, 1,900 children are placed
by court order in both open and closed facilities operated by the Youth Protection
Authority.

When referring to "residential care" in Israel today, most professionals and lay
people refer to the care provided in residential settings to children and youth placed
by child welfare services through the local welfare decision committees or court
orders. This chapter focuses on the 10,573 children and youth and the care provided them in the Israeli residential system.

The second section briefly relates some of the historical and social factors that
have influenced the development of residential care in Israel and the role of residential care within the continuum of child welfare services. The third section
describes the current situation of the residential care system in Israel and the children in care. The fourth section then elaborates on some recent developments and
changes in the Israeli residential system. We conclude by indicating some of the
major challenges and developing trends.

From Refuge to Rehabilitation: The Roots and Development of Residential Care in Israel

Any description of the residential care system in Israel should note that in Jewish
and Israeli society, raising and educating children away from home at a *yeshiva*
(Jewish religious school) was and is acceptable and even prestigious. This positive

perception was reinforced by Zionist ideology that strove to resocialize and reeducate youth as a means of creating a new society based on new values (Shlansky, 1994). Until very recently, children raised in the influential kibbutz movement lived and were educated communally; to this day, adolescents on kibbutzim usually live in group homes.

In the years before the establishment of the State of Israel in 1948, residential facilities played a critical role in providing a home, shelter, and education for youth who arrived without their parents, mostly from Europe. Many were orphans escaping massacres in Eastern Europe. Others were Zionist immigrants wishing to be a part of creating Israeli society. In addition, boarding schools were considered education facilities for the "elite," so many Israeli-born adolescents were sent to these schools by their parents.

Following the Second World War, boarding schools as well as kibbutzim continued to be homes for young, parentless refugees. During the mass immigration of the 1950s, residential settings continued to enjoy prestige and were considered ideal for helping newcomers, including children who arrived with their families, to become integrated into Israeli society.

In later decades, the role of both boarding schools and residential care gradually shifted. This shift was a result of many social factors including the reduction in immigration, the diminishing influence of ideologies, and the development of Israel and its economy. In addition, more pluralistic perceptions of immigration absorption began emerging in Israel, especially among activist groups that had been immigrants in the 1950s. These groups advocated more culturally sensitive approaches allowing for identification and continued preservation of unique cultural practices. Their defiance of the "melting pot" approach, characteristic of early Zionism, also entailed severe criticism of boarding schools and residential facilities as major institutions in the absorption of young immigrants. Residential care came to be seen by these activists as a means of preserving the dominant culture and depriving the youth of their own culture and families.

Residential care and education gradually lost its elite status in the eyes of most Israelis, although to some extent the prestige of residential educational settings has been preserved in the religious sector. Over time, then, residential facilities became homes for children and youth who did not adjust well to their community schools, to youth who had problems with their parents, and to those considered by child welfare professionals to be at risk of abuse and neglect (Shlansky, 1994).

Professional attitudes also changed, and out-of-home placement came to be seen as less desirable than community-based solutions for children. This shift in Israeli professional approaches can be attributed in part to the influence of professional approaches abroad as well as to infiltration of approaches underlying the United Nations Convention for the Rights of the Child (CRC), which was ratified by Israel in 1989. Thus, children who are placed in out-of-home care are often children who come from families that have already been offered community-based intervention (Dolev, Benbenishty, and Timar, 2001). This trend resulted in even more radical changes in the needs and characteristics of the children placed in residential care, as only those with more severe problems are being placed.

These shifts mean that residential facilities have had to adjust and transform their goals and practices to meet the needs of a changing population. Residential facilities that once aimed to provide quality education, resocialization, and life skills were forced to adjust to meeting the social and emotional needs of neglected and abused children, many with adjustment and behavioral problems and negative experiences in the educational system. This required a concomitant shift in values as well as in expertise. In addition, the fact that the once-prestigious facilities have become marginalized affected the extent of resources allocated to them and to the development of "state-of-the-art" practices within them. Thus, serious shortcomings began to emerge in the quality and level of care provided.

During the past decade, much concern has been expressed regarding the quality of care in residential facilities. In the late 1980s and early 1990s, several reports on poor living conditions and insufficient staff were published and received much public attention. In addition, the ratification of the CRC and the demands for more careful monitoring of the conditions of residential care contributed to these trends. This dissatisfaction with residential care brought about three parallel trends within the Israeli child welfare system:

1. Efforts to create alternatives for out-of-home care, including development of new services and models to provide more effective support for families in the community (Dolev et al., 2001) as well as more recent attempts to introduce new regulations and funding mechanisms aimed at providing incentives to prioritize community-based intervention.
2. Efforts to improve the foster care system and increase its capacity for providing out-of-home care (National Supervisor for Foster Care, personal communication 2005). Recent proposed legislation even suggests giving priority to foster and kinship care over residential solutions (Peled-Amir, 2003).
3. Accelerating changes introduced into the system of residential care.

These changes represent efforts to transform the goals and practices of the system such as to maintain its relevance and role within the system of out-of-home care in particular and within the system of child welfare services more generally.

The Current Israeli Residential System

Financing and Auspices

As indicated earlier, almost 9,000 children and youth reside in residential facilities where they were placed by local welfare decision committees or court order. The majority (8,214) are the responsibility of the Ministry of Social Affairs. These place-ments are allocated by the ministry and funded jointly by the ministry (75 percent) and the local authorities (25 percent).

Although most children under age 14 are placed in facilities that predomi-nantly serve children requiring out-of-home care, many of the children older than 14 are placed in boarding schools in which only few of the children have been removed from home, the rest being there voluntarily. There are over 300 residential facilities for children and youth removed from their homes, the vast majority of which are operated by private not-for-profit organizations.

Characteristics of the Residential Facilities

Residential facilities are classified and budgeted according to required level of care:

1. *Posthospitalization facilities*: These were established in the mid 1990s
   for children with very severe emotional and behavioral problems as
   an alternative to placement in mental health facilities. In 2003,
   243 children were placed in 14 facilities of this kind. Many
   posthospitalization facilities are units within larger therapeutic
   residential homes.
2. *Therapeutic settings*: A larger number of children (1,838) live in
   38 institutions for children with significant emotional or learning
   difficulties.
3. *Rehabilitative settings*: 3,395 children live in residential settings for
   children with milder difficulties.
4. *Educational settings*: 3,446 children live in settings for children with a
   normal level of functioning who need to be removed from their
   homes because of severe problems in the family. Most (2,677) are
   youth 14 or older.

The needs of the children in the various kinds of residential facilities determine the kinds of resources required, including the extent and composition of the staff, the interventions provided, and the location and type of education the children receive. Posthospitalization and therapeutic settings have the largest ratios of staff per child and employ a broader range of professional and paraprofessional clinicians. Children who reside in posthospitalization or therapeutic facilities usually attend a special education school on the premises whereas children who reside in a rehabilitative or educational setting usually attend a public school in the community.

Staff includes child care staff (generally referred to as counselors in the group model and as house parents in the family model). Educational and training require-ments for child care staff are minimal and often unmet. However, most residential facilities that exclusively or predominantly serve children and youth who were removed from their homes employ additional professional staff. All facilities include professional social workers (one full-time social worker for a group of 12–15 children) as well as additional therapists. The directors of most facilities are professionals in the areas of psychology, social work, or education. Boarding schools have much lower ratios of professional staff.

Most residential facilities in Israel are very large by the standards of such countries as the United States or England. Facilities for children age 14 and under generally serve 80–100 children (in groups of 12–15). Boarding schools attended by most youth ages 14–17 are frequently larger, many serving more than 100 youth. Most Israeli residential facilities are organized according to one of two major models: "the group model," in which children live in groups according to their age, and the "family model," in which children of different ages live with "house parents" (generally a young couple). All boarding schools are organized according to the family model.

QUALITY ASSURANCE AND SUPERVISION   According to the current legislation, all residential facilities are required by law to obtain a license from the Service for Children and Youth in the Ministry of Social Affairs. In practice, this agency places priority on providing intensive supervision of 85 residential facilities in which most residents are children and youth placed by the service. These include most facilities for children under age 14 and all private for-profit facilities. Most boarding schools are excluded from this category even if they serve youth who were removed from their homes. Thus, 90 percent of the children under age 14 live in facilities provided with intensive supervision, compared to only 34 percent of the youth ages 14 and over. In addition, the Ministry of Education provides intensive supervision of the facilities it operates.

In the early 1990s the Ministry of Social Affairs and the Ministry of Finance implemented the recommendations of a public committee aimed at addressing serious issues relating to the quality of residential care. These recommendations included the following:

- Formally defining the goals of residential facilities as services aimed at protecting children and addressing their daily emotional, social, and educational needs
- Setting new standards and regulations in areas such as child-to-staff ratios, therapeutic staff, and activities and enrichment
- A significant increase in the level of funding provided to help the residential facilities implement the new standards

These recommendations represent a shift in the perception of residential care in Israel, formally stating its role as a service for children who cannot continue to live with their parents, and defining its responsibility for their rehabilitation.

One of the major changes introduced into the Israeli residential care system as a consequence of implementing these recommendations was the development and adoption in 1995 of a new system for supervision and quality assurance. The RAF[2] supervisory system tracks, in two-year cycles, a set of well-defined outcomes considered important in the provision of good quality care, and the resources and procedures used to accomplish them. The RAF tracks, for example, low school achievement, aggression, depression, and anxiety; among process indicators, it also tracks availability of and participation in school support and availability of and participation in recreational or therapeutic activities aimed at dealing with anxiety. Thus, a comprehensive assessment of the quality of care and its outcomes is available for reexamining and redefining the most critical goals and practices of residential facilities and for detecting important trends and developments. Furthermore, the assessments provide a basis for the development of a national framework for improving quality of care.

Characteristics of Children and Youth in Residential Settings

Most children and youth placed in residential settings are placed because of severe problems in their families.[3] Many come from homes in which one or both parents have extreme problems in social functioning, such as drug addiction or mental illness. A significant proportion of children were subjected to abuse by their parents and usually also neglected physically or emotionally.

Most children in residential care (60 percent) are boys. Sixty-one percent of the children come from broken homes: Almost half of the children's parents (49 percent) are either divorced or separated, 10 percent are widowers, and 1 percent of the children have no parents. Almost 20 percent of the children come from families who have immigrated to Israel since 1990 (mostly from the former Soviet Union), and 5 percent are from the Israeli Arab community.[4]

Table 5.2 presents additional detail. More than half of these children have problems in their relationships with their families and are underachievers at school. Problems at school, as well as running away from the residential setting, physical self-neglect, theft, bed-wetting, drug use, depression and anxiety, and suicidal behavior are more prevalent among boys. Aggression and problems in the areas of social behavior, relations with family, and sexual behavior are more characteristic of girls. In addition, one-fourth of the children in residential care were diagnosed with ADHD or other learning disabilities; 15 percent regularly receive psychiatric medication.

Physical self-neglect and bed-wetting are most common in the younger ages (under 10); this age group also has a slightly higher proportion of problems with the family. Other problems are more typical of older ages. Teenagers aged 15 and above have a relatively high proportion of problems. This is especially true of alcohol and drug use, depression and anxiety, and problematic social behavior. In those areas the difference between the age groups is the largest. Finally, consistent with the classification of residential care in Israel, larger proportions of children in the more intensive facilities have problems in many of the areas.

Table 5.2. Percentage of Children Exhibiting Indicators of Problems by Age Group and Type of Setting

		Percentage by Age Group		
Problem Area	*Total Percentage*	*6–10*	*11–14*	*15–17*
Low scholastic achievements	55	48	58	55
Negative behavior at school	41	36	42	44
Running away	12	7	12	15
Physical self-neglect	24	30	24	19
Problematic relations with family	58	61	56	59
Aggression	34	32	36	33
Problematic social behavior	39	36	38	42
Theft	11	9	11	13
Bed-wetting	13	26	13	4
Alcohol abuse	5	0	2	12
Drug use	3	0	1	8
Depression and anxiety	43	36	43	49
Suicidal behavior	14	12	13.0	16
Total Number	4,768	1,122	2,080	1,558

Recent Developments in the Israeli Residential Care System

In addition to the introduction of the RAF quality assurance system, efforts are under way to adapt residential facilities and the residential system as a whole to more state-of-the-art professional practices as well as to adhere more to the guidelines established by the CRC. This included two major processes:

- Strengthening relationships between children in residential care and their families and communities
- Developing new and diverse models of residential care

Enhancing Contact and Intervention with Parents

Up until the 1980s, residential facilities in Israel did not view the relationship with parents as an important component of the care provided to children and youth. Moreover, for historical and ideological reasons, many residential care professionals viewed parents as the source of children's problems (Shlansky, 1994). The importance of parents' involvement in the lives of the children, as well as in the care provided in the residential facilities, began to be recognized during the 1980s as a result of changes in social values and norms, professional perceptions, and exposure to research findings that emphasized the importance of maintaining the relationship between children and their parents.

As awareness of the importance of the child-parent relationship grew, interest increased in efforts to maintain and strengthen this contact. Studies conducted during the 1990s revealed that most children in residential care maintain relatively intensive contact with their families and communities through visits to their homes on weekends and school holidays. In addition, most facilities allowed parent visits at all times or on special visitation days (Bendel and Katz, 1994; Dolev and Barnea, 1996; Fleishman et al., 1999).

Laufer (1991, 1994) reported that children's visits at home and parent visits at the residential settings were not used by the staff as opportunities to strengthen the relationship between the parents and children nor to form collaborative relationships between the parents and the residential staff. In addition, parents were not generally considered by the residential facilities as clients who required their intervention. Dolev and Barnea (1996) report that parents of only 4 percent of the children met regularly with a social worker at the residential setting, and an additional 14 percent met with a social worker approximately once a month. In addition to staff ambivalence toward parents, staff also lacked the skills and training required to effectively relate to parents. In addition, they felt overburdened by this requirement and tended to place responsibility for working with the parents on the local social welfare department (Dolev and Barnea, 1996).

The growing recognition of the importance of the parent-child relationship resulted in many initiatives aimed at enhancing this component in the residential care system. Many residential facilities have established programs for parents, including special activity days for parents and children, "visiting quarters" in which parents can spend weekends with their children in the residential facilities, and special intervention programs for parents and children. In addition, many are reimbursing parents for traveling to the facilities. New initiatives were also put into place to provide more intervention for parents. At the same time, new regulations recommending parent participation in decision-making processes relating to out-of-home placement were emphasized and enforced, and staff training was provided in this area. These measures were aimed at helping parents become an integral part of the decision process and thus more involved in their children's care.

Recent data indicate that over the past decade there has been significant improvement in parent involvement in residential care. Information on a representative sample of children in regular rehabilitative facilities indicates that in 2002, 41 percent of the parents visited their children at least once every two weeks compared to 27 percent in the 1996 survey. Moreover, in 2002 only 14 percent of the parents did not visit at all compared to 31 percent in 1996 (Ben Rabi and Hasin, 2006).

Developing New and Diverse Models of Residential Care

The changes in the residential care system have also resulted in the development of new models of residential care. The development of these models indicates four major trends:

1. *Establishing smaller, more intimate frameworks:* These include, for example, family group homes in which 12–15 children live with a

married couple, as well as independent family units within larger
residential frameworks.

2. *Developing facilities for specific population groups and purposes:* In
recent years the Israeli residential system has made an effort to
develop residential responses for population groups that were
previously neglected. An important example is the posthospitalization
residential care facilities established as an alternative to care in mental
health hospitals (see above). Short-term residential facilities,
established as "emergency centers" for children in extreme risk
situations, began to operate in the mid 1990s.

3. *Establishing residential facilities that are linked to the communities in
which they are situated:* A major new development in the Israeli
residential system is establishing community-based residential
facilities, or group homes. These are situated in the child's own
community and provide intervention for the family as a unit; maintain
contact between the child and his or her parents; involve the parents in
the care provided in the residential facility; maintain the child's links
with community institutions such as school, community center, and
health clinic; and return the child home after two to three years.

4. *Establishing "partial" residential models as alternatives to full
residential care:* Another development that may be considered outside
the realm of residential care is the implementation of day-residential
facilities providing a full range of intervention and care; however, the
children return home each night. A recent evaluation indicates that
they serve children with characteristics similar to those of children in
rehabilitative residential facilities and provide flexibility in the extent
of care provided (Ben Rabi and Hasin, 2006). A study conducted
among Israeli residential care professionals indicated that they
recommended day-residential care for 50 percent of a representative
sample of children currently in full-time residential facilities (Zilca
and Dolev, 2005). In addition, parents often do not view the
intervention as residential and are highly satisfied with the program.

Major Issues in Residential Care

Despite the numerous developments in the Israeli residential care system, many
issues uncovered by the earlier studies remain unresolved. In addition, the new
developments have highlighted new issues, some of which are currently the focus of
new initiatives.

Education in Residential Care

One area that has been a severe challenge to residential care is the provision of education and ensuring adequate educational achievement. The most recent data from

the RAF surveillance system indicate that half of the children in residential facilities have lower than standard achievements and 41 percent are not adjusting to the educational frameworks. Studies also indicated that despite the large educational gaps, residential facilities invest only limited resources in supporting the children's educational process (Dolev and Barnea, 1996; Fleishman et al., 1999).

Child Care Staff Qualifications and Training

Child care staff and qualifications present many challenges. As indicated earlier, education and training requirements for child care staff are minimal, and more than half of the staff members have a high school or lower level of education (Fleishman et al., 1999). In addition, directors reported difficulty recruiting and retaining staff (Bar, 1994; Fleishman et al., 1999). An underlying issue is the lack of a clear philosophy and definition of the roles and responsibilities of child care workers. Although they are often less educated, receive lower salaries, and have a lower professional status than the other professionals employed in the residential settings, their roles are loosely defined and tend to involve a broad range of diverse tasks and responsibilities (Dolev and Zilca, 2000).

Outcomes of Residential Care

Research related to the outcomes of residential care in Israel is only in its initial stages of development. We hope that data will be available soon from a number of sources. Two systematic studies of children and youth who have completed care in residential facilities are under way. In addition, the evaluation of community and day-residential facilities is providing, for the first time, information on the progress of children in rehabilitative facilities over a period of three years. Finally, many of the quality assurance and regulatory systems introduced into recent residential facilities provide systematic information on the progress of children in care and on their outcomes. This information needs to be analyzed and used.

Strengthening the Links with Community Services

Maintaining the children's relationships with their parents, developing community-based models of residential care, and providing more systematic regulation of entry and exit from care require collaborative work between government ministries and community services. Findings from studies conducted during the 1990s indicated that, in many cases, overburdened community services were happy to pass the responsibility for the child and his or her well-being over to the professionals at the residential facility while the geographical distance between many of the residential settings and the children's homes inhibited collaboration in intervention with the child or with the family (Dolev and Barnea, 1996).

One of the major principles of the community residential models is the importance of maintaining the responsibility for child welfare services in the community, as well as educational and other services central to the well-being of the child and his or her family. To achieve this goal, extensive efforts were invested in joint activities, learning processes, and individual case conferences for staff in the residential care settings and in the local communities. Evaluation findings indicate that the investment in structuring and maintaining these relationships brought about more extensive collaboration between the residential facilities and the local communities. However, in addition to needed investment in community-based care (which is not always available), the data indicate that much investment is needed in constructing joint working processes, conducting mutual learning, and overcoming differences in order to establish and strengthen such links.

Entering Residential Care, Leaving Care, and Length of Stay

The average length of stay of the children currently in care in intensively supervised residential settings is 2.7 years; a large proportion of the children in care (41 percent) are in care for 1–3 years, and only a few (16 percent) have been in care for more than five years (data from RAF surveillance system, 2003).

Disturbing findings from recent studies raised questions related to length of stay in residential facilities and to criteria for leaving care, as well as to allocation and patterns of use of residential care. A national study of local welfare decision-making committees exposed severe limitations of the decision-making processes concerning placement in out-of-home care, such as lack of systematic data in many of the cases, limited discussion of alternatives, and a lack of consistency in the decisions to place children out of the home, raising questions about the necessity of some out-of-home placements (Dolev et al., 2001). An additional study, in which experts were asked to review written case reports and recommend either community or out-of-home intervention, also raised doubts concerning some of the placement decisions. The experts recommended community-based intervention for almost 50 percent of a sample of cases on the basis of descriptions of children currently in residential care (Dolev and Zilca, 2001).

The national study also found that decision committees rarely review the situation of children already in residential care, and when a review is conducted, only a negligible proportion of the children are returned home (Dolev et al., 2001). More recent findings from the evaluation of community and day-residential facilities also indicated that reviewing children's situation as a basis for considering returning them home is not a standard procedure in most residential facilities (Ben-Rabi and Hasin, in progress).

A related concern is that there is evidence that a substantial proportion of children leave the residential care settings after a year or less in care, without systematic after-care planning. A recent study revealed that 9 percent of the children from regular rehabilitative facilities left care during the first year; half returned home without a care plan. Moreover, most of the children who left did so because of adjustment problems (Ben-Rabbi and Hasin, 2006). A national committee established to implement the CRC in Israel also made extensive recommendations to improve processes related to entry and completion of residential care (Government of Israel, 2003).

In response to these findings, new measures are currently being established to improve the decision processes and care planning around both entry to and departure from residential care. National initiatives that will improve the working processes and decisions of local decision-making committees are being planned and introduced. In addition, recent regulations were issued limiting the period of care to four years. In light of this decision, a structured process of returning children to their homes and planning for postresidential care is being developed, including the following:

- Introducing structured, annual review procedures for each child
- Discussing and formulating criteria for returning children
- Introducing structured care planning in collaboration with the services in the community
- Providing additional funds for community-based services to facilitate the child's transition from the residential facilities to the community

Residential Care in Israel—A Look to the Future?

As we have shown, the dominant role played by residential care in Israel has both social and historical roots. Changes in social values, economic growth, and professional approaches to residential care resulted in a significant transition in the role of residential care, in its status, and in its target population. Once considered valued and prestigious educational establishments, residential facilities met the challenge of caring for children "at risk." Residential facilities and their roles are also challenged by changing professional approaches, which emphasize preference for alternative responses, either in the community or in foster care.

During the past decade and a half, the residential care system redefined its role and the goals of its intervention, and upgraded and updated its practices in three major areas: improving and assuring the quality of care; diversifying the system of care to better address diverse needs; and strengthening the links between the residential system, the families, and communities. As indicated, challenges remain in all these areas, challenges that were noted by a recent report of the national subcommittee to implement the CRC (Government of Israel, 2003). More effort needs to be invested in improving educational achievement, recruiting and training child care staff, and studying the outcomes of residential care. Also needed are efforts to establish effective links with parents and communities and to review the efficacy of placement decisions, length of stay, and patterns for leaving care.

There are four additional factors that contribute to the debate concerning the role of residential care:

- *Foster care:* An initiative to reform foster care was implemented in 2001 and is supported by recently proposed legislation. Within the framework of this reform, the responsibility for recruiting and providing training and support for families was transferred from the government to specialized NGOs. This reform was aimed at increasing the ability to recruit, train, and support foster families and thus expand this service as an alternative to residential care. Within the past two years, the number of children in foster care has increased from 1,200 to 1,650. Although the numbers are still small compared to the extent of residential care, they represents a 25 percent increase in foster care during a relatively short period of time.

- *Day residential models:* The development, popularity, and apparent success of day residential models, offering comprehensive, intensive care within the community, seem to hold the potential for providing a compatible, less expensive solution for a large proportion of children currently placed in out-of-home care.
- *Community-based interventions:* The establishment of these models lagged behind developments in the residential care system. Most are still experimental, operating in only a few locations, and reaching the end of the experimental stages. The dissemination of these programs to additional locations will require a reallocation of funds.
- *Economic crisis:* As a result of a severe economic crisis in the country, budget allocations for social services were cut back dramatically between 2002 and 2003, and additional cutbacks were introduced in the 2004 budget. In an effort to more effectively use shrinking resources, the Ministry of Social Affairs issued a new regulation limiting the length of stay in residential facilities to a period of three years. The ministry is planning to allocate the funds saved through this process to developing community-based child welfare alternatives. However, the economic crisis and the cutbacks in social services and benefits may also increase the numbers of families having difficulties coping with their children and thus increase the need for out-of-home care.

These developments may indicate that Israel is headed toward a significant change in the role of residential care relative to both community-based services and foster care; however, it is difficult to foresee the extent, pace, or specific directions of this change. Predicting the future role of residential care in Israel must take into account the system's proven ability to transform itself to meet new challenges as well as its deep historical and cultural roots in Israeli society. The recent initiatives to decrease the role of residential care face fierce opposition from residential providers, who have gained substantial public support. The new initiatives, most of which have not yet been proven effective, need to compete with a well-established and valued professional alternative.

NOTES

1.   The Youth Protection Authority (YPA) operates residences along a continuum, which
     includes closed residences, open residences in the community, and diagnosis and crisis
     intervention centers. In addition, during the past decade the YPA established, together
     with other voluntary organizations such as ELEM and Ashalim, special "drop-in"
     residences for homeless and runaway youth.
2.   The system was developed by Myers-JDC-Brookdale Institute (Fleishman et al. 1999)
     and is based on the "tracer" approach (Kessner, Kalk, and James 1973) and the model
     of quality assurance (Donabedian 1991).
3.   Data are based on the Children and Youth Services database collected between
     September 2002 and January 2003, which includes 4,768 children aged 6–18 residing
     in the 85 residential homes that are intensively supervised by the Service.
4.   Among the total children's population in Israel, 25 percent are from the Israeli Arab
     community. Thus, Arab children are underrepresented among the children in
     residential care. This is due to both cultural and social characteristics of the Arab
     community in Israel, as well as to the limited number of available residential facilities
     for Moslem and Christian children. The scope of this paper does not allow an in-depth
     analysis of the situation and trends concerning residential care and child welfare
     services for Arab children and youth. Additional information can be found in
     Korazim, Dolev, and Abu-Asbah (2002).

REFERENCES

Bar, N. (1994). *Workers in residential care facilities for children at risk.* Jerusalem: Joint Israel.
Bendel, Y., and Katz, J. (1994). *Residential facilities for children at risk: Database on services.*
     Jerusalem: Unit for Children at Risk, Myers-JDC-Israel.
Ben-Rabi, D., and Hasin, T. (2006). *Community-based and day residential facilities: Intervention
     strategies and the status of the children and their parents—Summary of three years of
     study.* Jerusalem: Myers-JDC-Brookdale Institute.
Dolev, T., and Barnea, N. (1996). *Assessment of children's needs and of interventions provided
     in nine residential facilities for children up to the age of 14.* Jerusalem: Myers-JDC-
     Brookdale Institute.
Dolev, T., Benbenishty, R., and Timar, A. (2001). *Decision committees in Israel: Their organiza-
     tion, work processes, and outcomes: A summary report.* Jerusalem: Myers-JDC-Israel.
Dolev, T., and Zilca, I. (2000). *Childcare staff in residential care: Literature review.* Jerusalem:
     Myers-JDC-Brookdale Institute.
Dolev, T., and Zilca, I. (2001). *Residential facilities in Israel: Background paper for the Strategic
     Planning Committee.* Jerusalem: Myers-JDC-Brookdale Institute.
Donabedian, A. (1991). Reflection on the effectiveness of quality assurance. In R. J. Palmer,
     A. Donabedian, and G. J. Povar (Eds.), *Striving for quality care* (pp. 59–128). Ann Arbor,
     MI: Health Administration Press.
Fleishman, R., Barnea, N., Dolev, T., Ben-Zimra, T., and Hauslich. Z. 1999. *A survey of the
     boarding schools and their regulatory system under the supervision of the Children and
     Youth Services.* Jerusalem: Myers-JDC-Brookdale Institute.
Government of Israel, Ministry of Justice. (2003). Government Committee for Revising
     Legislation Concerning Children, Sub Committee on Out-of-Home Care, 2003.
     Jerusalem.

Kessner, D. M., Kalk, C. E., and James, S. (1973). Assessing health quality—The case for tracers. *New England Journal of Medicine, 288,*189–194.

Korazim, Y., Dolev, T., and Abu Asbah, K. (2002). *Arab children and youth at risk in the Northern District.* Jerusalem: Myers-JDC-Brookdale Institute and the Ministry of Labor and Social Affairs, Service for Children and Youth.

Laufer, Z. (1991). Maintaining family relationships at residential facilities for children ages 6–14. *Society and Welfare, 20,* 176–184.

Laufer, Z. (1994). The "no man's land" of home weekends for children in residential care. *Child Abuse and Neglect, 18*(11), 913–921.

Peled-Amir, T. (2003). *The Committee for Examination Principles in the Area of Children and Low and Their Implementation in Legislation: Sub-committee report on out-of-home placing.* Jerusalem: Israel Ministry of Justice.

Shlansky, S. (1994). The institution and the family between contradiction and complementarity: Changing perceptions in the Israeli youth villages. *Pnimiyot, 20,* 23.

Zilca, I., and Dolev, T. (2005). *Changes in patterns of use in Israeli residential care facilities.* Unpublished manuscript.

6

Residential Care for Children in Botswana

The Past, the Present, and the Future

TAPOLOGO MAUNDENI

Children in contemporary societies face numerous challenges that need diverse approaches. One of the approaches that has been tried in numerous countries is residential care. This is a relatively recent approach in Botswana, since for many years, children in need of care were absorbed by the extended family, a practice found in many African cultures. However, changes in the sociocultural and economic situations in Botswana have necessitated a new acceptance of residential care. There are three major types of residential care facilities for children in Botswana: centers for abused, dependent, neglected, orphans and abandoned children and youth; rehabilitation centers for juveniles; and centers for disabled children. The primary focus of this chapter is on the first type of setting.

It is important to mention from the outset that there are no institutions or orphanages for children in need of care in Botswana. What exist are small-scale residential facilities with house parents that provide a home-like setting. In other words, the types of residential facilities for children in need of care in Botswana do not fit the typical definition of institutions or orphanages for children found in other countries. In an orphanage or institution, there is a matron in charge of many children, who often wear uniforms and live in buildings resembling barracks. Children's homes use a family approach to the care of orphaned and abandoned children. They try to meet specific needs of children and youth. Special effort is made to keep siblings together in the same group home.

Also, there is no official definition of residential care in Botswana; rather, there is an official definition of "Approved Child Welfare Institutions." According to section 34, subsection 1 of the Botswana Children's Act, an approved child welfare institution refers to established homes, schools, and institutions for the reception of children. The subsection specifies that the minister[1] may establish and maintain the following:

- Any place of safety for the reception of children or juveniles under this act
- Any children's homes for the reception, care, and upbringing of children in need of care
- Any youth shelter for the reception of juveniles who have been arrested and are waiting to appear before a juvenile court
- Any school of industries for the reception, care, and training of juvenile delinquents in specific skills
- Any attendance center for the training of juvenile delinquents
- Such other place as the minister may consider necessary for the reception of children or juveniles under this act

The terms "residential care facilities" and "approved child welfare institutions" are used interchangeably in this chapter to refer to residential facilities for children in need of care.

A vital question to answer at this point is this: Who is a child in need of care in Botswana? Section 14 of the Botswana Children's Act of 1981 (currently under review) defines a child in need of care as a child who

- Has been abandoned or is without visible means of support
- Has no parent or guardian or has a parent or guardian who is unfit to exercise proper control over the child
- Engages in any form of street trading, unless he has been deputed by his parents to help in the distribution of merchandise of a family concern
- Is in the custody of a person who has been convicted of committing upon a child or in connection with a child any offense referred to in part IV of the act, or frequents the company of an immoral or violent person, or is otherwise living in circumstances calculated to cause or conduce his seduction, corruption, or prostitution

In summary, the term "children in need of care" refers to orphaned, abused, abandoned, and neglected children.

Background Information

Botswana is located in the southern part of Africa, sharing borders with South Africa, Zambia, Namibia, and Zimbabwe. The country is roughly the size of the state of Texas in the United States or of Kenya, but it has a far smaller population, approximately 1.7 million (Government of Botswana, 2001). Like most developing countries, Botswana has a young population. In 1991, for example, 43.6 percent of the population was between the ages of 0 and 14 years (Lesetedi and Ngcongco, 1995).

Botswana was one of the poorest countries in the world when it attained independence in 1966. However, it has now been transformed into the richest economy in southern Africa (excluding South Africa) and is one of the few African economies to be classified by the World Bank and the United Nations as an "upper middle-income" country (Hope, 1996; Maundeni, 2000). The economic success of Botswana has been attributed, among other things, to the country's resources and political stability. Diamond-generated wealth has given Botswana one of the strongest foreign reserves in the world. The country also exports beef to European countries.

Despite the progress that Botswana has made, the process of social change, which has been triggered by industrialization, urbanization, and the assimilation of Western values, has contributed to the emergence of a host of stressful social, cultural, and economic changes that undermine the capacity of many families to provide adequate care and support for their children (Jacques, 1998). Child welfare problems include child poverty (Pule, 2004), child abuse and neglect (Jacques, 1998), youth unemployment, domestic violence, children who have been orphaned, and street children, just to mention a few. However, until early 2005, there was no coherent child welfare policy in Botswana to guide organizations and groups that seek to intervene in the lives of children in need of care. At the time this chapter was written, the government had recently approved Children in Need of Care Regulations, but the regulations had not yet been implemented.

The largest child welfare problem faced by Botswana is that of orphaned children. As of December 1999, the government had identified, assessed, and registered 28,906 orphans throughout the country; however, it was estimated that the numbers could rise to 65,000 by the end of the year 2000 (*The Botswana Guardian,* December 1, 2000). There are several causes of orphanhood in Botswana but the major one is HIV/AIDS (Muchiru, 1998), followed by tuberculosis.

Orphans are confronted daily with a multitude of problems. Many live in poverty and their human rights are violated by their caregivers. Examples of such violations include sexual abuse of girls, the use of boys as cheap labor, and lack of access to basic needs such as food, clothing, and decent shelter. Orphans in Botswana also experience emotional stress, depression, anxiety, stigmatization, isolation, unintended pregnancies, early marriages, and deteriorating health conditions (Muchiru, 1998; *The Botswana Guardian*, December, 1, 2000; Raditedu, 2004).

Family violence is another child welfare problem, although no nationwide study has been conducted on children living with domestic violence. The scarcity of research is not surprising because the issue is rarely discussed in either the public or the private spheres. More is known about women and domestic violence than about children and domestic violence. Several scholars have noted that violence against women in Botswana is widespread and that many women stay in abusive relationships for years (Maundeni, 2002; Mogwe, 1988; Molokomme, 1990). Taking into account that a large percentage of the Botswana population is children, it is obvious that some children are exposed to violence in their homes.

A third set of problems also prevalent in the country includes child abuse and neglect, although research in these areas is still in its infancy in Botswana. The scant available literature indicates, however, that child maltreatment is increasing in the country (Ministry of Local Government, 2001).

Finally, there is a problem of abandoned babies in the country. This is not a new problem. Interviews with stakeholders (see the methodology section for a list of stakeholders who were interviewed) showed that between the late 1990s and 2005, incidents of infant abandonment increased. Unfortunately, no reliable figures exist for this phenomenon because some cases were not reported. Nevertheless, the media occasionally report such incidents. Perpetrators of this crime are usually mothers who have just given birth. They throw the babies in outlets such as pit latrines, garbage bags, or rivers; others just leave the babies in the care of strangers in public places such as churches and hospitals. For example, in April 2005, a local radio station reported about a woman leaving a newborn with a stranger in a church, saying that she was going to the toilet and would be back soon. In another incident, a woman left the baby in the arms of a patient who was in a queue at Princess Marina Hospital. Nearly a year later, that child was still residing in a hospital room with four other abandoned babies. Another woman abandoned a baby in a tree stump. The station commander who was interviewed by a staff member from *Mmegi* newspaper, reported:

> It looks like the mother tried to kill the baby by wedging its head between the sharp edges of the tree's stump, but fortunately God saved the child. He is alive and healthy at Selebi-phikwe government hospital. (Mmegi newspaper, May, 20, 2005, p. 17)

These stories show that a serious problem exists and that public hospitals are de facto becoming unofficial residential facilities. Yet society still denies that an increasing number of families are unable to take care of their children and that there is need to expand residential homes for such children.

Although there are numerous child welfare problems in the country, there are also numerous strategies both at policy and practice level that are in place to address them. Existing policies include the United Nations Convention on the Rights of the Child that Botswana ratified in 1995; the African Charter on the Rights and Welfare of the Child; the Children's Act of 1981; and the Adoption Act of 1952. A closer look at the dates of the laws shows that most are outdated. Consequently, many are currently under review by the Ministry of Local Government's Social Services Department.[2]

Several programs and services exist to address the needs of Orphans and Vulnerable Children. One of them is the National Orphan Care Program, which was established in 1999. The program is housed in the Social Services Department under the child welfare division. Its objectives are to review and develop policies, build and strengthen institutional capacity, provide social welfare services, and monitor and evaluate activities (UNICEF, undated).

Apart from services provided at the central government level, local authorities have departments of Social and Community Development, which are manned by social workers. The social workers, among other things, play a key role in the orphan care program. For instance, they identify and register orphans in their areas of jurisdiction, through home visits, schools, and churches; screen orphans using established criteria to identify the type of assistance they need; identify local groups purchasing food, clothing, and other necessities and distributing them to orphans. In a nutshell, they assist orphans with food, clothing, blankets, toiletries, counseling, school uniforms, and other educational needs.

The efforts of government are augmented by nongovernmental and community-based organizations such as Childline-Botswana, Botswana Christian Council, Botswana Christian AIDS Intervention Program, and Tirisanyo Catholic Mission. These organizations provide services to communities in various parts of the country, ranging from individual counseling, family counseling, recreational programs, life skills and day care for orphans to providing for basic needs such as food, clothing, and education. The organizations noted in this paragraph are funded by various local, regional, and international bodies, such as the government of Botswana and the Kellogg Foundation. They also engage in various fund-raising projects. Finally, the country also offers residential facilities for children in need of care. There is, however, no national foster care program in the country.

Although various child welfare services exist in Botswana, the psychosocial needs of some orphans and vulnerable children in the country continue to go unmet for several reasons: services offered by nongovernmental organizations (NGOs) and community-based organizations (CBOs) are not available in all areas of the country; social workers around the country are overwhelmed with providing material assistance to orphans and vulnerable children; and some social workers are not adequately trained to provide psychosocial support. These issues affect the need for residential care because when a number of children are housed in the same area, it can become relatively easy to make services available to them.

In addition, only in early 2005 were regulations passed to govern the establishment of residential care facilities. For many years, the kind of care provided within facilities varied from one institution to another; there was no monitoring tool.

A section on background information would not be complete without a discussion of the process that takes place before a child is put into a residential facility. According to the Botswana Children's Act, section 15:

1. Where any person observing a child has reasonable cause to believe that the child is in need of care he shall immediately make a report thereof to the social welfare officer or a police officer in the district in which the child is resident.
2. A social welfare officer or police officer to whom a report has been made under subsection (1) may remove or cause to be removed to a place of safety the child in question and shall as soon thereafter as may be, subject to the provisions of

section 17(5) bring the child or cause him to be brought before the children's court of the district in which the child is resident.

3. Where it appears to a commissioner that a child within the area of his jurisdiction is in need of care, he may by order in writing authorize a police officer to enter without a warrant any premises to search for the child and take him to a place of safety to be kept there until he can be brought before a children's court.

4. Where a child has been removed or taken to a place of safety, the social welfare officer in that district shall, before the child is taken to a children's court, enquire into and submit to the court a report containing such information on the general conduct, home environment, school records and medical history (if any) of the child, together with such recommendations thereon as he may consider necessary.

5. Any person who hinders or obstructs a social welfare officer or a police officer in the exercise of the powers conferred on him under this section shall be guilty of an offence.

The procedure outlined above sounds pretty straightforward and efficient. However, in reality, sometimes there are delays. One of the factors that cause delays in the process is that social workers in NGOs are not allowed by law to write court reports. Therefore, they cannot be directly involved in the process of removing the child from home; instead they must rely on local government social workers. This sometimes results in a long lapse before the cases are brought to court. Another issue that causes delay in the hearing of cases is the lack of magistrates who are designated to handle child welfare cases only; children's cases are combined with all others.

Children who are placed in care pass through the court process, or a court order must be made. In cases of emergencies, court orders are not made, but police reports are required, and court orders are then submitted within three days. Social workers with the local authorities as well as those working for residential centers pointed out that it is the responsibility of the local social worker to continue working with the children's families to rehabilitate them so that when the children are released from care, their families are more stable and better equipped to parent them. However, that is not always possible. In my own experience of working with social workers around the country as well as from social workers interviewed for this study, I have learned that in most cases, social workers are so overwhelmed with their day-to-day duties that they are unable to devote sufficient efforts to family rehabilitation, empowerment, and reunification programs.

Methodology

There is little documentation on residential centers for children in Botswana. The issues discussed in this chapter are based on several sources, one of which is in-depth, semistructured interviews with 12 respondents. The 12 respondents were two police officers (one of whom was trained in social work), two hospital social workers, four social workers who work for the local authorities, and four social workers who work in residential facilities.

My own experiences of providing community service to numerous child welfare organizations, my insights in teaching numerous social work courses at the University of Botswana for many years, as well as the very limited existing literature also informed the issues raised here. In addition to teaching and researching child welfare issues in the country, I have, for the past 12 years, offered expertise to numerous child welfare organizations. These include running workshops for workers in centers for orphans and vulnerable children, probation officers, and social workers in rehabilitation centers for juvenile offenders.[3] I am also a member of the reference group that reviewed the Botswana Children's Act, the National Child Welfare Committee, and the National Preschool Development Committee.

Interviews with stakeholders focused on, among other things, the history of residential homes for children in need of care in the country, factors that led to their establishment, the kinds of children admitted, reasons for admission, children's length of stay in the homes, services provided to children while in care, explicit and latent functions of the residential homes, and challenges.

History of Residential Care Settings for Abused, Neglected, Orphaned, and Abandoned Children in Botswana

The history of residential care facilities in Botswana is relatively recent. The first facility was established in 1987, followed by those established in 1998, 2000, 2003, and 2004. Although the first SOS (Save Our Souls) children's village was established in the 1980s, the SOS Children's Village has a long history. The first village was founded in 1949 in Imst, Austria. It was established to help children who had lost their homes, their security, and their families as a result of the Second World War. As time went on, SOS international received support from many donors and coworkers, and it grew to help children all over the world.

Although the first children's home in the country has existed for 18 years, there are only five residential care facilities for children in need of care in Botswana. Several factors account for this slow pace of growth. The first is lack of resources. Four out of the five facilities are owned and run by NGOs that often rely on the goodwill of donors. During the late 1990s, most NGOs in the country experienced cuts from donor agencies on the rationale that Botswana's economy is far better than that of many African countries. Therefore, donor agencies concluded that it is better to channel resources to countries that are more disadvantaged (Moatshe, 2004). Second, government has been quite reluctant to establish residential homes for children in need of care. Government continues to argue that care by relatives— the dominant cultural practice—is the logical option, as family members are better suited to provide care, love, and support to children. As such, the government does not play a key role in funding the facilities and only provides small grants to them. Nevertheless, government policy reflects a commitment to child welfare issues, as shown by the various laws regarding children in need of care.

Although government argues that the extended family is able to take care of children in need of care, numerous scholars have asserted that social and economic changes in the country have adversely affected the socioeconomic support base of the extended family. Therefore, the extended family is increasingly unable to adequately play its former rule before industrialization and urbanization, such as absorbing children in need of care (Himonga, 1985; Jacques, 1998; Kooijman, 1978; Maundeni, 2000, Raditedu, 2004). The process of social change has been accompanied by numerous shifts that have, among other things, weakened the communal production that existed in the past, bringing about the spirit of individualism and the emergence of the nuclear family that values helping only immediate family members.

Some of the difficulties that extended family members face in absorbing children in need of care are evidenced in the following words of one of the respondents who participated in Raditedu's (2004, p. 33) study of the psychosocial impact of orphanhood on a girl in Kalkfotein:

> People should understand that we have our own children and taking in other children in our homes results in us having so many dependents to take care of. This becomes very difficult; we don't have the resources to take care of so many children. Some of us are not working, we are suffering. This is why we share orphans in extended family.

These words indicate that although the popular belief is that the extended family is better suited to provide care, love, and support to children in need, doing so is not always easy. The current economic conditions make it difficult for unemployed relatives to provide care to orphans. Many orphans who participated in Raditedu's study felt that they experienced numerous problems because caregivers do not fully accept them (the orphans), but they keep the children because the caregivers want to benefit from the Orphan Care Program. These views held by orphans have far-reaching implications for their well-being, and as such stakeholders should take them seriously.

Factors That Led to the Establishment of Residential Facilities for Abused, Abandoned, and Neglected Children in Botswana

Among the reasons that led to the establishment of residential facilities for children in need of care in Botswana are the numerous problems that children experience as a result of urbanization and migration. These problems include child abuse and neglect as well as abandonment, parental divorce, orphanhood, incest, and rape, just to name a few (Maundeni and Levers, 2004). Although the process of social change contributed to numerous child welfare problems, it was only in the mid 1990s that publicity on child welfare problems intensified. This scrutiny was largely a result of the government ratification of international and regional treaties that protect children's rights, the existence of NGOs that focus on the well-being of children and women, and the massive public education programs on child welfare issues by stakeholders. Despite these trends, there is still controversy about what constitutes child abuse. In the numerous media talk shows and call-in radio programs that are occasionally aired, it is common to hear parents blame government and social workers for children's mischievous behaviors since government teaches children that they have rights. Many parents assert that they are unable to discipline their children out of fear that child welfare organizations will label their actions child abuse.

Second, since the late 1990s HIV/AIDS has led to a drastic increase in the numbers of orphans that are accommodated in residential facilities, particularly SOS facilities. Prior to 1997, for example, SOS used to admit approximately five children per year. This small number shows that during the first few years of their operation, the SOS villages were not fully embraced and utilized by the community. The major landmark in the history of residential care in the country took place between 1998 and 2004, when SOS started to admit 40 and 50 children per year. This drastic increase resulted from the high numbers of orphans whose parents had died of HIV/AIDS. In addition, since the extended family is no longer able to cope with the huge numbers of orphans, communities readily accepted the services of institutions such as SOS.

Characteristics of Residential Care in Botswana

Currently, there are five facilities for children in need of care in Botswana. These are the two Save Our Souls (SOS) villages,[4] which were established in 1987 and 1998; the facility that is run by Childline Botswana, which was established in 2003[5]; the Paolo Zanichille children's home, which was established in 2004[6]; and the Mpule Kwelagobe facility,[7] which started operating in 2000. Of these five facilities, only SOS has the ability to keep children on a long-term basis. This is so because its aim is to make children independent and self-supporting. Consequently, children who are accommodated in SOS villages are not eligible for adoption. Local authority social workers who were interviewed viewed this policy as problematic because it limits the facilities' capacity to take new children. They also believed that residential care for children should be temporary, not permanent.

Other facilities provide care to children on a short-term basis. The definition of short-term varies from one residential facility to another. For instance, the Childline facility keeps children for three months while the Paolo Zanichille facility keeps them until they reach the age of 14 years depending on regular review of the case by the social worker from the child's home town. The length of time that a child can stay in Childline, Mpule Kwelagobe, and Paolo Zanichille facilities also depends on the availability of adoptive parents as well as the readiness of both the child and the family to be united. The latter is discussed in detail in the section that focuses on challenges. However, sometimes children remain in these facilities for more than the stipulated periods.

The kinds of residential facilities in Botswana are small family-like facilities that cater to children in need of care. The SOS and Paolo Zanichille facilities are examples of how Botswana child care functions. One of the objectives of SOS children's homes is to build families for children in need of care as well as to help children shape their own future (SOS, undated). The objective of the Paolo Zanichille home reads as follows:

> Our objective is to grow the children in a safe and calm environment. We shall give them ethical and scholastic education, and provide them with the right of medical attention. We want to create a save haven, a big family, in which these children will be educated to learn values such as fraternity, solidarity, and finally learn how to be independent. It is of major importance that the children will not lose relations with friends and family. (Paolo Zanichille Children's Home, undated)

A common theme that runs across the objectives of the two homes (SOS and Paolo Zanichille) is the creation of "families" for the children during their stay in the homes. This goal is basically an extension of the traditional extended family that was common in many African cultures. It is a key feature that distinguishes children's homes in Botswana from large institutions for children in need that exist in some parts of the world.

The SOS concept of family is based on four principles: the mother; brothers and sisters; the house/family home; and the village. Each child has an SOS mother who lives with and tries to build a close relationship with the child. Girls and boys of different ages live together as brothers and sisters, with natural siblings always staying together within the same SOS family. The intent is for these children and their SOS mother to build emotional ties that are long lasting. The mothers and siblings live in family houses, which have their unique routines and rhythm. According to the reports of SOS officials, children enjoy a sense of security and home environment. They share responsibilities. Last, the SOS family is seen as part of the community. Residents attend schools in the community in the hope that they will be integrated into mainstream society. The families live together, with the intent of forming a supportive village environment where children enjoy a happy childhood. According to the SOS philosophy, it is through children's families, the village, and the community that children learn to participate actively in society (SOS, undated). SOS sees their villages as the best compromise between an "institution" and a dysfunctional poor family (Save Our Souls, 2004).

Childline and Mpule Kwelagobe facilities also use the approaches described above. The only difference is that they operate on a much smaller scale than SOS. In April 2005, the maximum number of children that could be absorbed by both the Child Line facility and the Paolo Zanichille facility was 20; Mpule Kwelagobe had a capacity of 50 children. The two SOS villages on the other hand had reached their full combined capacity of 425 children in April 2005.

The Current Situation of Residential Care in Botswana

At the time of this writing, approximately 475 children were housed in the five centers: 425 in the two SOS villages; 8 in Child line residential facility; 20 in Mpule Kwelagobe; and 7 in Paolo Zanichille. Each facility admitted children of various ages. For example, the Paolo Zanichille children's home admitted children between 1 and 7 years old, while Childline admitted infants as young as a week old. Even though the facilities had specified the ages of children they would accept, sometimes they took children above those ages because they preferred to keep siblings together rather than to separate them. The facilities' emphasis on keeping orphan siblings together is a welcome development because siblings have the potential to provide support to each other, particularly following traumatic experiences such as death of parents. Most orphans who stay with relatives are separated from their siblings, as the resources of the sheltering family are often inadequate to provide for large numbers of additional children. Despite the reasons that caregivers give for separating siblings, numerous researchers have found that separation adversely affects bonding among siblings (Raditedu, 2004). For instance, some of the respondents who participated in Raditedu's study lamented:

> Separation of orphan siblings is a common occurrence in this village. This is prob-
> lematic because it destroys the bonds that exist between them when their parents
> were still alive. This can have a long-term psychological effect on these children.
> The government must discourage that.

Functions of Residential Care in Botswana

Residential care facilities for children in need carry out various functions. They are doing their best, using available resources, to address children's psychosocial needs. All the five centers use a holistic approach to meeting children's needs. For instance, they provide for basic needs such as food and shelter, education, medical attention, and counseling (both to children and parents). This approach is facilitated by the various professionals (teachers, social workers, nurses, and housemothers) who are employed in the homes. The needs of children in residential care are addressed not only by staff of the facilities but also by various community members and volunteers. For example, some centers rely on volunteers from the community to provide tutoring services to children who do not perform well at school. Initially some community members and institutions stigmatized children residing in residential facilities, but with continued dialogue, the situation has improved.

The facilities also attempt, as much as possible, to help children become self-sufficient and independent. For example, some children who graduated from SOS are able to earn their own living; at the time interviews were conducted for this chapter, approximately 40 children had graduated into self-sufficiency. This group includes one who was working abroad, one who was a police officer, one who was an electrician, and 10 who were in the hotel industry. Others were attending various institutions of higher learning locally, regionally, and internationally. The SOS institutions continue to try to improve their 60 percent success rate for self-sufficiency, which it measured by factors such as the former residents' ability to hold a steady job and find suitable, affordable accommodation. Not all children who graduated from SOS manage to earn their own living. This is reflected in the statement below which appeared in the SOS (2004) newsflash:

> Some are struggling, both for accommodation and for employment, and it should be realized, that if you have no relatives it is a major struggle to find jobs and accommodation. Again it is up to SOS and the Youth to think laterally, to respect manual skills and break out of the dependency syndrome.

An unintended consequence of residential care that poses a challenge to moving children toward self-sufficiency is that some children become too dependent on the home, to the extent that they lose ties with their relatives. According to some staff of the homes, some youths have a tendency to believe that they must stay in the homes forever. Some are working, some are attending tertiary institutions, but they still stay in the children's homes. Children's dependency on the homes is often fostered by their relatives. Family members are encouraged to maintain contact with children, and most do so, but some do not. For some children, the contact between them and relatives is literally nonexistent. A director of one of the homes noted:

> I remember one day we (the staff members) had to play the roles of uncles and aunts when one of the youths who were staying here was getting married. You know in this country and in many African countries, it is very rare for a marriage to take place without the involvement of the extended family. So we went all the way to Selibi phikwe[8] to participate in the marriage negotiations, we even had to tell the groom's family how much dowry (bride price) they should pay,

The facilities also try to ensure that children in care get protection against all forms of abuse and enjoy their rights. In most cases when children are admitted to the facilities, they have already experienced traumatic situations that jeopardize their well-being. Consequently, children's homes try to shield children from additional trauma. In particular, the facilities try to protect and empower children by operating on a small scale they train housemothers in child care issues enhancing housemothers' ability to better respond to the needs of children, and they use a family approach, which they hope will enable children to develop strong and supportive relationships.

Challenges Faced by Residential Care Facilities

Although the facilities are managing to achieve many of their goals, they also experience numerous challenges. Some challenges are unique, and some are common to all five facilities. One of the challenges that cut across the five centers is that some children tend to stay in the facilities longer than was intended when they were placed. This trend is not only peculiar to Botswana but is well documented in other countries (cf. Sinclair and Gibbs, 1998). Several factors account for this trend in Botswana. First, quite often little attention is given to uniting children with families once the children are placed in care. Residential care facilities receive children who have experienced prolonged trauma; therefore, intense efforts are needed to rehabilitate them and their families. Such efforts are not always possible because, as indicated elsewhere in this chapter, local authority social workers are often faced with enormous workloads that include identifying, registering, and providing material assistance to the increasing number of orphans in the country. This leaves them with inadequate time to devote to family reunification.

The other reason that contributes to children's long stays in care is that some children are brought to the centers very late after internalizing the problems under which they grew up; therefore, rehabilitation is not only difficult but also takes longer. For instance, the effectiveness of therapy with a child who experienced sexual abuse for many years depends largely on the duration of such therapy.

Another reason that contributes to children's long stays in care is that there are very few places to absorb children who graduate from residential facilities. Besides family reunification, other options were placement with older siblings and extended family, and adoption. Foster care is rare in Botswana. Joining the extended family or being adopted are generally not viable options for all children graduating from care because of the reasons already mentioned. Adoption is not a popular option partly because some potential adoptive parents are reluctant to take children who are HIV positive. There are no statistics on the numbers of children in care who are HIV positive; however, with HIV/AIDS the major cause of death in Botswana, we cannot rule out the possibility that many children in care are HIV positive. Finally, some children overstay in care because their lack of skills and experience coupled with little support from family makes it difficult for them to be independent and self-sufficient.

How then do the facilities cope with children remaining in care for long periods? Respondents mentioned continued efforts to rehabilitate families as well as to trace relatives of abandoned children. In addition, staff in two facilities mentioned that they cope by using "youth houses." In such houses, youth are given individual allowances to run their house. It is not surprising that only two facilities mentioned youth houses because those facilities had a longer history than others, and they each accommodated a higher number of children.

The third challenge is follow-ups. According to the stakeholders interviewed, the residential facilities are doing a good job, but after-care programs are very weak, largely because staff members responsible for these programs have so many other duties.

The fourth challenge mentioned was to educate people to understand what constituted child abuse and children's rights as well as the role of child welfare organizations. Many people still have misconceptions about child welfare issues. Child welfare officers therefore still have a major and difficult task in sensitizing communities about the issues.

The fifth challenge is handling termination, particularly with young children whose vocabulary is very limited as well as with older children who are not willing to leave residential facilities. One of the major reasons some children are reluctant to leave care is the huge difference in the environment in residential centers and that in their natural homes. For example, the environment in residential homes is structured while that in most families is not. In addition, the standard of living in residential homes is higher than that in many natural homes of children.

The sixth challenge is that of children who continue to exhibit problem behaviors. Some of the problem behaviors reported included violence, use of vulgar language, early sexual activity, and poor school performance. This list is not exhaustive because only a few staff members and no residents of the facilities were interviewed for this chapter. Literature from abroad shows that one of the problems that residential homes for children face is children who run away. This problem did not arise in the interviews; instead, respondents reported that some children wanted to come back to stay in the residential homes.

Thus far we have focused on challenges that cut across all the five centers. Now attention focuses on challenges that are unique to some centers. One is that it takes time for communities to embrace the idea of residential homes for children in need of care. Consequently, some facilities are underutilized. However, residential care facilities are continuing to work to enlighten communities about their services.

Facilities run by NGOs also face financial constraints. As mentioned earlier, many international donors have reduced their support because Botswana is considered a middle-income country with less need for financial aid than other, poorer countries. In addition, most donors are reluctant to fund the ongoing operating costs of the facilities. The residential facilities run by NGOs are engaged in numerous fund-raising activities, but the money they generate from such activities is not sufficient. Financial constraints are not only peculiar to residential facilities for children in need of care; they are also experienced by NGOs that provide nonresidential services to women and children. For example, between 2001 and 2005, several such organizations closed down because of lack of funds. However, the government provides grants to NGOs that address child welfare issues. For example, in the year 2001–2002, the grant that was provided to SOS was about one million Pula[9] (equivalent to $153, 846).

The last challenge that is peculiar to some facilities is retaining housemothers, who leave for several reasons: jobs that pay better; personal situations such as pregnancy; criteria used to recruit them (e.g., one should not have young children); conditions of service (e.g., one must be able to spend most of the time in the facility). The inability of some facilities to retain mothers has serious implications for the facilities. For example, it is costly, as new mothers have to be trained when old ones are lost and losing a housemother creates instability in the lives of children.

The Future of Residential Care Facilities for Children in Need of Care in Botswana

So far I have discussed the history of residential facilities in Botswana, the current situation of such facilities, their explicit and latent functions as well as challenges they face. The chapter has shown among other things that a large percentage of the country's population is comprised of children; orphanhood is a major child welfare problem that is currently facing Botswana; stakeholders are embarking on various strategies to address the child welfare problems; and residential care facilities for children have explicit and latent functions. Finally, the facilities face a number of challenges. These include children's overstay in care; difficulties in reintegrating children into the community; scarcity of places to absorb children who graduate from care; financial constraints; inadequate contact between children and relatives; difficulties in following up graduates and in handling termination as well as in educating communities about issues affecting the welfare of children.

Now attention focuses on the future. Regulations governing children in need of care have recently been approved. Unlike Western countries, where foster parents are paid, Botswana would not pay foster parents. When the government approved the regulations, it deleted the recommendation that foster parents must be paid. Therefore, it remains to be seen whether in the absence of financial incentives, many people would express interest in fostering children. Small-scale residential care facilities for children will continue to be an option, particularly if existing facilities continue to receive funding from donors. The government of Botswana continues to believe that children are better cared for in their natural homes than in institutions; therefore, the chances are minimal that it would channel more resources into residential care in the near future.

Considering the challenges of child care in Botswana, I recommend the following: First, there is need for a national coordinating body for all institutions that will coordinate all residential facilities providing care for children through a databased system and explore ways of addressing challenges facing residential care facilities in the country. Second, the government should devote more funding to residential homes for children in need of care. The number of orphans only (excluding neglected, abused, and abandoned children) is increasing as HIV/AIDS continues to take the lives of many people. And since many NGO-run human service organizations experience financial hardships, it is reasonable to argue that the government should increase funds to such organizations. This move will go a long way in enabling existing residential homes to continue surviving as well as to expand their services so that they can care for more children. As the extended families' role in absorbing children in need of care continues to weaken because of the forces of social change, residential homes for children in need that reflect the Botswana culture could become the extended families for such children. This is particularly so if more efforts could be channeled to improving contact of children with their remaining relatives and stressing family reunification as well as community integration.

Finally, there is a need for research to explore good practices, opportunities, and challenges that face residential care facilities for children in need in Botswana. Such research must be comprehensive and representative of the views of residents themselves as well as all stakeholders.

NOTES

1. Minister here refers to the Minister of Local Government.
2. The review of various child welfare policies and laws in the country usually entails the engagement of consultants by the Social Services Department.
3. Five such centers exist in the country. All are owned by NGOs. They are funded by local and international organizations. They provide day care services to orphans (between 2 and 18 years of age) and their families. Such services include preschool facilities, psychosocial support, training in parenting skills and cooking skills, community outreach, home-based care support, recreational programs, and training in life skills.
4. These facilities are affiliated with the international organization SOS-Kinderdorf. One village is located in Tlokweng (approximately 4 kilometers from the capital city, Gaborone); the other one is located in Francistown (450 kilometers away from the capital city).
5. It operates from the capital city.
6. The facility is in Gantsi (720 kilometers from the capital city).
7. The Mpule Kwelagobe facility is in Jwaneng (201 kilometers from the capital city).
8. Selibiphikwe is a town that is located approximately 500 kilometers from the capital city where two of the residential facilities are found.
9. Pula is the currency for Botswana.

REFERENCES

Botswana Guardian, December 1, 2000.

Government of Botswana. (1981). The Botswana Children's Act. Gabarone: Government Printer.

Government of Botswana. (2001). Population and Housing Census. Gaborone: Central Statistics Office, Department of Printing and Publishing Services.

Himonga, C. N. (1985). *Family property disputes: The predicament of women and children in a Zambian urban community.* Unpublished doctoral dissertation, London School of Economic and Political Science.

Hope, K. R. (1996). Growth, unemployment and poverty in Botswana. *Journal of Contemporary African Studies, 14*(1), 53–67.

Jacques, G. (1998, July 5–9). *Back to the future: AIDS, orphans and alternative care in Botswana.* Paper presented at the Joint World Congress of the International Federation of Social Workers (IFSW) and the International Association of Schools of Social Work (IASSW), Jerusalem, Israel.

Kooijman, K. F. M. (1978). *Social and economic change in a Tswana village.* Leiden: Afrika-Studiecentrum.

Lesetedi, G. N., and Ngcongco, N. L. (1995), A demographic and socio-economic profile of women and men in Botswana: A review of summary indicators of population composition and distribution, mortality, migration and economic ability. In *Ministry of Finance and Development Planning* (pp. 176–188). Gaborone, Botswana: Central Statistics Office.

Maundeni, T. (2000). *Children's experiences of divorce in Botswana.* Unpublished doctoral dissertation, University of Glasgow.

Maundeni, T. (2002). Wife abuse among a sample of divorced women in Botswana: A research note. *Violence Against Women, 8*(2), 257–274.

Maundeni, T., and Levers, L. L. (2004, September). *Concerns about child subject research in Botswana: A call for establishing structures and guidelines that protect children.* Paper presented at the Department of Social Work Seminar.

Ministry of Local Government. (2001). *Initial report to the United Nations Committee for the Convention on the Rights of the Child.* Gaborone: Government Printer.

Moatshe, B. (2004). *The impact of declining donor support on the sustainability of non governmental organizations in Botswana: Insights from some NGO managers in Botswana.* Unpublished bachelor's thesis, University of Botswana.

Mogwe, A. (1988). *Battered women in Gaborone.* Unpublished master's thesis, University of Cape Town.

Molokomme, A. (1990). Women's law in Botswana, laws and research needs. In J. Stewart and J. Armstrong (Eds.), *The legal situation of women in Southern Africa* (pp. 7–46). Harare: University of Zimbabwe Publications.

Mmegi newspaper, May 20, 2005.

Muchiru, S. M. (1998). The rapid assessment on the situation of orphans in Botswana. Gaborone: AIDS/STD Unit, Ministry of Health.

Paolo Zanichille Children's Home. (undated). Gantsi.

Pule, M. M. (2004). *The consequences of growing up poor: Some thoughts on Botswana.* Unpublished master's thesis, Department of Social Work, University of Botswana.

Raditedu, B. L. (2004). *Psychosocial impact of orphanhood on the girl-child: A study of Kalkfotein.* Unpublished bachelor's degree project, Department of Social Work, University of Botswana.

Save Our Souls. (2004). Newsflash, SOS Children's Village Association of Botswana.

Sinclair, I., and Gibbs, I. (1998). *Children's homes: A study in diversity.* New York: John Wiley.

7

Residential Care in South Africa

Changing the Perspective from Social Welfare to Social Development

BRIAN STOUT

Residential care for children in South Africa is one of the aspects of social policy that has been significantly affected by the two most prominent aspects of the country's recent history: the transition from apartheid to a democratic state and the HIV/AIDS pandemic. South Africa is shifting its social care emphasis from social welfare to social development, and this has an effect on the place of residential care within the system. The apartheid legislation has already been amended and reinterpreted in light of the new dispensation, and a new Children's Act is being enacted in 2008.

This chapter first places the current situation of residential care into the context of the history of social care provision in South Africa. It then describes the current situation of residential care for children. The final section outlines the future prospects under the new Children's Act for children in need of residential care, with a particular focus on provision for children affected by HIV/AIDS.

Social Welfare before South Africa's Transition to Democracy

Social work and social welfare throughout most of South Africa's history were characterized by a focus on provision for the needs of poor white citizens, with at times an almost total neglect for the welfare needs of the majority black population. This makes any discussion of the history of the provision of residential care to children difficult because there is an absence of both academic writing and official figures for the black population. However, an understanding of the history of social welfare in general is valuable in considering the current provision of residential services for children and future plans.

Social welfare in South Africa began in 1657 with the distribution of relief to poor white farmers. Social services developed during that time, with provision made for children with disabilities, but no help was given to the indigenous population. Throughout the nineteenth century the development of the mining industry led to the breakup of many families. Black people set up their own self-help and voluntary organizations (Brown and Neku, 2002).

Until the 1920s social work as a distinct profession did not exist in South Africa; social welfare needs were addressed through family and community (Drower, 2002). A study of the history of social work in the country shows that it emerged to meet the needs of poor whites and was not inclined to work for the empowerment of the black population (Noyoo, 2000). Any interventions that were made were uncoordinated, short term, and focused on the white community (Drower, 2002). Legislation that was designed to protect children, such as the Children's Protection Act of 1913, applied only to white children. Following a government investigation and report into the "poor white problem," social welfare departments were introduced in the 1930s, and social workers started to receive training. The first Department of Welfare was established in 1937 (Sewpaul and Lombard, 2004). Also in that year, the Children's Act of 1937 was passed, a "liberal and progressive" (Van der Spuy et al., 2004, p. 172) piece of legislation that used the language of education and rehabilitation to discuss children and provided a legislative framework for future developments in child welfare.

Schools of social work were introduced at the University of Cape Town (UCT) in the 1920s and Wits University, Johannesburg, in the 1930s, but it was only in the 1940s and 1950s that training for other racial groups was introduced (Mazibuko and Gray, 2002). Although this ended social work's status as an all-white profession, it remained deeply divided (Sewpaul and Lombard, 2004). There were, however, at that time voices in the universities and at conferences that acknowledged the many black children who were living in desperate conditions. For example, the Conference on Urban Juvenile Delinquency in 1938 called on the government to extend its social welfare program to all children, regardless of race (Van der Spuy et al., 2004).

The political development of South Africa in the second half of the twentieth century was dominated by the apartheid regime. Apartheid, a policy of racial segregation and "separate development," was introduced in 1948, and over five decades black people in South Africa were subjected to systematic discrimination in every sphere (Burger, 2003). Children in particular suffered violence, abuse, and other trauma as a consequence of apartheid (Rock, 1997). Apartheid segregation was reflected in welfare policy and the delivery of social services. Rather than heeding the call to extend social welfare services to black children, the government decided to increasingly keep the two races separate so the social problems of black young people would not affect the white population (Van der Spuy et al., 2004). Social work reinforced Afrikaner nationalism and served to maintain the authority of the National Party government (Noyoo, 2000). For this reason the funding of social work posts was based on the nature of the population served, and the methods followed favored therapeutic group work (Noyoo, 2000) and social casework (Sewpaul and Lombard, 2004). The separation of services according to race perpetuated discrimination. Black people, who had the greatest need, received the smallest proportion of the welfare budget and were least likely to have access to essential infrastructure (Brown and Neku, 2002). Training reflected Western methodologies emphasizing individual and family intervention and rehabilitative approaches (Drower, 2002).

In the 1980s the first statutory council for social work was developed, with a view to regulating social work conduct and education (Drower, 2002). However, social work at that time still remained blind to the needs of the disadvantaged majority population and continued to be committed to individual, psychotherapeutic interventions.

Throughout the entire period of apartheid, discriminatory policies were opposed by a resistance movement led by the African National Congress (ANC). This national and international campaign culminated in eventual success in the 1990s with the release of Nelson Mandela, the unbanning of the ANC, and the first democratic elections in 1994 (Burger, 2003). At this time, the social work profession joined with other parts of society in making admissions to the Truth and Reconciliation Commission (TRC), acknowledging complicity with apartheid (Sacco and Hoffman, 2002). Social work educators at Wits University joined with practitioners in making submissions to the TRC. They admitted that clinical practice was allowed to dominate, to the exclusion of social and community development; the radical perspective was neglected and students were insufficiently educated in social action; and social work educators had not challenged apartheid policies vigorously enough (Sacco and Hoffman, 2002).

Residential Child Care in Transition: 1994–2006

The Current Legislation

Since the introduction of democracy, South Africa has made changes to almost every aspect of its social policy and legislative framework. The child and youth care sector is one of the areas transformed over this period; important legislation has been rewritten and national minimum standards have been introduced (Coughlan, 2000). This section describes the changes over this period, and the following section outlines changes in the forthcoming Children's Act. Before this, however, the previous legislation regarding children in need of residential care will be outlined.

Forty percent (16 million) of the South African population are children. Eighty-one percent of these are African, 9 percent are "colored," 8 percent are white, and 2 percent are Indian Asian. Seven out of 10 of these children live in poverty, and children in rural areas are more likely to live in poverty than those in urban areas. So providing for children in need is an important and necessary task for the South

African state. Until the full enactment of the new Children's Act, the law for children in need of care is still contained in the Child Care Act (74 of 1983). Children in need of care are dealt with by the Children's Court. The Child Care Act 1983 made provision for six forms of residential care (SALC 2002a):

- A "place of safety," which falls under the Department of Social Development, is defined as any place suitable for the reception of a child, into which the owner, occupier, or person in charge is willing to receive a child. The court has the power to remove a child to a place of safety if the child is thought to be in grave danger. A place of safety needs to be registered with the Department of Social Development, but the broad definition can include a children's home or even a private individual (Skelton, 1998).
- A "shelter" is any premises used for the temporary care of more than six children in "especially difficult circumstances." Those circumstances are defined by the act as those that deny children their basic needs, such as when they are living on the streets or exposed to violence. Children can self-refer to shelters, which are required to be registered.
- A "children's home" can be run by a church, welfare organizations, or the private sector but must be registered with the Department of Social Development. It is a residence for the protection and care of more than six children. Children's homes should have trained staff to work with children on a long-term basis. Child and youth workers will work with the child, and social workers will provide a link with the family.
- A "reform school" falls under the Department of Education and is defined as a school maintained for the care and training of children sent there under the Criminal Procedure Act 1977. This is the most restrictive type of residential facility.
- "Schools of industries" also fall under the Department of Education and are maintained for the care and education of children. They are usually used when a child needs more supervision than is available in a children's home.
- "Secure care facilities" fall under the Department of Social Development; they offer children an environment for their care, safety, and development.

Except for an emergency situation, a court order was required before a child could be lawfully removed from his or her home. As the Children's Court plays a central role in the placement of a child in care, the Court will have a crucial role to play in the move away from a dependence on residential care (Snyman, 2003). At a Children's Court Enquiry the court had a number of options: the child could remain with his or her parent or guardian, or the child could be placed with a foster parent, in a children's home, or in a school of industries. A child could not be sent to a reform school by a Children's Court, only by a criminal court. A child could, however, be transferred to a reform school from a children's home by administrative transfer, a practice that has been criticized as an infringement of the child's rights (Skelton, 1998).

Similar to the children who are in residential care under the auspices of the Departments of Education and Social Development, many South African children are cared for within the prison system, by the Department of Correctional Services (DCS). This group of children can be divided into two categories: those who are in custody because they have committed or been charged with offenses, and those who are in custody because their mothers are remanded or sentenced prisoners. The policy of the DCS is that the admission of young children is permissible only when no other suitable accommodation and care are available (DCS, 2004). Mother and Child units are expected to provide an environment conducive to the care and development of young children, and the DCS should provide basic health care services. The DCS acknowledges that Mother and Child units are not ideal facilities at any time and that overcrowding negatively affects service delivery (DCS, 2004).

The Shift to a Social Development Perspective

The recent changes in the legislation relating to the provision of residential care for children will be outlined, but before that, they will be put into the context of the changes in overall social welfare provision in South Africa.

Both the existing and future changes in South African residential child and youth care need to be understood within the context of the changing conceptualization of social work and social care. Since 1994 social work has been influenced by the GEAR (Growth, Employment, and Redistribution) policy that is based on the idea that long-term poverty reduction requires economic growth and private investment (Drower, 2002). The government set as one of its priorities the objective that basic welfare rights could be provided to all citizens (Brown and Neku, 2002). The construction of this developmental social welfare policy was an answer to the difficulty in meeting the expectations of the millions of poor people in South Africa when an institutional welfare state was unaffordable (Bak, 2002).

The White Paper on Social Welfare (Ministry for Welfare and Population Development [MWPD], 1997) is pivotal to the new conceptualization of social work in South Africa:

> The goal of developmental social welfare is a humane, peaceful, just and caring society which will uphold welfare rights, facilitate the meaning of basic human needs, release people's creative energies, help achieve their aspirations, build human capacity and self-reliance, and participate fully in all spheres of social, economic and political life.

This white paper contained a section on residential care providing that children could be placed in residential facilities but only as a last resort. It indicated that such facilities would be much more multipurpose and that child care and youth care workers would be adequately trained. The 1999 Social Welfare Action Plan was devised to put the recommendations of the white paper into practice.

The Social Work Amendment Act (102 of 1998) repealed previous legislation regarding social work. Future attempts to define social work in South Africa are required to underline the communal dimension of human existence. The focus should be on the relationship between people and their environments and a concern about poverty, oppression, and the need for empowerment. Developmental social work has roots in the Black Consciousness movement and is a recognition of the unequal distribution in individualized services (Bak, 2002). The previous case-work approach and the social work education system that supported it were rejected as not suitable for South Africa's needs: "The case work method commonly used by the country's social workers has become outmoded, expensive, irrelevant and west-ern and is not productive for alleviating poverty" (Brown and Neku, 2002, p. 306).

Social welfare is the third-largest spending program in South Africa, after health and education (Triegaardt, 2002). The key shift in social welfare has been to link developmental and antipoverty policies to economic policy, although it is not always clear what the link between social work and economic policy should be (Bak, 2002). The financing policy has shifted the emphasis from a top-down delivery to a participatory approach:

> These shifts of policy reflect congruency with the developmental paradigm which emphasizes: community participation; resources being shifted to the most needy, that is urban to rural; non-discriminatory, inter-provincial disparities; holistic aims with specialized components, and integrated programmes, not per head services. (Triegaardt, 2002, p. 328)

Changes in Provision for Residential Child Care

The shift from a welfare perspective to a developmental perspective has been just one of the influences on the changes in residential provision for children in South Africa. The Child Care Act of 1983 was introduced by the apartheid government, so following the shift to a democratic state it had to be reinterpreted in light of first the Constitution (Act 108 of 1996) and the United Nations Convention on the Rights of the Child (UNCRC). The Constitution provides special rights to children, and legislation relating to children must be interpreted in light of this. Section 28 of the Constitution provides for children's rights, and §28 (2) states the general prin-ciple that a child's best interests are of paramount importance in every matter con-cerning a child. South Africa is committed to international instruments that enshrine children's rights. It ratified the UNCRC in 1995 and is committed to upholding the broad range of rights it contains.

It is with regard to the treatment of children in custody that South Africa has attracted the most criticism. The state has struggled to meet the high standards set by the Constitution and by international law. The detention of children in custody is regularly criticized both within South Africa and by international monitoring bodies (Fagan, 2004; Human Rights Watch, 2005; McClain-Nhlapo, 2004). Human Rights Watch (2005) puts the number of children in the country who are in detention awaiting trial at more than 2,000. Research of the DCS itself also found that children of prisoners in its care were not exposed to activities and opportunities that promote normal development (DCS, 2004). The children experienced various forms of maternal deprivation and displayed aggressive and hostile behavior. The children's development was impaired, leading to destruction of attachment to and trust of other people at a later stage.

In 1995 an Inter-Ministerial Committee on Young People at Risk (IMC) was set up to develop a policy framework for the transformation of the child and youth care system. Their Interim Policy Recommendations indicated that too many children were going into residential care and recommended that the system facilitate the provision of services at an earlier stage to allow more children to stay with their families. The report further recommended an improvement in the situation of children who were admitted to residential care, suggesting greater emphasis on assessment and integration. The report considered child care workers to be central to the system and emphasized the importance of their training and development.

The IMC in 1996 carried out an investigation into places of safety, schools of industries, and reform schools and found widespread human rights abuses in those facilities. Their report recommended the appropriate placement of children, the establishment of appropriate programs, the eradication of abuse, and the transfer of the management of the facilities to the Department of Social Development (SALC, 2002a).

The Child Care Act was amended by the Child Care Amendment Act 96 of 1996. This brought changes to the criteria on which a finding that a child is in need of care must be based and ensured that a social worker's report was obligatory at a Children's Court Inquiry. The Amendment Act changed the test of whether a child is in need of care from one of the unfitness of the parent to the child-centered test of whether the child is in need of care. Skelton (1998) summarized the conditions when a child is determined to be in need of care:

- The child needs to be removed from an adult who has custody because of serious neglect or abuse.
- The child has to appear in the Children's Court because of the death or disappearance of his or her only parent figure.
- The child is described by the current caregiver as demonstrating uncontrollable behavior.

The 1998 publication of the Draft Minimum Standards for the South African Child and Youth Care system saw amendments to regulations and to subsidiary legislation. These amendments brought international law standards to the welfare system, including prohibition of corporal punishment in children's facilities and tighter procedures for review and extension of placements (Sloth-Nielsen, 2003b).

The Child Care Amendment (Act 14 of 1999) abolished the capacity of the Minister of Welfare (now known as the Minister of Social Development) to transfer children to reform schools without a court order. This act also gave a child a limited right of appeal against orders made under section 15 of the Child Care Act, including placement of a child in a children's home or school of industry (Sloth-Nielsen, 2003b).

It is not always easy to see how a developmental approach has actually been implemented in South African social work (Bak, 2002). One example might be the "Eyes on the Child" child protection project in Cape Town. Under the provisions of this project, community volunteers act to protect vulnerable children, including using a family home in the community as a safety home (Bak, 2002). With regard to how the changes in social welfare and wider society have affected residential care for children, Coughlan (2000) presents a case study of one children's home, in the Eastern Cape town of King William's Town. Before 1996, what is now known as King William's Town Child and Youth Care Centre was a traditional children's home serving mainly white children. In 1996 it merged with a Catholic children's home that served black children. Changes that needed to be made to facilitate this merger included the introduction of policies to address racism and promote cultural sensitivity among children and staff. This cultural sensitivity included promoting the first-language needs of staff. There needed to be an increased representation of black staff in management and an increased participation of stakeholders in the community. The home's constitution needed to be rewritten, as did some staff policies and job descriptions. Communication channels needed to be reconsidered to give less-powerful groups an avenue for dissent (Coughlan, 2000).

In 2004 the Western Cape Provincial Government commissioned a review of its child care facilities. This review produced varied results, and the criticisms included a finding that children were not engaged in meaningful activity and in some facilities were lying in bed until midday, with no programs in evidence. The work environment seemed to be designed for the benefit of the staff, not the children, and the training provided did not appear to have been internalized or applied (Gallinetti, 2004). The only facility providing an economical service compatible with child rights was the outsourced facility, New Horizons (Gallinetti, 2004).

Full consideration of the provision of residential care for children, in an international context, was provided at a world conference held in Sweden in 2003, "Children and Residential Care—New Strategies for a New Millennium." This conference was held in the spirit of the UNCRC, which requires international cooperation in development. The UNCRC requires that special protection and assistance be provided for children in residential care. The premise of the conference was that growing up in residential care is detrimental for children and that good practices for finding alternatives that are in operation in some countries can be repeated in others. The Swedish conference referred to the entitlement that a child has been granted by the UNCRC to grow up in a family, stating that institutional care should be seen as the last resort. This is reflected in the forthcoming South African

Children's Act 2008. A move away from residential care requires a greater reliance on the alternatives such as family preservation, adoption, professional foster care, or a system of reception, assessment, and referral.

In southern Africa, broadly speaking, the reasons that parents place their children in institutional care are poverty or the desire to educate their children. Parents in developing countries will often see institutions as a survival strategy allowing children to escape from a desperate situation. These institutions are also attractive to donors. Although 13 million children in southern Africa lost one or both parents to AIDS in 2000, only 1 percent of those children ended up on the street or in institutions. The impact of HIV/AIDS on the residential care sector in South Africa will be considered in the next section.

HIV/AIDS

The need to provide for AIDS orphans is such a crucial part of South Africa's future child care plans that the issue requires particular attention. The scale of the problem is immense and is projected to increase. Rosa (2003) suggests that unless there are major health interventions there will be 3 million South African children who will have lost their mother to AIDS by 2015. In 2001 that figure was around 900,000, and the Minister for Social Development, Zola Skweyiya, estimated that 35 percent of those children lived with foster parents, 0.1 percent were adopted, and only 0.25 percent were in residential care. The remaining 65 percent remained in families, communities, or so-called child-headed households (Rosa, 2003).

AIDS has affected the whole population, but the impact that it has had on children is particularly severe. Children suffer in a multitude of ways including through parent-child transmission, chronic illness, abandonment, trauma, orphanhood, and interrupted schooling (Richter, 2003). Mbambo (2005) suggests that orphaned children are vulnerable from three perspectives: survival, psychosocial, and developmental. Such children are less likely to be at school, more likely to suffer emotional problems such as depression, and likely to suffer discrimination due to the stigma attached to HIV. They have little or no access to appropriate support (Mbambo, 2005).

The provision of residential care is a part of the government's strategy for dealing with the impact of AIDS on children, but it is not central to this strategy. The government has a duty under §28 (1) (c) of the Constitution to provide the resources necessary for the survival and development of AIDS orphans. It has begun to take steps to fulfill its obligations by the adoption of a National Integrated Plan for Children and Youth Infected and Affected with HIV/AIDS (NIP) (Sloth-Nielsen, 2003a). This plan endorses a community- and home-based care approach, advocating that orphaned children should not be institutionalized but should, wherever possible, grow up in some sort of family environment (Sloth-Nielsen, 2003a). The NIP provides a limited budget for community- and home-based care, counseling and testing for HIV, teaching of life skills, and community programs. Following this plan, it is clear that the South African government does not intend residential care to be the primary provision for children orphaned by AIDS. It is only one of the models currently in use; children can also live in independent orphaned households with no formal assistance, receive informal care from community members, be placed in foster families, or participate in home-based programs (Sloth-Nielsen, 2003a).

Exact data on children affected by AIDS who are cared for in residential facilities is hard to gather as many small facilities have opened to house AIDS orphans (Richter, 2003). Prior to the new legislation, these institutions often were not registered, did not receive a government subsidy, and were not subject to official supervision. The desire to respond to the AIDS crisis by institutionalizing children is driven by the lack of coordination provided by the government (Richter, 2003). Nongovernmental organizations therefore respond with compassion but lack of direction and follow historical precedents of relying on mass institutionalization.

Mass institutionalization of children is not an effective way to deal with children who have been made vulnerable by AIDS (Richter, 2003). It is difficult to create residential care environments that are not damaging to children's development. Residential care is expensive, and if institutions are not financially sound then children are made doubly vulnerable if they subsequently close. In addition, in a very poor country such as South Africa, the existence of residential care facilities may result in some poor families rejecting their children in favor of institutionalization.

Recent research (Meintjes et al., 2007) has found that 34 percent of children in residential homes whose status was known were HIV positive. Although this figure is qualified by the fact that the status of 40 percent of the children is unknown, it still contrasts with the prevalence of 1.9 percent among children in the general population. However, contrary to the stereotypical picture of the state caring for "AIDS orphans," the primary reason for the admission of these children to care was not the death or illness of a parent but rather abuse and/or neglect. The impact of HIV/AIDS on the residential sector is primarily to require residential units to develop the skills to care for HIV positive children.

Residential Care in South Africa beyond 2008

In 2006 and 2008 the South African Parliament enacted new legislation, the Children's Act, as the previous legislation, the Child Care Act (1983) was considered to be incompatible with the Constitution and the UNCRC (Burger, 2003; Sloth-Nielsen, 2003b). The legislation was split into two parts and the Children's Act (2005) was signed into law in 2006. Parts of this act are already in force, but the rest of it will come into effect at the same time as the Children's Amendment Bill. At the time of writing the Children's Amendment Bill has been passed by Parliament but is still awaiting presidential signature and the completion of accompanying regulations. It is expected that the full Children's Act will be in place before the end of 2008 (Jamieson et al., 2008).

The Children's Act brings legislation in line with the South African Constitution, with international law, and with the move to a social development approach. It makes a fundamental conceptual shift from parents having power over children to children having rights of their own. It emphasizes mediation and family group conferences ahead of formal court proceedings (Jamieson et al., 2008). The legislation is closely based on a discussion paper (SALC, 2002a) and report (SALC, 2002b) produced by the South African Law Commission as a review of the Child Care Act 2003. Issues covered in the Law Commission's comprehensive report and the eventual legislation include provisions to deem childhood to begin at birth, to lower the age of majority to 18, and to establish and administer Child and Family Courts at the regional level. Although the report advocates keeping children in the community as far as possible, it accepts residential care as an essential part of the system and acknowledges that there are occasions when institutionalization is the most suitable option for a particular child. The report recommends that to ensure appropriate use of residential options, only the courts should be allowed to place children in residential care.

The SALC also recommended that a child be placed in a care center as close as possible to his or her home. The national strategy should allow for the development of small units. This is to allow the child to continue to receive support from parents, family, and friends as well as continuity in the services offered by child care professionals. Placement in a residential program should not exceed two years' duration without a court review. The court must also be involved if a child is to be transferred to a more restrictive facility.

The commission recommended that a chapter on child rights be included in the bill. This was linked to the responsibilities that the children would have. The report advocated a holistic approach to the protection of children in residential care that would entail children being made aware of their rights and responsibilities; service providers being aware of the rights and responsibilities of children, as well as their own rights and responsibilities; and user-friendly grievance procedures and a system of monitoring.

The center of the Children's Act is the need to adapt a national social development policy framework. It constitutes a programmatic plan to address and advance children's material conditions. This policy is based on the premise that resources should be directed at the youngest and most vulnerable children, decreasing the possibility that they will become victims of social ills such as neglect, abuse, or malnutrition (Sloth-Nielsen, 2003b).

The Children's Act focuses on providing protection to groups of the most vulnerable children, such as those affected by HIV/AIDS, children with disabilities and chronic illnesses, those living in child-headed households, and those living on the streets (Sloth-Nielsen, 2003b). The act provides for the delivery of social services to strengthen and support families, with the state becoming involved only as a last resort. Prevention and early intervention programs as well as nurseries and early childhood development programs are provided for in the legislation and will be delivered either by nonprofit organizations or directly by the government.

The Children's Act envisages interdepartmental cooperation and the use of a range of social providers. Residential care centers are now called Child and Youth Care Centers and are required to be registered. Children's homes, places of safety, secure care facilities, schools of industry, and reform schools have all also been redesignated as Child and Youth Care Centers and must reregister. Registration applications must be considered within six months of submission: this new provision will greatly assist the many unregistered homes currently seeking registration. The Child and Youth Care Centers are required to provide therapeutic programs as appropriate to the child's developmental needs. They are conceived therefore as a last resort, but one that is expected to meet more than just a child's basic needs. The programs provided must be assessed by a suitably qualified person. In addition to services for their own residents, these Centers are also able to provide services in the community, including to children in conflict with the law (Meintjes et al., 2007).

Recent Research into Residential Care in South Africa

Perhaps the best way to understand the implications of the changes in legislation and approach on residential care in South Africa beyond 2008 is to consider two recent pieces of research, both of which considered current provision in the light of forthcoming legislation. The first of these is the research by Meintjes et al. (2007), which examined residential care, particularly for children affected by HIV/AIDS. These researchers investigated both registered and unregistered homes and found substantial variety in the nature and quality of service provision. However, the picture was more complex than a simple case of registered homes being good and unregistered homes being poor as the researchers found that the legal status of the home revealed little about it. They recommended that the future registration permit good, family-based indigenous providers to have access to straightforward mechanisms that would allow them to gain legal status and access to funding. The researchers recommended that a less rigid approach to registration needed to be adopted; in some instances, the very factors that led to children's suffering, such as lack of electricity in a particular region, also led to a provider's registration being refused. With regard to children affected by HIV/AIDS, despite the prevalence of this disease and the importance of this issue, the researchers found that knowledge about it was uneven and good practice was not universal. The key areas that this report recommended strengthening included awareness of the prevention of mother to child transmission and the relationships between residential services and children's homes.

The Built Environment Support Group (BESG), an NGO that supports the poor and vulnerable in finding suitable accommodation, also carried out recent research into residential care provision (BESG, 2007). The researchers did case study–based research into six institutions, some registered and some unregistered. They were initially interested in investigating the implications of any policy misalignment between the Departments of Social Development and Housing—for example, through the provision of housing grants to unregistered homes. They actually found a more complex picture whereby registration created expectations of funding that were not always met, and some unregistered homes were able to access international funding. This research again found that there was good and bad practice in both registered and unregistered homes. It showed that in some instances both registered and unregistered homes demonstrated very poor practice, constituting misuse of funds and neglect of children. Unregistered homes did serve a need and managers were eager to achieve registration. The report recommended that all these children's homes be under strict control but that a flexible approach be instituted that would allow unregistered homes to achieve registration.

Taken together, these research reports portray a great need for residential care for children that the state is struggling to meet adequately. Many homes, some of which are well-established parts of their communities, have not yet been registered, and some of those that are registered continue to demonstrate poor child care practice. Excellent practice by committed, trained, and experienced workers is evident in both registered and unregistered homes but is not easily replicable. International donors can complicate the situation, as large institutions targeted at "AIDS orphans" are most successful at attracting international funding but do not necessarily meet the needs of children or demonstrate best practice. The challenge for the government in implementing new legislation is to bring the social development approach into effect, strictly monitoring all provision; and registering, rewarding, and replicating best practice.

Conclusion

The introduction and implementation of the Children's Act means that residential child care in South Africa faces a hopeful future, with positive indications that provision will comply with national and international standards. South African children face many challenges, and it appears likely that the provision of residential care will play a part in meeting those challenges, without being central to the child care regime. It is crucial, as new policies are introduced and the challenges of poverty, AIDS, and abuse of children continue to be faced, that policy makers and academics continue to reflect on what constitutes best practice in the specific situation that confronts South African children.

REFERENCES

Bak, M. (2002). Can developmental social welfare change an unfair world? *International Social Work, 47*(1), 81–94.

Brown, M., and Neku, R. J. (2002). A historical review of the South African social welfare system and social work practitioners' views on its current status, *International Social Work, 48*(3), 301–312.

Built Environment Support Group (BESG). (2007). *No place like home.* Durban: Author.

Burger, D. (Ed.). (2003). *South Africa yearbook 2003/4.* Pretoria: Government Communications/STE Publishers.

Coughlan, F. (2000, September 10–13). *Promoting organisational change in South Africa.* Paper presented at Action Learning and Action Research Conference, University of Ballarat, Australia. Retrieved June 1, 2005 from http://www.ballarat.edu.au/alarpm/index.shtml.

Department of Correctional Services. (2004). *Briefing to the Social Development Portfolio Committee, 25 August.* Department of Correctional Services. Retrieved June 1, 2005 from http://www.pmg.org.za (subscription only).

Drower, S. (2002). Conceptualizing social work in a changed South Africa. *International Social Work, 45*(1), 7–20.

Fagan, J. J. (2004). Juveniles in prison. *Article 40, 6*(2), 1–2.

Gallinetti, J. (2004). PAWC commissions a review of facilities. *Article 40, 6*(4), 4–7.

Human Rights Watch. (2005). *World report: South Africa,* New York: Author. Retrieved June 1, 2005 from http://hrw.org.

Jamieson, L., Proudlock, P., and Waterhouse, S. (2008). Key legislative developments affecting children in 2007. In P. Proudlock, M. Dutschke, L. Jamieson, J. Monson, and C. Smith (Eds.), *South African child gauge 2007/2008.* Cape Town: Children's Institute, University of Cape Town.

Mazibuko, F., and Gray, M. (2002). Social work professional associations in South Africa. *International Social Work, 47*(1), 129–142.

Mbambo, B. (2005). HIV/AIDS—Thief of childhood. *Children First, 59.*

McClain-Nhlapo, C. (2004). *Briefing by the South African Human Rights Commission to the Parliamentary Portfolio Committee on Correctional Services: 7 September 2004.* South African Human Rights Commission. Retrieved November 15, 2004 from http://www.pmg.org.za (subscription only).

Meintjes, H., Moses, S., Berry, L., and Manpane, R. (2007). *Home truths: The phenomenon of residential care for children in a time of AIDS.* Cape Town: Children's Institute, University of Cape Town and Centre for the Study of AIDS, University of Pretoria.

Ministry for Welfare and Population Development. (1997). *White paper for social welfare.* Retrieved June 1, 2005 from http://www.polity.org.za/html/govdocs/white_papers/social971.html?rebookmark=1.

Noyoo, N. (2000). Social development in sub-Saharan Africa. *International Social Work, 45*(3), 453–465.

Richter, L. (2003, May 12–15). *Institutionalisation of children in South Africa in the wake of the HIV/AIDS epidemic.* Paper presented at Children and Residential Care—New Strategies for a New Millennium Conference, University of Stockholm, Sweden. Retrieved June 1, 2005 from http://www.children-strategies.org.

Rock, B. (Ed.). (1997). *Spirals of suffering.* Pretoria: HSRC.

Rosa, S. (2003, August/September). State duty to children without parents. *Children First.* Retrieved May 16, 2005 from http://www.childrenfirst.org.za.

Sacco, T., and Hoffmann, W. (2002). Seeking truth and reconciliation in South Africa. *International Social Work, 47*(2), 157–167.

Sewpaul, V., and Lombard, A. (2004). Social work education, training and standards in Africa, *Social Work Education, 23*(5), 537–554.

Skelton, A. (1998). *Children and the law.* Pietermaritzburg: Lawyers for Human Rights.

Sloth-Nielsen, J. (2003a). Too little, too late? The implications of the Grootboom case for state response to child-headed households. *Law Democracy and Development, 1,* 113–136.

Sloth-Nielsen, J. (2003b). Promoting children's socio-economic rights through law reform— the proposed Children's Bill. *ESR Review, 4*(2), 2–4.

Snyman, S. (2003, May 12–15). *The role of the Children's Court in moving away from residential care towards family based care.* Paper presented at Children and Residential Care—New Strategies for a New Millennium Conference, University of Stockholm, Sweden. Retrieved June 1, 2005 from http://www.children-strategies.org.

South African Law Commission (SALC). (2002a). Project 100: Review of the Child Care Act: Discussion paper 103. Retrieved June 1, 2005 from http://www.law.wits.ac.za/salc/salc. html.

South African Law Commission (SALC). (2002b). Project 110: Review of the Child Care Act: Report. Retrieved June 1, 2005 from http://www.law.wits.ac.za/salc/salc.html.

Triegaardt, J. (2002). Social policy domains. *International Social Work, 45*(3), 325–336.

Van der Spuy, E., Scharf, W., and Lever, J. (2004). The politics of youth crime and justice in South Africa. In C. Summer (Ed.), *The Blackwell companion to criminology* (pp. 162–179). Oxford: Blackwell.

8

Residential Care in Korea

Past, Present, and Future

BONG JOO LEE

Since the opening of the Myung-Dong Catholic Church Orphanage in 1868, the country's first modern residential child welfare facility, residential care has been an integral part of child welfare systems in Korea. In fact, during most of its child welfare service history, residential care has been the predominant form of care for children who need protection and care outside of homes. Only in recent years have policy makers and the general public begun to recognize that long-term residential care may be detrimental to children and that more "family-like" care should be considered as a policy option (Kim, 1997).

The primary purposes of this chapter are to examine how residential care is defined and how it has evolved over time in Korea. The chapter also provides a discussion of major sociodemographic, ideological, and cultural factors that have contributed to the development of residential care. After a detailed description of the current situation of residential care, the chapter concludes with an exploration of future directions and potential concerns about residential care in Korea.

Definition of Residential Care in Korea

The first modern child welfare law acknowledging that providing care for at-risk children was society's responsibility was enacted in 1961 in Korea. Before the Child Welfare Law in 1961, Korea's child welfare system was predominantly geared for providing relief services to Korean War orphans and children in extreme destitution, who often lived in the streets. These relief activities were mainly organized by international charity organizations (Choi, 1995). The passage of this landmark law marked a turning point in the history of Korean child welfare policy development after which child welfare programs began to be supported financially by the government and shaped by national laws and regulations. Through several revisions of the law, most recently in 2000, child welfare in Korea has come to be defined as care supported by public resources that is provided to children who need "protection." The Child Welfare Law in Korea further defines children in need of protection as

- Children who have been abandoned or lost by their parents or guardian
- Children who cannot be cared for by their families
- Children who are abused and/or neglected by their parents or guardians
- Children whose parents are deemed to have inadequate capacity to provide care

The law also specifies that it is society's responsibility to provide adequate care for those children. To provide this care, the Korean child welfare service system is divided into two areas: in-home care services and residential care services (Ministry of Health and Human Services, 1996). In-home care services are further categorized as households headed by children (supported by the government), adoption services, and foster family care services. Residential care is generally defined as care provided in out-of-home institutions for those children who cannot be cared for in home settings and/or who need special treatment services. There are six broadly defined types of institutions that are considered part of the child residential care system in Korea:

- Child bringing-up institutions: to provide care for children who cannot be cared for by their families due to parents' death, abandonment of the child, and/or maltreatment of the child.
- Temporary care welfare institutions for children: to provide temporary care for runaway and delinquent youths. The primary purpose of this type of institution is to provide referral and screening services to plan for more permanent placement services while providing temporary residence for a child.
- Child vocational training institutions: to provide education and job skill training services for children older than 12 years of age who are cared for in child welfare institutions.
- Juvenile detention centers: to provide care for delinquent youths by court orders.
- Self-independence assistance institutions: to provide room and board services on a short-term basis for children who are aging out of child welfare institutions during the period when they are seeking a job and undergoing initial job placement.

Of these broadly defined types of residential care institutions in Korea, the juvenile detention centers were not included in the chapter discussion because they are mainly viewed from a law enforcement perspective and are operated by a different government division under different legislative provisions.

A Brief History of Residential Care in Korea

Throughout the century before the passage of the 1961 Child Welfare Law, orphanages supported by religious organizations and international charity organizations dominated the structure of child welfare in Korea. The early modern child welfare institutions in Korea were orphanages established by religious organizations.[1] The first modern orphanage was established in 1868 by Father Blanc in the center of downtown Seoul as an affiliated institution of Myung-Dong Catholic Church. It was followed by of another Catholic Church–affiliated orphanage near Inchon—a harbor city about 20 miles from Seoul. The protestant churches soon followed, opening their own residential care facilities. The first protestant church–affiliated orphanage was opened in Seoul in 1906 (Lee, 1993). The establishment and activities of these institutions represent not only their efforts to provide necessary relief to children who could not be cared for in their homes but also missionary activities of foreign religious organizations.

In the nearly 60 years following establishment of the first residential care facility in Korea, the development of the early child welfare system was supported mainly by religious organizations without explicit government policy attention or guidance. It was only in 1921 that the Korean government under Japanese colonial rule established a social welfare division as a central government unit, marking the beginning of a national child welfare policy governing child welfare programs. By 1934, there were 23 child welfare residential facilities caring for 2,192 children (Ku, 1969). For some time even after the establishment of the independent Korean government in 1948, the old regulations and laws continued to guide the operations of residential care institutions in Korea. Throughout this period, both the number of child welfare institutions and children cared in those institutions continued to increase. By 1950, there were 116 child welfare residential care facilities caring for 8,908 children (Ku, 1969).

In response to the increase in the number of residential care facilities and public concern about the poor quality of those institutions, the Korean government enacted new regulations in 1950 to provide standards for residential care. The unique feature of this 1950 child welfare legislation was that it first expressed the belief that highly institutional, large residential facilities might be detrimental to children and youth. It recommended the creation of more "family-like" institutions comprised of small cottages, with each cottage serving a maximum of 20 children (Sung and Kim, 2001).

The 1950 Korean War brought a tremendous increase in the demand for residential care facilities providing care for war orphans and refugees. The 1950 regulation of child welfare facilities was still in effect during the war and guided the establishment and operation of many new residential care facilities. By the end of the Korean War in 1953, the number of residential care facilities had increased to 440 institutions serving about 54,000 children. Many more children were living in the streets and their livelihood was largely dependent on outdoor relief provided by international charity organizations (Choi, 1995). At this time, the government was struggling to recover from the aftermath of the Korean War and weaknesses in the economy, and most Korean child welfare services had to depend on private charity mostly from international organizations. With support from these organizations, the number of residential care facilities continued to increase during this period, reaching 542 institutions caring for over 60,000 children in 1960.

The passage of the Child Welfare Law in 1961 marked a turning point in the history of Korean child welfare policy development as child welfare programs began to be supported financially by the government and shaped by national laws and regulations. The landmark legislation for the first time spelled out the definition of a child needing protection by society and the means to provide different types of services according to the specified needs. However, while the law specified several types of child welfare service programs, the main one continued to be residential care for children who could not be looked after in their homes due to extreme poverty, parents' death, or abandonment by their parents. The revision of the Child Welfare Law in 1981 broadened the scope of the government's child welfare policy from focusing only on children in need of "protection" to promoting the well-being of all Korean children. The legislation, in principle, shifted the focus of child welfare policy from providing services to selected groups of children at risk to promoting family and child well-being and preventing problems from occurring. However, careful examination of the law reveals that the declaration stopped short of implementing any actual programs or policies directed at accomplishing the declared policy goal (Kim, 1998). Rather, the revised law's main emphasis was still to provide necessary substitute care for children who could not be cared by their own families, and the main vehicle for providing such care was residential facilities.

A major revision of the Child Welfare Law was passed in 2000 in response to growing public concern about the abuse and neglect of children. Before the legislation, there was no law mandating the reporting of suspected child abuse and neglect. Selected services were provided to abused children and their families by private agencies and advocacy groups on a voluntary basis. With several incidents of severe abuse and neglect cases reported in the mass media in the late 1990s, advocacy groups and child welfare experts pushed the revision of the law to include mandatory reporting requirements. Their efforts ultimately led to the 2000 revision that placed into law the requirement of reporting child abuse and neglect. As a result, the law defined child abuse and neglect, mandated reporting systems including establishment of a 24-hour hot-line, instituted regional child abuse/neglect prevention centers, and provided a legal basis for government intervention in cases of suspected child abuse and neglect.

The revision of the Child Welfare Law in 2000 was a particularly important piece of legislation in that it specified abuse and neglect as a condition when a child needed protection that requires government intervention. Consequently, this law could have had the effect of enlarging the pool of children needing care in residential facilities because of abuse and neglect. However, after revision of the law, the mandated reporting had not brought a large increase in the number of children needing care in out-of-home settings because its implementation has been problematic for various reasons. Even though the law required mandatory reporting, it failed to specify the procedures and legal authority for intervention, especially when an out-of-home placement is required. As a result, there have been very few out-of-home placements even for cases of abuse and neglect reported and substantiated (Chang, 2003). The revision was also very ambiguous about resources and guidelines to enable the newly established abuse/neglect prevention centers to deal more effectively with children and families needing intervention.

Along with the administrative difficulties, a key barrier has been the cultural tradition in Korean society that places a strong emphasis on family cohesion and autonomy. Confucianism has been the dominant philosophy affecting individual behaviors and family processes in Korean society for several hundred years, and the core value of Confucianism revolves around the family. According to Confucianism, the family takes precedence over its individual members. Maintaining the dignity and honor of a family has traditionally been regarded as far more important than seeking an individual family member's well-being. Thus, a matter such as allegation of child abuse has been strictly regarded as a family matter, leaving no room for intervention from society. "Saving face" is a very important concept with regard to keeping family matters within the family. This cultural tradition explains why Korean families generally tend not to seek help from outside the family, such as from social service agencies. Because of this cultural tradition, neighbors suspecting child abuse have been very reluctant to report it because they fear that they are violating the suspected family's dignity and the family members prefer solving the "family problem" by themselves instead of seeking help outside the family.

Even though the revision of the law that added abuse and neglect as conditions requiring child protection has not had major effects on the demand for residential care in its early implementation, its long-term effect still can be significant. As more program measures are implemented to improve the intervention side of child protective services in coming years, the pool of children needing out-of-home placements will likely increase. Such a trend will increase the demand for residential care services in the absence of any meaningful alternative options, such as family foster care.

Recent Trends in Residential Care

Before we turn our attention to recent trends in residential care in Korea, it is necessary to understand the relative status of residential care in the context of the overall child welfare service system in Korea. Table 8.1 shows the number of children needing protection each year from 1990 to 2000 and how they were cared

Table 8.1. Number of Children Needing Protection by Type of Care, 1990–2000, in Korea

Year	Number of Children Needing Protection*	Residential Care	Foster Family Care	Adoption	Households Headed by Child
1990	5,721	65%	20%	15%	0%
1991	5,095	67%	20%	13%	0%
1992	5,020	62%	24%	14%	0%
1993	4,451	66%	21%	13%	0%
1994	5,023	59%	18%	15%	8%
1995	4,576	62%	11%	10%	17%
1996	4,951	64%	15%	10%	12%
1997	6,734	58%	18%	13%	11%
1998	9,292	55%	25%	14%	6%
1999	7,693	61%	16%	15%	8%
2000	7,760	57%	18%	17%	7%

* The numbers represent children needing protection each year.
Source: Ministry of Health and Human Services, 1990–2000, Yearly Report.

for across different child welfare service settings. The number of children who needed protection had been stable at around 5,000 during the first half of the 1990s and then increased to over 7,000 by the end of 2000. This growth reflects the increased poverty rates brought on by the Asian financial crisis during that period. The data show that residential care is the primary service for the majority of children removed from their homes as a result of concern for their well-being in Korea. Throughout the decade, residential care was the service provided for 55 percent to 67 percent of the children who needed out-of-home protection.

Even though there is no government policy favoring foster care over residential placement, family-type care is generally considered more beneficial to children in need. As a result, a few demonstration programs for recruiting foster care families have been implemented in recent years (Ministry of Health and Human Services, 2002). However, expanding "in-home" services such as foster care or adoption has been difficult because of the Korean society's cultural orientation regarding the importance of blood-relatedness in preserving family cohesion and continuity. Thus, there is a significant stigma related to adopting someone as a family member who is not related by blood. Bae (1995) points to this cultural belief about the importance of "blood" family as a main reason that adoption is so rare among Korean families and is done in secrecy when it happens. By the same token, becoming a foster parent to the children of strangers has been a very foreign idea in Korean society.

Historically, the use of foster family care has been limited and occurs only as a temporary placement option, mostly in preadoption services; but current policy direction suggests that increasing measures will be employed to strengthen and improve the foster family care system in Korea. However, the pace of change will be probably slow and residential care will be an integral part of child welfare systems in the foreseeable future in Korea.

Table 8.2 presents the data on recent trends of residential care by facility types in Korea. The vast majority of the residential care facilities are child bringing-up institutions, and those institutions care for the vast majority of children in out-of-home settings. The fact that the predominant form of residential care is child bringing-up institutions suggests that the primary function of residential care in Korea is to provide residence and protection services for those children who cannot be cared for in their own homes rather than to provide any specialized treatment or therapeutic services.

Examination of the long-term trend in the child bringing-up institutions shows that both the number of facilities and the children cared for in those facilities decreased significantly during the 1970s. The number of child bringing-up institutions declined about 50 percent from 504 institutions in 1970 to 253 institutions in 1980. The number of children cared for in those institutions was also reduced by 60 percent from around 50,000 children in 1970 to about 20,000 children in 1980. After the substantial decline during the 1970s, the number of child bringing-up institutions has remained stable in recent years, but the number of children in those institutions continued to decline during the 1990s. The most recent data show that only about 17,000 children were being cared for in residential care facilities in 2000.[2]

Table 8.2. Trends in Residential Care by Facility Type in Korea, 1980–2000

Year	Child Bringing-Up Institutions	Temporary Care Welfare Institutions	Child Vocational Training Institutions	Self-Independence Assistance Institutions
	Number of Facilities			
1970	504	N/A	19	N/A
1980	253	N/A	16	N/A
1985	233	N/A	11	3
1990	223	N/A	7	10
1995	215	11	5	13
2000	235	8	5	12
	Number of Children (as of end of each year)			
1970	49,891	N/A	1,710	N/A
1980	20,908	N/A	1,246	N/A
1985	21,697	N/A	994	197
1990	20,147	N/A	444	471
1995	15,105	609	231	620
2000	16,293	387	184	222
	Average Number of Children per Facility			
1970	99	N/A	90	N/A
1980	83	N/A	78	N/A
1985	93	N/A	90	66
1990	90	N/A	63	47
1995	70	55	46	48
2000	69	48	37	19

Source: Ministry of Health and Human Services, each year, Yearly Report.

Several factors contributed to the decline in children served in residential care—child bringing-up institutions in particular—in Korea. First, the large decline from 1970 to 1980 reflects the shrinking pool of Korean War orphans who needed residence care as they aged and left the system during the 1970s. Second, fertility patterns changed dramatically during the period. As shown in Figure 8.1, both the number of births and crude birth rate declined during the period. The crude birth rate, which measures the number of births per 1,000 individuals, decreased almost 60 percent, from 31.2 births per 1,000 in 1970 to about 11.6 births per 1,000 in 2001. The number of total births also declined during the same period from about a million births in 1970 to about 500,000 births in 2001. The decline in the birth rate resulted in a smaller child population (see Table 8.3). From 1960 to the mid 1970s, the child population (under 20 years old) stayed at more than 50 percent of the total population. With the continued drop in birth rate, the proportion of the child population has declined since 1975. In 2000, only about 30 percent of the total population was made up of children compared to over 50 percent in earlier periods. The smaller share of the child population suggests less demand for child-related services.

Third, the period since the 1970s also represents unprecedented economic development in Korea. As shown in Figure 8.2, per capita gross national income increased almost 40 times during the 30-year period from 1970 to 2002.[3] During this time, the Korean society finally escaped the absolute destitution it had suffered since the beginning of the country's modernization. With the decrease in the numbers of children in the country and the improvement in the economy, there has been steady decline in the demand for residential care for poverty-related reasons.

The decline in the number of children cared for in residential facilities during the 1990s, in particular, reflects continued changes in the characteristics of the population that need residential care services. Table 8.4 shows the distribution of children needing protection and the reason by year in that decade. Note that the

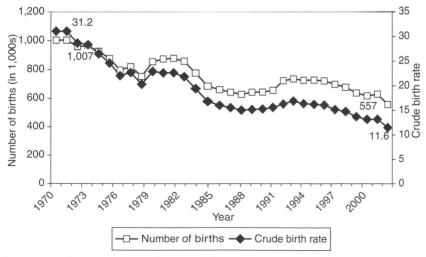

Figure 8.1. Trends in Births, 1970–2001, Korea
Source: National Statistical Office.

Table 8.3. Trends in Population Size, 1960–2000 (numbers in 1,000s), Korea

Year	Total	Age 0 to 19	Age 20 and Over	% of Ages 0–19
1960	24,989	12,537	12,453	50.2%
1966	29,160	15,392	13,768	52.8%
1970	31,435	16,330	15,106	51.9%
1975	34,679	17,355	17,324	50.0%
1980	37,407	16,896	20,511	45.2%
1985	40,420	16,411	24,008	40.6%
1990	43,390	15,583	27,807	35.9%
1995	44,554	14,099	30,455	31.6%
2000	45,985	13,330	32,655	29.0%

sharp increase in the number of children needing protection in 1997 and 1998 reflects the added demand for child welfare services caused by the Asian financial crisis at that time. Even with the increase in the total number of children needing protection in the later years of the 1990s, the clear pattern shown in Table 8.4 is declines in abandoned and lost children needing protection. Historically, children needing protection because they were abandoned or lost indicated that parents were experiencing material difficulties and were giving up their children to child welfare institutions because they could not care for them.

In 1990–2000, on the other hand, both out-of-wedlock and runaway (and other) problems increased as the causes for children needing protection. The changing trends suggest that the need for child protection is shifting from poverty-related issues to changes in family structure and other child-parent issues.

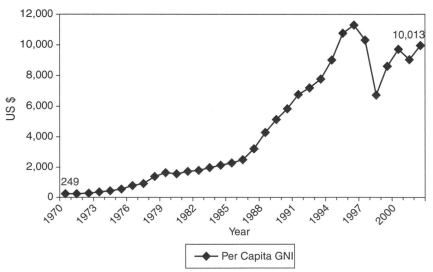

Figure 8.2. Per Capita GNI, 1970–2002, Korea
Source: National Statistical Office.

Table 8.4. Number of Children Needing Protection by Reason, 1990–2000, Korea

Year	Total*	Abandoned	Out-of-Wedlock	Lost Children	Runaway, Other
1990	5,721	32%	41%	6%	20%
1991	5,095	32%	40%	4%	25%
1992	5,020	30%	36%	5%	30%
1993	4,451	30%	43%	3%	24%
1994	5,023	28%	35%	4%	33%
1995	4,576	27%	28%	3%	42%
1996	4,951	26%	28%	4%	43%
1997	6,734	20%	27%	5%	47%
1998	9,292	18%	44%	3%	35%
1999	7,693	19%	40%	3%	39%
2000	7,760	16%	38%	2%	43%

* The numbers represent children identified by the government as needing protection each year.
Source: Ministry of Health and Human Services, each year, Yearly Report.

Changes in family structure have been suggested as one of the recent reasons for children needing residential care protection (Yoon, 2002). Historically, divorce has been rare in Korea due to a high stigma associated with broken families. However, family dissolution through divorce has become much more common in Korea in recent years. The crude divorce rate (measured as the number of divorces per 1,000 individuals) increased by almost 200 percent from about 1 per 1,000 in 1990 to about 2.8 per 1,000 in 2001 (see Figure 8.3). With increases in the number of divorces and accompanying family dissolutions, it is often the children who suffer most. Especially when the divorcing parents do not have adequate financial or personal resources to deal with the consequences of family dissolution, children often end up needing residence and protection services in out-of-home settings

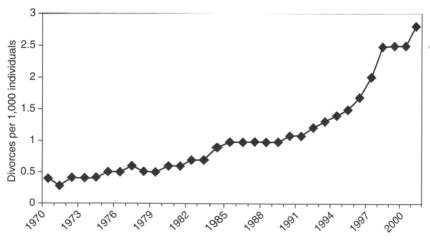

Figure 8.3. Trends in Crude Divorce Rate, 1970–2001, Korea
Source: National Statistical Office.

because they are no longer cared for within the family. Currently, a residential facility represents a likely option for those children.

Current Situation of Residential Care

In this section, I examine the current situation of residential care in Korea.[4] The discussion focuses the child bringing-up institutions because they are the predominant form of residential care in Korea. Explored first are the characteristics of the child bringing-up institutions, followed by examination of the children cared for in those facilities.

Characteristics of Child Bringing-Up Institutions

SIZE   The belief that large residential facilities might be detrimental to children and youth has guided the government's effort to encourage transition to smaller settings in recent years in Korea. As early as 1950, the government recommended establishment of more "family-like" institutions comprised of small cottages with each cottage serving a maximum of 20 children.

Figure 8.4 shows the distribution of the child bringing-up institutions by the maximum number of children they could serve in 1998. The data show that most facilities are large, with more than 95 percent serving more than 60 children. About one-fifth of all institutions are intended to serve more than 120 children. The current data suggest that the norm of residential care in Korea is large institutions despite the stated policy preference for smaller settings. The discrepancy between the stated policy preference and the current situation is largely due to the lack of incentives for

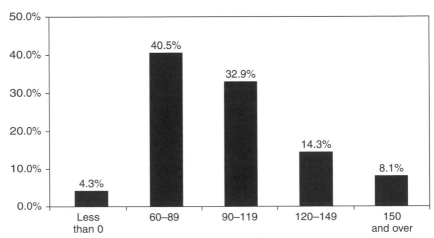

Figure 8.4.   Distribution of Child Bringing-Up Institutions by Maximum Number of Beds, Korea, 1997
Source: Byun and Lee (1998).

the residential care providers to move toward smaller facilities. Even though the preference has been for smaller facilities for some time, the government has been very slow to implement any concrete policy measures to achieve the stated goal.

UTILIZATION OF CURRENT CAPACITY   The data in Figure 8.5 suggest that many facilities are not utilized to their full capacity. Only about 40 percent had more than 70 percent of the available beds filled. The majority (51 percent) were at somewhere between 50 and 69 percent of maximum capacity. The findings suggest that most residential facilities are underutilized and probably experience over-capacity problems. The facilities that were developed in the 1960s and 1970s to meet the increasing demand are now struggling to fill their capacities, indicating that the speed of decrease in the child population in need of services far outpaced the residential care providers' efforts to restructure their supply capacity.

FINANCE   The average total revenue for the child bringing-up institutions was about $300,000 in 1998. Figure 8.6 presents the average revenue sources for the institutions indicating that the facilities rely heavily on the government, which provides about 78 percent of their support. By the late 1990s, most international organizations had stopped their charity operations in Korea. Currently a very small share (less than 1 percent) of the revenue comes from international charity organizations.

STAFF   The quality and qualifications of staff in the residential facilities are a major factor in determining the level of care in each institution. One quality indicator used frequently is the ratio of children in care to caregivers. Figure 8.7 shows that the majority of the facilities had a ratio of five to six children to each staff member. Very few facilities (about 3 percent) reported a ratio of nine or more

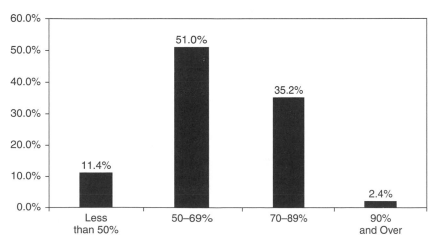

Figure 8.5.   Distribution of Maximum Capacity Utilization Rates in Korean Residential Child Care Facilities, 1997
Source: Byun and Lee (1998).

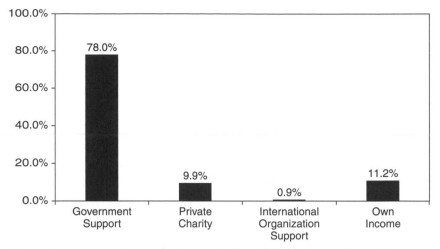

Figure 8.6.   Revenue Sources for Korean Residential Child Care Facilities, 1997
Source: Byun and Lee (1998).

children to one staff member. The data suggest that most facilities maintain the ratio recommended by the government (8 children per worker).

While the number of workers caring for children in the residential facilities appears to be adequate, data on the quality of the staff present a different picture. As an indicator of quality I considered the education level of the workers and whether they have child welfare service–related licenses. Data in Figure 8.8 show that the level of education among the staff is relatively low. Almost half of all workers (about 47 percent) had only a high school diploma and one-fifth had less than this level of education. The license data show a similar pattern. Byun and Lee

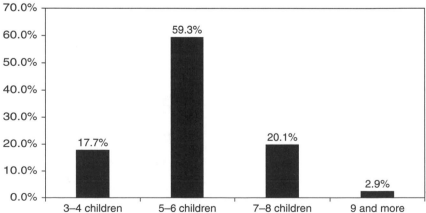

Figure 8.7.   Average Child-to-Staff Ratios in Korean Residential Child Care Facilities, 1997
Source: Byun and Lee (1998).

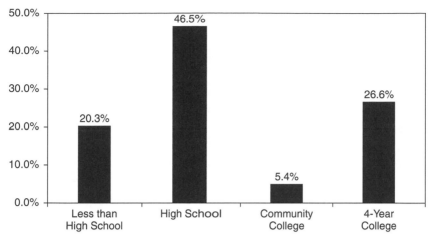

Figure 8.8. Level of Staff Education in Korean Child Care Facilities, 1997
Source: Byun and Lee (1998).

(1998) found that only about 31 percent of the staff reported having a child welfare service–related license.

Characteristics of Children in Care

AGE OF CHILDREN IN CARE   As shown in Figure 8.9, the vast majority of children in care (about 80 percent) are 10 years of age or older, but the records show that their age at placement was much younger. About one-fourth of the total children in

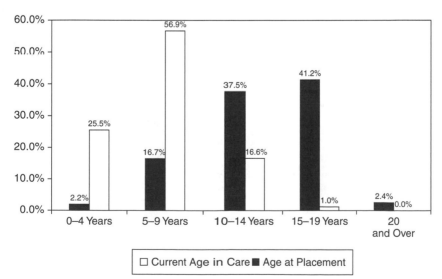

Figure 8.9. Age Distribution of Children in Korean Child Care Facilities, 1997
Source: Byun and Lee (1998).

care were placed when they were younger than 4 years of age and an additional 60 percent were between 5 and 9 years old at placement, indicating that many children stay at these facilities for a long period of time.

REASONS FOR PLACEMENT   Most children were placed in residential facilities because of family dissolution through parents' divorce or child abandonment. The current data suggest that these residential facilities are no longer acting as orphanages, as did their counterparts in the 1950s and 1960s. As shown in Figure 8.10, only about 8 percent of the children were placed because of the death of both parents; a much larger share of the children (about 41 percent) were placed because of parents' divorce. The findings on the reasons for needing residential services suggest that many children are not orphans as they used to be and they were placed in the facilities due to family dissolution.

LENGTH OF PLACEMENT   Figure 8.11 presents the age distribution of children at the time of their discharge from a residential facility. The data suggest that many children stay in the facilities until they reach adulthood. The majority of children (about 70 percent) were 15 years of age or older at the time of their discharge and a significant proportion (about 16 percent) left these facilities at age 20 or older. Combined with age at initial placement, these data show that children often stay at these facilities for many years and until they age out of the child welfare system. Next, the data on the duration of stay for the children who left the residential facilities were examined in Figure 8.12.[5] As expected, the vast majority of the

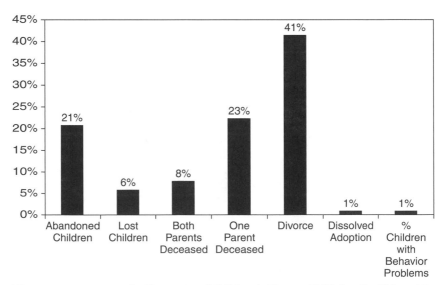

Figure 8.10.   Reasons for Placement of Children in Korean Child Care Facilities, 1997 Source: Byun and Lee (1998).

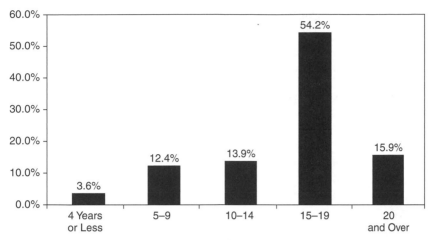

Figure 8.11. Age of Children at Discharge from Korean Child Care Facilities, 1997
Source: Byun and Lee (1998).

children (about 70 percent) were in care for longer than five years at the time of discharge. More than one-third of the children stayed in care for more than 10 years. The data on age at discharge and length of placement suggest that the norm in Korean residential facilities is for children to enter them at a relatively young age and to stay for long time—quite often until they reach adulthood.

Salient Issues and Future Directions

Residential care has been and will remain an essential part of the child welfare system in Korea for the foreseeable future. However, there is growing dissatisfaction with the current residential care system among the public and policy makers. In this

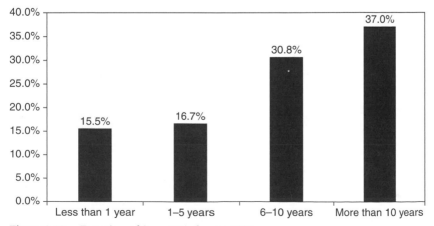

Figure 8.12. Duration of Stay at Discharge, 1997

section, I discuss several challenges facing residential care in Korea and offer recommendations for future development.

Redefining Purposes of Residential Care

There clearly is need for redefining the primary goal of residential care in Korea. In its early history, its primary function was to provide long-term residence services mostly for orphans. The current situation, reflected in the changing target populations and nature of their problems, requires redefining the goal of residential care. The old purpose of providing longer term residence services until children age out of the system was probably appropriate when the primary target population was war orphans at a time of great destitution in the country. There is need for a distinction between facilities for short-term stays and those intended for longer term residence. With more children needing residential services for various family-related problems, greater emphasis needs to be placed on preserving and rehabilitating the children's relationship with their families. Residential facilities should provide short-term residential services with the policy goal of family reunification based in local communities. The ultimate goal of residential institutions should change from merely protecting children from harm to improving and ensuring their well-being and development.

Improving Quality of Care

Currently, most residential facilities are large institutions intended to serve many children. There clearly is need for transition to smaller settings that are based in the community. There should be policy and financial incentives to transform large facilities into smaller ones. Since 1997, there have been several demonstration programs using small group homes of five to seven children as residential facilities based in the community. These demonstration projects should undergo rigorous evaluation to determine whether their use is a viable policy option.

Another critical need is to improve the quality and qualifications of the staff in the residential facilities. As the residential facilities move toward providing more specialized treatment services and shorter stays for the children, professional staff will be needed. The education and licensing policy of staff need to be reexamined to ensure that staff members are providing a sufficiently high quality of care.

Outcomes of Residential Care

While there has been much discussion and growing interest in the outcomes of residential care in Korea, there is very little empirical research in this area. As residential care seeks a new mission and implements policy measures to improve quality, more emphasis on monitoring outcomes is needed. Researchers should examine how well residential care fosters children's development and well-being compared to other program alternatives.

NOTES

1. The literature on how the orphans and abandoned children were cared for before these modern institutions is very scant. It is generally known that most of the responsibility was placed on relatives and charities provided by religious institutions such as Buddhist temples in neighborhoods. However, there also is some evidence to suggest that the government recognized the problem and, at times, assumed some responsibility in taking care of those children in need of protection. For example, a law proclaimed in 1783 during the Cho Sun Dynasty laid out providing shelter, food, and clothing for orphans and abandoned children when they could not be taken care of by their relatives as the responsibility of local governments (Choi, 1989).
2. The decline was not only in the absolute numbers but also in the rates of children being cared for in residential care. There were about 325 children in residential care per 100,000 children in 1970 in Korea. The rate declined about 1/3 to 128 children in residential care per 100,000 by 2000.
3. The significant dip in the growth of per capita GNI in late 1990s was due to the Asian financial crisis at the time. Since then, the Korean economy has been on a recovery tract approaching the pre-crisis level by 2002.
4. This section draws heavily from the findings in Byun and Lee (1998). Their study is the most recent study of the residential care in Korea that was based on a large scale survey of the institutions.
5. One would ideally like to use the duration data based on the entry cohort definition rather than the exit cohort one. However, only the exit cohort data were available in the study by Byun and Lee (1998) that I drew the data from for the discussion in this section.

REFERENCES

Bae, Tae-soon. (1995). Toward improving adoption services in Korea: Challenges and efforts. *Study of Korean Child Welfare, 3*, 107–126.

Byun, Yong-chan, and Lee, Sang-hum, (1998). *Survey of child welfare residential facilities: A report.* Seoul: Korea Institute for Health and Social Affairs.

Chang, Wha-jung. (2003, May 21). *Analysis of current situation of child protective services and their challenges.* A discussion paper presented at the public discussion for improving the CPS system. Seoul.

Choi, Won-kyu. (1989). Child welfare during the late Cho Sun Dynasty. In Sang-rak Ha (Ed.), *The history of Korean social welfare.* Seoul: Bakyoung-Sa.

Choi, Won-kyu. (1995). *Activities of international charity organizations and their influences on the development of Korean social work.* Unpublished doctoral dissertation, Seoul National University.

Kim, Hyun-shook. (1997). A study of better policy options for caring for children in need of protection in changing social environment. *Social Welfare Study, 20*, 87–95.

Kim, Hyun-yong. (1998). The review and proposal of the institutional child care program in the revision of the Child Welfare Law. *Study of Korean Child Welfare, 7*, 95–125.

Ku, Ja-hun. (1969). *Child welfare.* Seoul: Center for Korean Social Welfare Research.

Lee, Bae-kuen. (1993). Current situations and challenges of child welfare residential facilities. *Study of Korean Child Welfare, 1*, 46–57.

Ministry of Health and Human Services. (1996). *Child welfare service guidelines.* Seoul: Ministry of Health and Human Services.

Ministry of Health and Human Services. (various years). *Yearly statistical report.* Seoul: Ministry of Health and Human Services.

Ministry of Health and Human Services. (2002). *Report of foster care services in year 2001.* Seoul: Ministry of Health and Human Services.

Sung, Young-hae, and Kim, Yun-jin. (2001). *Child welfare.* Seoul: Dong-moon Sa.

National Statistical Office. (2003). Korean Information Statistical System. Retrieved March 5, 2003, from http://www.kosis.kr/.

Yoon, He-mi. (2002, October 10). *Issues and professionalization of child welfare services in Korea.* A paper presented at the 18th annual conference of the Korean Society of Child Welfare. Seoul.

9

Residential Programs for Children and Young People

Their Current Status and Use in Australia

FRANK AINSWORTH AND PATRICIA HANSEN

This first part of this chapter provides the statistical data on the status and usage, within the child welfare system, of residential programs for children and young people in Australia. In doing so, it highlights the extent to which Australia, unlike other Western-type economies, has significantly reduced the usage, not necessarily successfully, of these types of programs.

What the Figures Say

The Australian population as of December 31, 2004, was 20,229,800 (ABS, 2005). Slightly later figures from June 30, 2005, show that of this population, 4.9 per 1,000, or 23,695, were children and young people aged 0–17 in out-of-home care placements under the auspices of child protection authorities (AIHW, 2006a). The departments with responsibility for child protection services are variously titled community services, community development, heath and human services, human services, child and family services, and child safety. The in-care figures vary between 5.8 per 1,000 children in New South Wales (NSW) and Queensland (QLD) to 3.8 per 1,000 children in Western Australia (WA) and Victoria (VIC). Table 9.1 shows the distribution of children in out-of-home care for these and other states and territories (South Australia, Victoria, Tasmania, Australian Capital Territory, and Northern Territory) (AIWH, 2006a).

These figures cover all placements provided directly by state and territory child care and protection services or indirectly by nongovernment child and family

Table 9.1. Rates of Children and Young People Aged 0–17 Years in Out-of-Home Care, per 1,000, by State and Territory, June 30, 2005

State/Territory	Rate	Actual Number
NSW	5.8	9,230
Vic	3.8	4,408
Qld	5.8	5,657
WA	3.8	1,829
SA	3.9	1,329
Tas	4.9	576
ACT	4.5	342
NT	5.5	324
Total	4.9	23,695

Source: AIWH, *Child Protection Australia 2004–05*, 2006a.

service organizations. They also cover all forms of out-of-home care; that is, non-relative foster care, kinship care, and some limited forms of residential group living. Worthy of special note, of the 23,695 children in out-of-home care, 22,427, or almost 96 percent, are in regular home-based foster care (54 percent), kinship care (40 percent), or some form of independent living (2 percent).

Only 1,094, or 4.6 percent, of children and young people in out-of-home care as of June 30, 2005, were in residential placements. This includes 155 in small (usually fewer than six places) group homes, which are more realistically viewed as multiple fostering. Of the remaining 939 placements, there were 61 (1%) in Queensland and 365 (8%) in Victoria. Tasmania reports no children and young people in residential placement at all. Most of the children and young people in residential placements are school age, with 42 percent aged 10–14 years and 42 percent aged 15–17 years (AIHW, 2006a). Table 9.2 lists the numbers in care by state and territory.

Only 37, or 3.9 percent, of the 939 children in residential placement were under age 5 (AIHW, 2006a). It is possible that these children are siblings of older children

Table 9.2. Children and Young People in Residential Placement* by Age and State and Territory, June 30, 2005

State/ Territory	Under 1	1–4	5–9	10–14	15–17	Unknown	Total	% of in-care population
NSW	1	2	17	117	129	2	268	2.9
Vic	–	4	40	129	192	–	365	8.3
Qld	–	–	6	29	26	–	61	1.0
WA	1	17	50	62	37	–	167	9.1
SA	–	1	7	47	39	–	94	7.0
Tas	–	7	10	34	7	–	58	10.1
ACT	–	–	–	27	29	–	56	16.4
NT	2	2	2	14	5	–	25	7.7
Total	4	33	132	459	464	2	1,094	

* Includes family group homes.
Source: AIWH, *Child Protection Australia 2004–05*, 2006a, p. 61.

placed in residential facilities as foster care placements that allow children from one family to stay together are difficult to find (Ainsworth and Maluccio, 2002)

Indigenous Children in Out-of-Home Care

The June 30, 2005, figure of 23,695 children and young people in out-of-home care in Australia includes 5,678 children of Aboriginal and Torres Strait Islander descent. This is a rate of 26.4 per 1,000 children aged 0–17 years for that population (AIWH, 2006a). The rate is more than six times higher than for other Australian children. Table 9.3 lists the numbers in care by state and territory.

The variation in both number and rate shown in Table 9.3 reflects the uneven distribution of the indigenous population across the states and territories. These figures should be considered in the light of the Aboriginal Child Placement Principle (ACPP), which establishes a preference for placing Aboriginal and Torres Strait Islander children with Aboriginal and Torres Strait Islander people. This principle indicates that placement should be with a child's extended family as a best option, or if that option is not possible, then within the child's indigenous community or with other Aboriginal people. All jurisdictions adhere to this principle by way of either legislation or policy (AIWH, 2005).

In New South Wales, 87 percent, and in Western Australia 83 percent, of Aboriginal children were placed in accordance with this principle, which elevates kinship care to a priority position; as a result, very few Aboriginal children are placed in residential programs. In fact, the AIWH child protection data for 2004–2005 show only 47 Aboriginal children in indigenous residential programs and 119 in non–indigenous residential programs throughout Australia. Of a total Aboriginal out-of-home care population of 5,678, only 166 Aboriginal children are in residential programs, or less than 2.9 percent of that population group (AIWH, 2006a).

Table 9.3. Number and Rate per 1,000 Children Aged 0–17, by Indigenous and Nonindigenous Status, and Ratio of Indigenous to Nonindigenous Children and Young People by State and Territory, June 30, 2005

State/Territory	Number of Children			Rate per 1,000 Children		
	Indigenous	*Other*	*Total*	*Indigenous*	*Other*	*Total*
NSW	2,543	6,687	9,230	39.7	4.4	5.8
Vic	526	3,882	4,408	40.7	3.4	3.8
Qld	1,275	4,382	5,657	20.8	4.8	5.8
WA	692	1,137	1,829	22.6	2.5	3.8
SA	286	1,043	1,329	24.3	3.1	3.9
Tas	78	498	576	9.5	4.6	4.9
ACT	60	282	342	32.0	5.8	4.5
NT	218	106	324	8.9	3.1	5.5
Total	5,678	18,017	23,695	26.4	3.9	4.9

Source: AIWH, *Child Protection Australia 2003–04,* 2006a, p. 51.

Other Out-of Home Care Placements

Nationally, the number of young people aged 10–17 years held in juvenile corrective institutions declined from 1,352 in 1981 to 635 in 2000, the latest date for which data are available (Productivity Commission, 2005). Given the similarity of the age range between these children and young people and those in the AIWH 2005 child protection data, it is reasonable to assume that these young people are part of the out-of-home care population, even though they are in the care of the juvenile justice authorities. Some youth in out-of-home care become engaged in delinquent activities and migrate into juvenile corrective institutions while still in the care of the child protection authorities. In NSW in 1993–1994, a ward of the state who was under the supervision of the child care and protection authorities was 15 times more likely to enter a juvenile justice center than the rest of the juvenile population (Community Services Commission, 1996a). Table 9.4 lists 2000 data for each state and territory and Table 9.5 lists the same data but for indigenous youth.

A comparison of the data in Tables 9.4 and 9.5 reveals that, as with the data on out-of-home care from child care and protection sources (see Table 9.3), Aboriginal and Torres Strait Islander youth (295.4/100,000) are significantly more likely to be detained than nonindigenous youth (29.8/100,000) (Productivity Commission, 2005).

In 2006, the Australian Institute for Health and Welfare issued the first report from the juvenile justice national minimum data set (JJNMDS) (AIHW, 2006b). This report finds that in 2003–2004, nationally there were 5,357 young people aged 10–17 in juvenile detention facilities. This is approximately 2 per 1,000 of young people in that age range. This report does not show national figures by age, gender, or Aboriginality. Given the age of these young people, many, if not all, are probably known to the child protection authority in their respective state or territory. Some will be state wards. Detention facilities in the juvenile justice system are, to all intents and purposes, residential programs.

Table 9.4. Average* Daily Population and Annual Rate of Detention of Juveniles (per 100,000) Aged 10–17 Years in State and Territory Juvenile Corrective Institutions in 2000

State	Number	Annual Rate
NSW	244.5	34.6
Vic	55.8	10.9
Qld	98.0	23.8
WA	113.3	51.1
SA	54.5	33.6
Tas	37.8	67.8
ACT	14.5	40.8
NT	17.0	68.8
National average population number = 658.3. National average detention rate = 29.8.		

*Average based on population of juvenile correction institutions on the last day of each quarter.
Source: Productivity Commission, 2005, *Report on Government Services 2002*, pp. 630–631.

Table 9.5. Average* Daily Population and Annual Rate of Detention of Indigenous Juveniles (per 100,000) Aged 10–17 Years in State and Territory Juvenile Corrective Institutions in 2000

State	Number	Annual Rate
NSW	90.5	330.5
Vic	6.5	138.8
Qld	57.0	232.2
WA	73.3	576.6
SA	14.0	284.2
Tas	8.3	193.5
ACT	3.0	361.5
NT	11.8	116.2
National average number 264.3. National average rate 295.4.		

*Average based on population of juvenile correction institutions on the last day of each quarter.
Source: Productivity Commission *(2005) Report on Government Services*, 2002, p. 632.

Unfortunately, data about children and young people in residential health facilities, including those for substance abuse and mental health conditions, are not readily available. The same is true for residential boarding schools that cater to children and youth, some of whom are there by virtue of welfare issues. This chapter, as a result, focuses on residential programs in the Australian child protection sector.

The Decline in the Use of Residential Placements

Bath (1997) finds a continuous decline the use of residential placements from 2,416 in 1993 to 1,818 in 1996, or a reduction of 24.8 percent. By June 30, 2005, there were only 939 residential placements, a decline of more than 48 percent since 1993 (AIHW, 2006a). During this time, there has been no substantial development of foster care treatment (Chamberlain, 2004) or other programs to provide for children and young people with challenging or antisocial behaviors. Instead, regular foster care is expected to provide for all types of need.

In the Australian child care and protection context, the term "residential placement" is synonymous with "residential care," which refers to

> placement in a residential building whose purpose is to provide placements for children and where staff personnel are paid. This category includes facilities where there are rostered staff, where there is a live-in carer (including family group homes), and where staff are off-site (for example, a lead tenant or supported residence arrangement), as well as other facility-based arrangements. (AIHW, 2006a, p. 42)

All these facilities are very small. In NSW, the Children and Young Persons (Care and Protection) Act of 1998 sets the legal limit for such facilities at no more

Table 9.6. Classification of Residential Programs in Australia

Classification	Characteristics
1. Residential care	Care and supported accommodation only
2. Residential education	Care, accommodation, and in-house education services
3. Residential treatment	Care, accommodation, and in-house treatment services

than six places per facility. The NSW Children's Guardian (NSW Office of the Children's Guardian, 2006), an office established under the 1998 Act, specifies the small size as a condition of accreditation of out-of home care agencies (not specific programs). This is also confirmed by a recent survey of residential care in NSW (Flynn et al., 2005). Increasingly, the small size is being accepted as a national practice standard, although other states and territories may not have legislative support or regulation in place to reinforce it. These facilities provide care and supported accommodation only and are rightly classified, in a three-part classification system of residential programs, as residential care (type 1). In this classification (see Table 9.6), programs that provide an integrated accommodation, support, and in-house education are classified as residential education (type 2). Similarly, programs that provide integrated accommodation, support, and in-house treatment are classified as residential treatment (type 3). Unfortunately, residential education and residential treatment programs for children and youth barely exist in Australia as a consequence of their abandonment over the last decade or more by the child care and protection services.

Institutional Care and Impact on Residential Programs

A number of historical and contemporary events in Australia have contributed to the closure of residential programs by the child care and protection services. First among them is the history of the "stolen generation" of Aboriginal children who were removed from their parents solely because of their race, a practice that has had a serious impact on Aboriginal communities.

These children were not removed because of any finding of abuse or neglect but solely on racial grounds. They were then subjected to a regimen of institutional education and training mainly by religious missionaries. This practice was commonplace until the 1970s (Australian Law Reform Commission, 1997; Human Rights and Equal Opportunity Commission, 1997; McDonald, 1996). The aim was to separate Aboriginal children from their culture and integrate them into white society. To this day, the Aboriginal community considers institutional care and any mention of residential programs deeply offensive.

The equally abhorrent practice of forced child migration that affected primarily white children from Britain and Ireland represents another phenomenon that tainted residential programs for children and youth. Child migration, namely the practice of sending unaccompanied children to counties such as Canada,

South Africa and Australia, was common in the immediate post–World War II period and continued spasmodically until the 1960s. This approach was supported by British authorities, including nongovernment organizations such as Barnardos, the Church of England Children's Society, and various Catholic orders (Bean and Melville, 1989; Gill, 1997; Humphreys, 1995). Particularly distressing are the carefully documented accounts of the physical and sexual abuse of some of the children placed in residential institutions, including orphanages sponsored by religious orders (Gill, 1997; Humphreys, 1995). For these children, now referred to as the "lost innocents" (Senate Community Affairs Reference Committee, 2001) who were sent to populate the British Empire in South Africa, Canada, and Australia (Gill, 1997) and to benefit from a new life, they were victims of a gross deception. Forced separation from family and community has affected all those children and youth who were subjected to these practices. The abuse they suffered while in care continues to haunt many of them and, not surprisingly, many are critics of institutional care and all residential programs (Senate Community Affairs Reference Committee, 2001). Tied to all of this are reports of abuse in institutional care and other residential programs run by both government and nongovernment organizations that affected Australian born children who were neither Aboriginal nor unaccompanied child migrants (Community Services Commission, 1996b; Forde, 1999; Senate Community Affairs Reference Committee, 2004).

Partially as a result of the reports of abuse, all state and territory governments began to move against the use of residential programs in the 1970s. The policy aimed to close residential programs regardless of their purpose or the results they achieved. The view was that, by definition, residential programs were harmful.

Today, the picture of abuse is very different. With the decline in residential placements, the reporting of abuse from such venues does not even warrant a separate mention in the AIHW annual *Child Protection* report for 2004–2005 (AIHW, 2006a). In contrast, family foster care includes 194 substantiated abuse cases (approximately 12 percent of all substantiations). In a more detailed analysis for the WA Department of Community Development, Murray (2005) reports 59 instances of substantiated abuse (all categories) of children in departmental care between July 2003 and 2005. This analysis identifies 35 percent of relative or foster caregivers and 1 percent of residential staff as the person responsible for the abuse. The remainder of the incidents are attributed to parents, other children including siblings, and unrelated adult visitors. Comparable data for other states and territories are unavailable.

Furthermore, the major international social policy ideologies of the last two decades or more—deinstitutionalization, normalization, least restrictive environment, mainstreaming, and diversion—supported the move away from residential programs, even though none of these principles originated in the child welfare sector (Ainsworth, 1999, 2001). These ideologies, much more than the United Nations Convention on the Rights of the Child (UN, 1989), combined with an increased interest in the effectiveness and cost of service programs during the 1980s and 1990s, made residential programs a prime target for cost cutting. Broadly accepted throughout this time was the view that various forms of foster care (family foster care, kinship care) were the preferred and less expensive option (Fulcher and Ainsworth, 1994). Yet in fiscal year 2003–2004 in NSW, the Department of Community Services, the statutory authority for child care and protection services in that state, spent $58.5 million (Australian) on individual service contacts for 169 children and youth (about $346,000 per child) for whom foster care placements could not be found (Horin 2004). In part, this shows that the policy of eliminating residential programs has failed when evaluated on the cost criteria that were used to promote foster care as the cheaper and preferred service option. More rigorous and comprehensive examinations of the comparative cost of foster care and residential programs do not exist in Australia.

Profile of the Residential In-Care Population

The problem is that some of the difficult and disturbed youth who find their way into the child care and protection system continue to be referred to the few remaining type 1 residential care programs. As the data show, the children and young people in these programs are predominantly aged 10–17. This group engages in disruptive and delinquent activities or more serious aggressive and violent behaviors, including behaviors linked to mental health and substance abuse problems arising in many instances from earlier abuse and neglect (Ainsworth, 1999, 2001). Invariably, these children and young people demonstrate an inability to live peaceably with others, either in their immediate family or with foster caregivers. They rarely attend day school as they have usually been suspended or expelled. A history of multiple disrupted foster care placements is commonplace. They are so alienated from others that without effective intervention to steer them to an alternative outcome, they face long-term unemployment and homelessness, with the potential to drift into a life of social isolation, adult crime, and poverty. Unfortunately, type 1 residential care programs are inappropriate for these children and young people as they are not designed nor resourced to meet their educational or treatment needs. Consequently, some of these young people, due to the absence of 24 hour a day, 7 day a week residential education and treatment services, are accommodated under individual service contracts (as noted above) for significant periods of time in specially rented houses, hotel, and motel rooms where they are supervised by mainly untrained youth workers.

Barber and Delfabbro (2004), in a recent Australian study of foster care, state that it is possible to predict which children on entry to out-of-home care will not settle into a stable foster care placement. In their sample of 235 children, 20 percent, or 47 young people, fit their description. The most critical variable in this prediction is a prior disrupted foster care placement. These are the likely subset of children and young people in out-of-home care in Australia who are reported as being in a residential care placement (AIWH, 2006a). As noted, 42 percent of these children and young people were 10–14 years of age and a further 42 percent were 15–17.

Other Related Developments

Australian children and young people who might well have been placed by child care and protective services in residential programs are in desperate circumstances when foster care fails, as no other alternatives exist. They are often referred to programs for homeless youth, as this is the only other option. Since 1985, when a national jointly funded Commonwealth-State Supported Accommodation Assistance Program (SAAP) for homeless youth was established, services for homeless youth have been used to accommodate seriously troubled children and young people. This program was initially promoted as a "safety net" program for these youth. The program has since broadened its mandate and now aims to "provide transitional supported accommodation and related support services to help homeless people (of all ages) achieve the maximum possible degree of self reliance and independence" (National Strategic Plan, 1997).

The importance of this program becomes apparent in light of the national profile of SAAP clients. In 2003–2004, of the clients who used this program, 1,900, or 1.9 percent, were under age 15, while another 9,300, or 9.3 percent, were between ages 15 and 17. These figures include both male and female youth and account for 11,200, or 11.2 percent, of the total program clients in that year (AIWH, 2005). In one state, NSW, in 2003–2004, 3,200 clients were under age 17, or 12.8 percent of all clients. Clients under age 15 numbered 550, or 2.2 percent of all clients (AIHW, 2005).

There is evidence from SAAP agencies that 52,700 children aged 0–17 were accompanying a parent or guardian when the parent requested SAAP services (AIHW, 2005). Unfortunately, while these figures are broken down by child age, they are not correlated with parental age. As a result, it is impossible to know how many of the SAAP clients aged 15–17 had young children with them. What is known is that for every 10,000 youth aged 0–17 in the Australian general population, 106 children accompanied a parent or guardian who used SAAP services. The highest rate of use was among those aged 0–4, with 186 per 10,000 children in this age bracket accompanying a SAAP client (AIHW, 2005). In NSW, because of the mandatory reporting requirements, any child in a refuge for the homeless as a result of domestic violence will be known to the child protection authority.

What these figures indicate is that the SAAP population contains a significant number of children and young people who under current protective legislation and are the legal responsibility of the child care and protection services. Moreover, there is evidence that the Department of Community Services in NSW actively seeks to place wards and other young people for whom they have responsibility into SAAP programs (Community Services Commission, 2001). Indeed, it can be argued that state and territory authorities have off loaded many of the most disturbed and difficult children and youth who should be in out-of-home care to SAAP programs that are meant to be short-term transitional facilities (Community Services Commission, 2001). In that sense, SAAP facilities have become the de facto residential programs of the child care and protection system.

The SAAP programs, which in NSW alone cost $110.8 million (Australian dollars) and nationally $321.3 million in 2003–2004 (AIWH, 2005), are generally staffed by a largely untrained workforce, with little if any prior professional background in child care and protection services. The SAAP programs are what they were created to be—short-term emergency accommodation. The federal act that provides the mandate for SAAP programs does not authorize them to provide education or treatment services per se. Given the short duration of accommodation envisioned for SAAP programs, it is impossible to provide such services.

A recent inquiry and the resulting recommendations into access and exit policies in SAAP programs by the NSW Ombudsman (2004) undermines attempts to work selectively with particular children and young people. This is because the Ombudsman in this report draws attention to the SAAP mandate to provide services to all homeless youth and declares that the exclusion of specified categories of youth contravenes antidiscrimination legislation. This means that in NSW, SAAP programs cannot exclude youth with mental health problems, substance abuse issues, those who are violent, and individuals who do not pay residential accommodation fees.

Many SAAP programs are now populated with vulnerable children and young people who in the 1970s and 1980s would have been in residential programs run under the auspices of nongovernment or government child care and protection agencies. It is possible that the recommendations in the NSW Ombudsman's report (2004) will make SAAP programs unsafe places for these children and young people.

National, State, and Territory Expenditures

Another issue of interest and concern is the cost of out-of-home care services. Data on costs are hard to find, not least of all because of variation in the way the state and territory expenditures are classified. Limited data on this issue can be found in the Productivity Commission's report (2005) on government services, which provides information for 1998–1999. National expenditures on community services totaled $16.8 billion (Australian dollars) in that year, and 22.7 percent was on family and children services—or $2.4 billion. This sizable figure covers a vast range of services other than out-of-home care. Expenditures on only out-of-home care are difficult to find because the states and territories vary in how they assign similar items to different cost centers. One glimmer of light on this issue is to be found in the NSW Department of Community Services Corporate Plan issued in 2005. That plan includes data on the cost of delivering these services. In 2004, costs were approximately $30,000 per child per annum. Given that NSW had an in-care population on June 30, 2004, of 9,145 children, this results in an estimated annual expenditure of $27.4 million on these services. Nationally, assuming other states and territories have a similar cost structure, the cost of providing out-of-home care for 21,795 children is an estimated $653.8 million. This is almost 25 percent of the total national expenditures on family and children services.

Out-of-Home Care Research

One interesting development in 2004 was the publication of an *Audit of Australian Out-of-Home Care Research* (Cashmore and Ainsworth, 2004). This audit, undertaken for the Child and Family Welfare Association of Australia (CAFWAA) and the Association of Children's Welfare Agencies (ACWA) in NSW, sought to catalogue all out-of-home care research projects undertaken between 1995 and 2004. The audit identified only 94 such projects. Most were conducted either by university-based researchers or nongovernment agencies, either alone or in partnership. To quote:

- The main gaps in the research were shown to relate to both the content area and the type of research.
- There were no national research or evaluation projects and only one multi-site cross-state project.
- Few studies replicated the findings of earlier research or from research in other jurisdictions.
- Just over half the projects use qualitative research methodology and half are based on small non-random samples, often in single agency services.
- Most of the current Australian out-of-home care research projects focus on aspects of family foster care and only two on aspects of residential or other forms of alternative care.
- There is little substantial research on kinship care although more children are entering kinship care and it is already the most prevalent form of care in some states.
- There is little research in Australia on:
  - Permanency planning (from family reunification to adoption)
  - Treatment foster care or wrap-around services
  - The evaluation of policy and legislative changes
  - The educational needs and outcomes of children and young people in care
  - There are few studies on care for indigenous children, children from other cultural backgrounds or children with disabilities.

(Cashmore and Ainsworth, 2004, pp. 9–10)

Equally devastating are these audit findings:

- Overall, total funding for out-of-home care research for the 10 years (1995–2004) from all sources was estimated at just over $3.9 million.
- Overall, expenditure for out-of-home care services for the same period is estimated at $3 billion. This works out to only about 13 cents for research for every $100 of expenditures on out-of-home care services.

(Cashmore and Ainsworth, 2004, p. 10)

Given this information, it is hardly surprising that studies of the outcomes of residential services, of children's perspectives, or the costs of residential programs are not even on the research horizon.

The Stockholm Declaration Reviewed

The 2003 Stockholm Declaration on Children and Residential Care begins with the following statement.

> There is indisputable evidence that institutional care has negative consequences for both individual children and society at large. The negative consequences could be prevented through the adoption of national strategies to support families and children, by exploring the benefits of various types of community based care, by reducing the use of institutions, by setting standards of public care and for the monitoring of the remaining institutions. (Stockholm Declaration, no date, p. 1)

These noble ideas were pursued in Australia long before 2003 (Ainsworth and Hansen, 2005). Now the consequences of this approach are clear. In every state and territory foster care is in crisis (McHugh, 2004; Overington, 2006). Indeed, the number of foster carers has dropped from 14,000 to less than 9,000 in the last five years (Overington, 2006). In no small measure this is the result of placing children and youth whose behaviors are unmanageable in regular foster care that is, in normal home environments. These are children and young people who need type 2 (education) and type 3 (treatment) services that are 24 hours per day 7 days per week, the kind that only residential programs can provide. As a recent NSW survey shows (Flynn et al., 2005) these types of programs do not exist in Australia because of the almost total closure of residential programs in favor of home-based services and an emphasis on the use of foster care.

It is of course important to note that foster care has not failed these difficult and disruptive children and young people—foster care was never designed for them. Foster care services are important and deserve an honored place, but they need to be preserved for those children and young people for whom foster care is best suited. Most states in Australia have tried to rely solely on foster care. This strategy has not worked. It has simply created a crisis within the foster care system. The result is that many of the nation's most difficult and disruptive young people have been transferred out of mainstream child care and protection services to emergency accommodation programs (SAAP), to residential programs in the juvenile justice system, or to life in individual care arrangements where a young person is inadequately looked after in an apartment by unqualified staff.

Indeed, even the most ardent exponents of foster care, who see it as capable of covering all service eventualities, indicate that when treatment foster care (Chamberlain, 2004) or foster care as an alternative to remanding a child fails (Lipscombe, 2006; Walker, Hill, and Triseliotis, 2002), residential programs are the only alternative. This shows that despite our reluctance to concede the case, residential programs have a place in the child care and protection system. There is a need to develop these services rather than allow difficult and disruptive young people to take the first steps into the less desirable homeless accommodation or juvenile justice arenas. By failing to invest in a new generation of residential programs Australian child care and protection authorities are allowing the history of past abusive institutional practices (Forde, 1999) to determine the future (Ainsworth, 2007).

A major issue is how to design, resource, and implement a range of progressive, nonabusive residential education and treatment programs that operate 24 hours per day, 7 days per week. Australia also needs a direct care workforce, similar to those in parts of North America, Britain, and some counties in Europe (Clough, Bullock, and Ward, 2006; Fulcher and Ainsworth, 2006; Petrie, Boddy, Cameron, Wigfall, and Simon, 2006), who are trained specifically for work in residential and other group settings.

The Australian experience now shows that a mature child care and protection system has to have some residential education and residential treatment facilities that are capable of working with disturbed youth with difficult-to-manage behaviors. It is against this experience that the Stockholm declaration needs to be reviewed. Somewhat surprisingly, it appears that Australia is more compliant and further down the Stockholm declaration track than most other countries. Australia has demonstrated that home-based foster care services in all their various forms are not enough. Innovative residential education and treatment programs should be developed to serve a specialized and highly selected group of children and young people for whom home-based services are inappropriate. Residential programs are likely to remain contentious, costly, and difficult to staff and manage. They may also achieve only modest changes in behavior, not least of all because they are often used as a last resort rather than a placement of first choice. Without such programs the responsibility for vulnerable youth is all too easily transferred from the child care and protection sector to other less appropriate services in other systems. This can hardly be a sensible way of dealing with difficult and disruptive young people.

REFERENCES

Ainsworth, F. (1981). The training of personnel for group care with children. In F. Ainsworth and L. C. Fulcher (Eds.), *Group care for children. Concept and issues* (pp. 225–244). London: Tavistock.

Ainsworth, F. (1997). *Family centred group care: Model building.* Avebury: Aldershot.

Ainsworth, F. (1998). The precarious state of residential child care in Australia. *Social Work Education, 17*(3), 301–308.

Ainsworth, F. (1999). Social injustice for "at risk" adolescents and their families. *Children Australia, 24*(1), 14–18.

Ainsworth, F. (2001). After ideology. The effectiveness of residential programs for "at risk" adolescents. *Children Australia, 26*(2), 11–18.

Ainsworth, F. (2006). Group care practitioners as family workers. In L. C. Fulcher and F. Ainsworth (Eds.), *The best of group care practice with children.* New York: Haworth.

Ainsworth, F. (2007). Residential programs for children and young people. What we need and what we don't need. *Children Australia, 32*(1), 32–36.

Ainsworth F., and Hansen, P. (2005). A dream come true—no more residential care: A corrective note. *International Journal of Social Welfare, 14*(3), 195–199.

Ainsworth F., and Hansen, P. (2006). Five tumultuous years in Australian child protection: Little progress. *Child and Family Social Work, 11*(1), 33–41.

Ainsworth F., and Maluccio, A. N. (2002). Siblings in out-of-home care. Time to rethink? *Children Australia, 27*(2), 4–8.

Australian Bureau of Statistics (ABS). (2005). *Census data.* Available at http//www.abs.gov.au.

Australian Institute for Health and Welfare (AIHW). (2005). *Supported Accommodation Assistance Program. National data collection. Statistics 2002–03.* Canberra. Available at http//www.aihw.gov.au/housing.

Australian Institute for Health and Welfare (AIHW). (2006a). *Child protection Australia 2004–05.* Canberra. Available at http//www.aihw.gov.au.

Australian Institute for Health and Welfare (AIHW). (2006b). *Juvenile justice in Australia 2000–01 to 2003–04.* Canberra. Available at http//www.aihw.gov.au.

Australian Law Reform Commission. (1997). *Seen and heard: Priority for children in the legal process.* Sydney: Author.

Barber J. G., and Delfabbro, P. H. (2004). *Children in foster care.* London: Routledge.

Bath, H. (1997). Recent trends in the out-of-home care of children in Australia. *Children Australia, 22*(2), 4–8.

Bath, H. (1998). *Therapeutic crisis management: Training manual.* Canberra: Marymead Child and Family Centre.

Bean, P., and Melville, J. (1989). *The lost children of the empire.* London: Unwin Hyman.

Cashmore, J., and Ainsworth, F. (2004). *Audit of Australian out-of-home care research.* Sydney: Child and Family Welfare Association of Australia/Association of Children's Welfare Agencies.

Chamberlain, P. (2004). *Treating chronic juvenile offenders. Advances made through the Oregon multidimensional treatment foster care model.* Washington, DC: American Psychological Association.

Clough R., Bullock R., and Ward A. (2006). *What works in residential child care? A review of research evidence and the practical considerations.* London: National Children's Bureau. National Centre for Excellence in Residential Child Care.

Community Services Commission (1996a). *The drift of children in care into the juvenile justice system. Turning victims into criminals.* Sydney, December.

Community Services Commission. (1996b). *Just solutions – wards and juvenile justice.* Sydney, March.

Community Services Commission. (2001, September). *Issues paper 1. Out-of-home care and the role of SAAP.* Sydney: Author.

Fecser, A. F., and Long, N. J. (2000). *Life space crisis intervention.* Hagerstown, MD: Institute for Psychoeducational Training. Available at http//www.air.org/cecp.

Flynn, C., Ludowici, S., Scott, E., and Spence N. (2005). *Residential care in NSW.* Sydney: Association of Children's Welfare Agencies.

Forde, L. (1999). *Commission of inquiry into abuse of children in Queensland institutions.* Brisban: Queensland Government.

Fulcher, L., and Ainsworth, F. (1994). Child welfare abandoned? The ideology and economics of contemporary service reform in New Zealand. *Social Work Review, 6*(5/6), 2–13.

Fulcher, L., and Ainsworth, F. (2006). *Group care practice with children and young people revisited.* New York: Haworth Press.

Gibbs, J. C., Potter, G. B., and Goldstein, A. R. (1995). *The EQUIP program. Teaching youth to think and act responsibly through a peer-helping approach.* Champaign, IL: Research Press.

Gill, A. (1997). *Orphans of the empire.* Sydney: Millennium Books.

Horin, A. (2004, March 19). The kids that cost DoCS $800,000 a year—each. *Sydney Morning Herald,* p. 1.

Human Rights and Equal Opportunity Commission. (1997). *Bringing them home. National inquiry into the separation of Aboriginal and Torres Strait Islander children from their families.* Sydney: Author.

Humphreys, B. (1995). *The empty cradle.* London: Corgi Books.

Lipscombe J. (2006). *Care or control? Foster care for young people on remand.* London: British Association for Adoption and Fostering.

McDonald, C. N. (1996). *When you grow up.* Broome: Magabala Books.

McHugh, M. (2004, May). *Availability of foster carers.* Sydney: Social Policy Research Centre, University of New South Wales.

Murray, G. (2005). *A duty of care to children and young people in Western Australia.* Perth: Department of Community Development.

National Strategic Plan. (1997). *Supported accommodation assistance program. Second update.* Canberra: SAAP Coordination and Development Committee.

NSW Department of Community Services. (2005). *DoCS Corporate Plan.* Sydney. Available at http//www.community.nsw.gov.au.

NSW Office of the Children's Guardian. (2006). *Accreditation benchmark policy statement.* Available at http//www.kidsguardian.nsw.gov.au.

NSW Ombudsman. (2004, May). *Assisting homeless people: The need to improve their access to accommodation and support services. Final report arising from an inquiry into access to, and exiting from, the Supported Accommodation Assistance Program.* Sydney. Available at http//www.csc.nsw.gov.au/publication.

Overington, C. (2006, September 27). Foster parents "deserve payment." *The Australian,* p. 3.

Petrie P., Boddy, J., Cameron, C., Wigfall ,V. and Simon, A. (2006). *Working with children in care. European perspectives.* Maidenhead: Open University Press.

Productivity Commission. (2005). *Report on government services 2002.* Canberra. Available at http//www.pc.gov.au.

Senate Community Affairs Reference Committee. (2001). *Lost innocents: Righting the record. Report on child migration.* Canberra: Senate Secretariat, Parliament House. Available at www.aph.gov.au/senate_ca.

Senate Community Affairs Reference Committee. (2004). *Forgotten Australians. A report on Australians who experienced institutional or out-of-home care as children.* Canberra: Senate Secretariat, Parliament House. Available at www.aph.gov.au/senate_ca.

The Stockholm Declaration on Children and Residential Care. (no date). Available at http://www.children-stracgics.org/declaration. Accessed December 12, 2005.

United Nations (UN). (1989). *Convention on the Rights of the Child.* New York.

Vorrath, H. H., and Brendtro, L. (1985). *Positive peer culture* (2nd ed.). New York: Aldine de Gruyter.

Walker, M., Hill, M., and Triseliotis, J. (2002). *Testing the limits of foster care. Fostering as an alternative to secure accommodation.* London: British Association for Adoption and Fostering.

10

Children and Youth in Institutional Care in Brazil

Historical Perspectives and Current Overview

IRENE RIZZINI AND IRMA RIZZINI

Institutions for Children in Brazil

This chapter discusses the institutionalization of children and adolescents in Brazil and places current debates about institutional care in a historical context. The institutional care of children is deeply rooted in the Brazilian governmental and religious response to needy children. Up to the mid-twentieth century some of the Brazilian elite also sent their children to boarding schools to train them to take their place among the next generation of the elite.[1] The primary use of institutions has been for children who were orphaned, abandoned, or delinquent or whose parents could not or would not take care of them. A major formal shift in attitudes toward institutional care occurred in 1990 with the passage of the Statute of the Child and Adolescent (Law 8.069, July 13, 1990)—a law that articulated the fundamental

Irene Rizzini is a professor and a researcher at the Pontifical Catholic University of Rio de Janeiro, Brazil, and director of the International Center for Research on Childhood (CIESPI). Professor Rizzini serves as president of Childwatch International Research Network. Irma Rizzini is a professor at the Federal University of Rio de Janeiro, Department of Education. This text is based on the book *The Institutionalization of Children in Brazil: Historical Perspectives and Current Challenges* (CIESPI/UNICEF, 2004). A portion of the research conducted was supported by the University of Chicago, Chapin Hall Center for Children, with the participation of Paula Caldeira, Alexandre Bárbara Soares, Thereza Cristina Silva (CIESPI), and students from PUC-Rio (Social Service Department): Bianca Lessa, Denise Marçal de Oliveira, Emely Teixeira Pontes, Fátima da Silva Teixeira, and Francisca Paiva Ribeiro. The authors are grateful to Anjali Akaur and Mariana Menezes who translated the original manuscript from Portuguese and to Malcolm Bush, from the Chapin Hall Center at the University of Chicago for valuable comments on the text.

rights children and youth should enjoy. The section of that law on children and youth in special circumstances redefines institutional care as shelter care, describing it as care that should be temporary and that should be structured in ways to maintain children's connections to their community and family of origin. In contrast, the deliberate isolation of the nineteenth-century institution, which survived deep into the last century, was regarded as a desirable characteristic either because it shielded the child from bad influences and permitted the supposedly good influences of the institution the maximum chance to shape that child or because it protected society against "dangerous" children.

The dilemma of the current situation in Brazil is that while intentions about the use of institutions have changed, it is not clear how much practice has changed. And this dilemma is made more acute by the dearth of comprehensive data about institutionalized children past and present. Not only do we not have historical censuses of children in institutions but we do not even know how many children are in what kinds of institutions in Brazil now. So while there is fragmented evidence about change and continuity in the use of institutions for children and youth, there is little comprehensive data. Even partial data, however, will give the reader general idea of the scope of the current institutionalization practices. The Brazilian research institute IPEA did a study on children in institutional care for whom the federal government granted a per diem contribution to the cost of their care and where the children entered care through the formal guardianship system; it counted 630 institutions with 808 facilities which cared for about 20,000 children and adolescents (IPEA/CONANDA, 2004). Because of the lack of other formal data, we do not know the percentage of all children in institutions that are represented in this survey.

What we do know is that a variety of pressures, some economic and some philosophical, have resulted in the demise of large orphanages, some of which housed as many as 500 children. But pressure for institutional care of some kind persists for several reasons. One reason is that the gross demand may have increased because of the urbanization of rural populations and growing urban poverty. Such poverty has resulted in a high percentage of single-family homes and the frequent inability of a single parent to cope, leading the parent or the child to seek help that results in institutional care. Urban poverty breeds urban crime, and urban crime results in pressure to remove children and youth who spend their days on the streets, to keep them out of sight. But poverty and crime have not resulted in broad government policies to provide economic, educational, and social support for families to reduce the risks of children entering care and ending up in institutions. This failure to create alternatives occurred even though during the years after the military dictatorship (which formally ended in 1985) many important reform proposals were made based on the international movement to guarantee the rights of the child. In Brazil, the pressure to change policies toward children was one of the consequences of the broad social movements to restore democracy and human rights.

In Brazil, widespread poverty that affects the majority of the population is one of the reasons for the persistence of institutional care. Increased family and community violence results in children leaving home for their own protection, and some of these children end up in some part of the institutional care system. The persistence of institutional care is surviving a major change in public discourse, which now emphasizes the principle of placing children in institutions as a last resort. Given this change in discourse, we need to examine political and ideological factors to understand why we have not experienced significant reforms to improve the care of children living away from home or to improve the standard of living of the general population, thus reducing the need for out of home care.

It is important to add that the Statute of the Child and Adolescent (1990) was formulated in full knowledge of, and respect for, the principles enshrined in the United Nations Convention on the Rights of the Child (1989). In fact, the statute was inspired by the convention and reflects several of its articles on the rights of children. The statute expressly prohibits placing children in institutions when their only problem is their poverty. The statute also mandates supporting children at risk at home and in their communities whenever possible. If that is not possible, the statute encourages the search for alternatives to institutions.

In the rest of the chapter, we briefly describe children in residential care, the landmark characteristics of the ways Brazil has treated needy children in the past and the present, the pivotal changes in attitude and law in the 1980s and 1990s, the contemporary reality of institutional care, and challenges for the future.

Children in Residential Care in Brazil

The current practice of placing children and adolescents in institutions and the ways of treating them cannot be understood just by reference to past practices. Although the backgrounds of contemporary children and adolescents and some of the reasons for their institutionalization are similar to those in the past, there are important differences. Even in the absence of comprehensive information about the current population of such children, we know from available information that today the majority of children in institutions move frequently among their home, the streets, and shelters. The high mobility that characterizes the lives of these children and adolescents seems to be connected to the high levels of urban violence in the country, and particularly violence linked to drug trafficking. It is a reality quite different from the past, when, for example, many of the "clientele" of these institutions were placed there by their own families.

Most of the children and adolescents interviewed during the research carried out by CIESPI in the city of Rio de Janeiro have a similar trajectory:[2] They left their homes, had the experience of living on the streets, and passed through various institutions. In addition to the breakdown of families, which used to be seen as the only reason children were left in orphanages and shelters, today there is another important factor to be considered: the children´s rejection of their families. Many children who now leave their homes do so feeling that they are a burden in their homes. Despite the value placed on the idea of *family* and especially of the *mother*, many of the children said when they were telling their stories that they did not desire to or could not return home, for reasons such as familial conflicts or to avoid involvement in the world of drug trafficking.[3]

This analysis is about children and adolescents who are currently in institutional care. We are concerned in this chapter mainly about poor children. So we do not take into consideration those institutions that specifically serve juvenile delinquents and children with special needs.

Brazil has a large number of poor children. According to the national census, approximately a third of the 60 million youth between the ages of 0 and 19 in the year 2000 lived in families whose household income is below the poverty line. Some of these youth ended up moving between home, the streets, and a variety of institutions because their families did not have the resources to support them. We should note that most poor youth do not end up in this cycle of unstable living conditions, but for those who do, poverty is a key reason propelling them away from their homes. Before we describe these children in the present, we would like to sketch the history of such children in Brazil.

Significant Patterns in the History of Institutional Care in Brazil: Continuity and Change

It is difficult in the limited scope of this text to synthesize a history as complex as that of the institutionalization of children in Brazil. We will focus on a few principal concepts that mark the history of this practice.

Below we have identified patterns that are important for understanding the history of child welfare in Brazil, particularly as they influenced the models for providing asylum for poor children and the continuities and changes in the models up to the present.

The "Institutional Culture"

Brazil has maintained a long tradition of placing children and youth in institutions based on the model of seclusion and isolation. Many children, particularly from poor families, have gone through the experience of being educated away from their families and communities. From the colonial period children were raised in boarding schools, seminaries, reformatories, and other types of institutions created in accordance with the educational and welfare theories of the time. Some of the most interesting strands of this history relate to helping and controlling the population of children characterized as dangerous in the context of the growth of large cities and the development of the nation state.

The broad judicial category of "menores" ("minors"), particularly as it related to children from the poorer classes in the second half of the nineteenth century, had an essentially social and political character.[4] These youth became the specific target for intervention by the state and other sectors of society, such as religious and philanthropic institutions. After the second half of the twentieth century the model of institutional placement for wealthy children fell into disuse and its practice has been nonexistent in Brazil for many years. So institutions as a model for raising and educating children have been preserved for specific groups of the young population.

The Construction of Ideologies that Justify Institutional Care

In the specialized institutional services at the end of the nineteenth century and part of the twentieth century, the children of the poor became categorized as "menores desvalidos" (literally children without value), abandoned, orphans, delinquents, and other designations that substituted for older terms as new service practices and ideologies developed.

In the twentieth century, emerging charitable organizations for the protection of disadvantaged children questioned the institutional model. But after the establishment of the "National Policy for the Well-Being of Minors" by the military government (which took power in 1964), the institutional model was reinforced and was justified on the grounds of national security. The ideology of detaining children who lived or spent their time on the streets was justified on the grounds of protecting children from "the danger he/she presents to him/herself and society," since "they lacked affection and economic support" (FUNABEM, 1974).

While we do not have a census of children in institutions, our observations of several institutions and statements from educators as well as from children placed in these facilities indicate the continuing usage of these institutions despite all arguments made against institutional care. The main argument for institutions is the lack of alternatives to support the children and their families.

The Social Construction of the Category "Minor" ("Menor")

The judicial category "minor" historically identified individuals to whom special laws were applied because they were not able to exercise their rights as citizens and were considered to be under the legal control of the family or other responsible persons.

In the second half of the nineteenth century various Brazilian metropolitan areas became preoccupied with the education of the young vagabonds and the indigents who seemed to escape family control and/or wandered on the streets. The former legal term (*menor de idade*) was replaced by the new socially constructed category "minor." A "minor" was identified as a special target for state paternalism, so the policies about them turned even more to social control and restraint, especially after the inauguration of the Republic (1889). The state institutions, created after the inauguration of the republican regime, had a decisive role in the judicial and social construction of the category "minor."[5] In the beginning the judicial sector identified the term and divided it into subcategories that were needed to account for the complexity of the universe of assistance and control. Solidifying this process, the welfare establishment and social science were drafted to contribute to the theoretical definition of new terms and methodologies. For each category there was a service modality, thus creating specialization among institutions. Interventions became divided into therapeutic and preventive, in accordance to particular categories of "minor."

In more recent times new conceptual paradigms of childhood based on the notion of the child and adolescent as subjects of rights were written into the United Nations Convention for the Rights of the Child (1989) and in the Statute of the Child and Adolescent (1990), creating a new vision for assisting low-income children. Two important changes were the rejection (in principle) of the practices of depriving children of their liberty and separating them from their families and communities. One sign of the changing climate is that organizations that previously only offered closed institutional care started to serve children on a more open basis by offering day services or sending residential children at home for weekends. This change was an indication of the growing distaste for the closed system characterized by the orphanage. Now the watchword was that the segregation of the child should always be avoided. The Statute of the Child and Adolescent provides that the shelter constitutes an exceptional and provisional measure (Article 101) and that institutionalization is forbidden except for adolescents who have clearly committed criminal acts (Article 106). We should point out, however, that these new developments have not significantly reduced the stigmatization and discrimination suffered by poor children. Recent research conducted by CIESPI with children and adolescents who have gone through various institutions in Rio de Janeiro has shown that practically all of them consider society to be prejudiced against them. "What do they think of me? Failure, marginal, vagabond, glue sniffer . . ." (Rizzini et al, 2003, pp. 236).

The Culpability of Family and the Reduction of the Parental Role

The developing, specialized knowledge confirmed the concept of the incapacity of families, especially the poorest ones, to take care of and raise their own children. This concept justified the transfer to the State of the responsibility to take care of these children. Institutionalization involved a temporary suspension of parental power so that it was the judiciary that decided how the children should be raised and when they could return to their environment. The concept was shared by some parents who saw themselves as incapable of looking after their children. In consequence, they sometimes approach the Guardianship Councils or other public bodies such as the juvenile courts to request those bodies to take over the care of their children.[6]

Current practice still demonstrates a paternalistic attitude that ignores the underlying factors that weaken parents. But the authoritarian social welfare systems in which the families were dismissed from their parental role because of their incapacity are not valued as much now as they were in the past. Decisions about children's lives that exclude the key participants are increasingly rejected, especially by the children. Moreover, more attention is being paid to the underlying circumstances that bring children to the attention of the authorities. The movement toward concentrating decision making at the municipal level and establishing civic review of municipal actions allows a more hopeful view of the future treatment of low-income children and youth. However the main actors—children, families, and their communities—should not be marginal to the reform process. Their participation, which has historically been denied, should be encouraged to provide a critical perspective to the debate about improving their lives.

Dependency Relationships Engendered by the System

An analysis of the existing historical documentation reveals the spread of *clientalism* in public assistance encouraged by the State at various levels. *Clientalism* is a Brazilian term that refers to a system of relationships between the powerful or rich and ordinary citizens whereby legitimate transactions are expanded into transactions that benefit the rich and exploit the poor. The structure of assistance toward children as a project of the centralized State explicitly identified with the protection of national security, permitted, for example, elites to request the placement of particular children such as their servants' children into institutions even if some people saw those placements as adulterating the institutions' mission. (Such children were institutionalized not as a favor to them or their parents but to prevent servants from bringing the children to work with them.) *Clientalism* of this sort was denounced during the institutional reforms as a practice that filled institutions with children who did not need to be placed and for whom institutional programs had not been designed. The absence of data makes it hard to be sure if these practices have diminished, but the civic oversight that is part of municipalization through the operation of the Guardianship Councils is likely to have discouraged the tradition.

The Circulation of Children

Records from the nineteenth century show that children and adolescents wandering on the streets of Rio de Janeiro were picked up by the police and designated as vagrant, vicious, or criminal. There were institutions near the city center that allowed for immediate placement of these children, and the correctional institutions on the islands permitted their complete isolation, thus reducing the risk of rebellions and escapes. The official policies created in Rio de Janeiro for the placement of *abandoned, minor, vicious, and criminal* children were modeled on the theory of separating undesirables from the city.

The placement of children labeled as criminals or vagabonds and their unplanned circulation around different institutions still occurs today. These children, who by the end of the twentieth century were being called *girls or boys of the street,* have become a part of the urban scene in almost every country. In Brazil, the problem of children surviving in the streets has gained considerable visibility in the last 20 years along with knowledge of the poverty of their families and the lack of alternatives for improving their material conditions. The children, along with other members of their families, try to survive using a variety of strategies. Illegal activities such as drug trafficking is a profitable way of earning a living, and children engage in the drug trade even though they know it may shorten their lives. According to statements by the children and adolescents caught in these circumstances, their life trajectory is characterized by the intense mobility from home to the streets and to various types of institutions such as shelters, detoxification clinics (for drug abusers), and detention centers.[7]

As this narrative shows, the predominant causes of institutionalization have not changed in the long term. They continue to be linked to parents' lack of financial resources to raise their children. What seems to be new today is that the children and adolescents themselves are taking a more active role in their lives. Their movements are not restricted to those mandated or arranged by organizations or public authorities. The children consciously use institutions for different purposes—for example, to rest, nourish themselves, sleep, get away from the streets, and protect themselves from threats that they may be facing where they live or on the streets (from rival drug gang "comandos" [commands] or from the police and others).

Assisting Children in Need Rather than Helping Families

Brazil opted to invest in a "policy to assist minors" by institutionalizing them rather than making a comprehensive attempt to improve the life conditions of children and youth in their homes and communities. This only began to change in the 1980s. Brazil had and has one of the most unequal income distributions in the world. The problem that dates first from the failure to abolish slavery until the late 1880s, from massive inequalities in land distribution, and the failure to break up large plantations was exacerbated by the absence of federal programs to redistribute income for the benefit of the urban poor. In the cities, the extreme contrast between the urban poor living in favelas (slums) and the rest of the population—as well as the segregation of these poor—at once made it extraordinarily difficult for the poor to move into the economic mainstream and made it easy for other city dwellers to ignore their plight except as problems of crime and violence.

There are, however, signs that different attitudes are developing toward poor families. The federal government is increasing programs to reduce poverty, but the challenges of endemic violence related to drug trafficking and the systematic exclusion of a significant percentage of the population from the economic mainstream remains immense.

Focusing on Recent History: Overview and Challenges

The Debate about the Institutionalization of Children in the 1980s and the Participation of Citizens in that Debate

Silence and censorship combined to maintain the policy of institutionalization even in the appalling conditions that existed in these institutions and to guard the truth from the eyes and ears of the population.[8] But in the 1980s, fresh energy and ideas entered the debate, brought there by the unprecedented involvement of diverse citizens' groups. The history of the institutionalization of children and adolescents took a new direction in the middle of the 1980s resulting in the passage in 1990 of the Statute of the Child and Adolescent, a sweeping legislative reform of the Code of Minors (1927, 1979). The reform codified into law the essence of the U.N. Convention on the Rights of the Child, but it went far beyond that convention.

The national security policies in force during the military dictatorship had used isolation as a method to repress any citizen who threatened the social order and official institutions. In the 1970s and 1980s, the maltreatment of low-income children became more visible mainly because the number of children on the streets increased—a result of urban migration and concentrated urban poverty.[9] Since the 1980s, a combination of grassroots movements, nongovernmental organizations, the Catholic Church, and progressive factions within the government started to work together to improve the conditions of children's institutions in Brazil. With the country's return to a democratic government in 1985, a number of social issues began to emerge that the military government had kept from public attention or that activists had put on hold while civil society joined forces to advocate the end of military rule. Among these was a focus on the special needs of low-income children and youth, particularly street children.

By the mid 1980s, media reports on the often abysmal conditions in existing children's institutions and the treatment of street children by police, plus advocacy efforts by nongovernmental organizations, resulted in a considerable national outcry on behalf of these children. This advocacy included (1) popular participation in political debates after the military dictatorship ended, (2) the publication, from the beginning of the 1980s, of diverse studies about the consequences of institutionalization on the development of children and adolescents and the high costs of maintaining institutional placements (Altoé, 1990; Campos, 1984; Guirado, 1980; Rizzini, 1985; Rizzini and Altoé, 1985); and (3) the interest of professionals from diverse disciplinary backgrounds in this area that contributed to much more profound understanding, reflection, and writing on the topic.

Children and youth became involved with this movement as well. The protests of children in placement expressed in acts of rebellion and criticisms also contributed to complaints by the press and public statements in various publications (Collen, 1987; Herzer, 1982; Luppi, 1987). In 1986, more than 500 children and youth participated in the First National Meeting of Street Children in Brazil, and some of the youthful participants also spoke on the floor of Brazil's Congress. In 1986, the government established the National Commission on the Child and the Constitution, which had the role of collecting information on the needs of children and proposing constitutional changes. Those proposed changes went through numerous revisions with constant input from broad sectors of Brazilian society before they became law in October 1990. Among the key principles in the code are guarantees of full human rights for children, special assistance and protection for children and youth, and special codes for children who need special care. The law also decentralized decision making on children and built in citizen participation through the creation of municipal and state Children's Rights Councils; these councils are made up of representatives of public and private organizations charged with setting and implementing children's and youth policy at the local level and administering all public funds for children and youth services.

New Paradigms for Placing Children in Residential Care in the 1990s

The 1990s were shaped by efforts to implement the Statute of the Child and Adolescent. The reigning discourse for children in need of care in this era was about the search for alternatives, widely understood as alternatives to institutionalization. The logic of this new discourse was to preserve the links that children have with their families and communities. The vehicle for a more family- and community-oriented approach to care was the substitution in many situations of shelter care for institutional care. The Statute of the Child and Adolescent reads as follows:

> The entities that develop shelter programs should adopt the following principles: I – preservation of family bonds; II – integration in a foster family, when the maintenance resources of the family of origin have been exhausted; III – personalized treatment in small groups; IV – development of activities in a context of coeducation; VI – whenever possible, avoid the transfer of sheltered children to other entities; VII – participation in local community life; VIII – gradual preparation for severance from the entity; IX – participation of persons from the community in the educational process.
>
> For all purposes of law, the director of the shelter entity is considered as equivalent to the guardian. (The Statute of the Child and Adolescent, Chapter II, Section 1, Article 92, pp. 38)

While the shelter was seen as a temporary measure for the protection of children in situations considered to be personally and socially risky, institutional care was still retained for delinquent youth. But in both cases, the law included mechanisms that guarantee the rights of the child and adolescent.

The approach toward residential care today is different in important respects from the past: There is a growing awareness of the necessity to focus on the causes of the problems that propel children and adolescents toward shelters or institutions. On the other hand, there is a new emphasis on identifying forms of support that could help the children remain permanently with their families and in the communities in which they were raised.

Despite the clarity of the statute, however, there is still confusion in practice about the changes in the philosophy of care on which the law is based. The statute, in article 101, refers to "shelters" meaning a place that engages in the "act of sheltering." However, the term is still used in practice to refer to any institution, as confirmed by an educator who works in one of these institutions: "When they feel threatened they (the adolescents) know that going to a "shelter" is an alternative. As a result this entity has been transformed into a place where children and adolescents go when

they need to hide in order to get out of sight for a period of time."[10] The children
and adolescents also call the institutions "shelters." "In the shelter, I sleep one day,
two days . . . afterwards I leave again, I go back to the streets. That's how I am"
(Luiza, 15 years old).

Asked why any type of institution is labeled a "shelter," a group of workers
responded that such nomenclature conforms to the principles of the Statute of the
Child and Adolescent. So the new term might cause people to rethink attitudes and
practices that were deeply engrained or it might just encourage a change of label to
appear that current practices are in compliance with the new law.

It should be pointed out that efforts are being made to ensure that the intent
of the new law is not simply ignored. In 2001, for example, the Human Rights
Commission from the House of Deputies, accompanied by journalists, visited 18
institutions for children and adolescents in five states. They verified that most institutions operated according to the old models of residential care, contrary to the
Statute of the Child and Adolescent. They found incompetent staff as well as government officials who were simply ignoring bad conditions in institutions.
According to the report, it is clear that there is enormous distance between the
intentions of the new law and the reality of the treatment dispensed particularly
toward adolescents deprived of their liberty.

We will now focus on the services of the institutions directed to children and
adolescents, highlighting some of their characteristics considering their plurality
and complexity.

Children and Adolescents Placed in Residential Care

There are still a number of different types of institutions that house children and
adolescents in Brazil. We will start by focusing on which children and adolescents
arrive at these institutions.

1. Orphan or abandoned children and adolescents are those who do not
   have any bonds with their original families or have been abandoned
   by their parents. Included in this group are also orphan children who
   have no other family members who could be responsible for raising
   them.
2. Children and adolescents "at risk"[11] are those who, due to violence,
   family crises, or natural disasters, are unable to return to their
   communities and need temporarily to be cared for out of their own
   homes. Often these are children and adolescents who have left the
   streets or left their homes because of domestic violence, or who are
   involved in gangs and need to protect themselves from other gang
   members.
3. Children and adolescents in poverty: As in the past, families seek out
   the courts and institutions to get their children placed either because
   of poverty or because they have difficulty disciplining them. One of
   the workers recently interviewed in Rio de Janeiro, stated that from

2001 to 2002 there was a 20 percent increase in the number of inquiries about placing children because of extreme poverty; these were parents who have strong affectionate links with their children but who cannot afford to feed them.[12]

Pathways into Residential Care

How do children arrive at these institutions? We should note that there are public and private institutions. In general the public ones are associated with municipal or state programs. The private ones are initiatives connected to various churches and nongovernmental organizations. Often the nongovernmental institutions receive public resources to support their work.

The children and adolescents arrive at the institutions in different ways. The most common are these:

1. Brought by their own families when parents lack the resources to provide for their children's basic needs
2. Brought by the juvenile court. These are often children abandoned as babies. Others are placed because they need to be protected from violence.
3. Appearing by themselves, searching for help or shelter due to violence, extreme family poverty, or other risks often linked to the drug trade.
4. Referred by other agents of the state and municipal governments. For example, children and adolescents found on the streets are forced into institutions by social workers, the police, or other officials. The children and adults interviewed remember these events as quite violent.
5. Brought by the Police Department for Protection of the Child and Adolescent when they have committed some type of crime.
6. Brought by the Guardianship Council. The cases arrive through complaints from a local police force, governmental and nongovernmental institutions that attend children and adolescents, their own families, and eventually the Police Department for Protection of the Child and Adolescent.

While we know about these various entry points into institutions, we do not have a detailed understanding of how the professionals and institutions interact with the children and adolescents and how these interactions contribute to the sequences of broken ties and instability the children experience.

Types of Institutions that House Children and Adolescents

There are many different kinds of institutions for children and adolescents in Brazil but there is no integrated system of care based on children's needs. This lack reflects the absence of a national policy to promote the healthy development of children and youth, a serious deficiency in a country in which half the population is less than 20 years old. Below, we categorize institutions mainly by the length of time children and adolescents typically spend in them.

INSTITUTIONS THAT HOUSE CHILDREN FOR A SHORT PERIOD OF TIME   These institutions are aimed at children and adolescents considered at risk. There are various institutions in this group and they are meant to provide temporary care. Consequently, they lack investment in educational and social activities and do not reflect a child development perspective. In the city of Rio de Janeiro, these institutions are called "abrigos" (temporary shelters. Term adopted by the Statute of the Child and the Adolescent, articles 90, 92, 93, 101).[13]

In general, these institutions receive children and adolescents while they wait for their cases to be evaluated by the juvenile court. Ideally, a child or adolescent should stay in a shelter for a maximum of three months, until they can return to their families or to the community, or can go to a substitute family. In practice, however, there is a different outcome. Either children end up staying at the shelter for years with grossly inadequate care or they do not stay in any one institution but keep wandering between the streets, their family homes, and multiple institutions.

With time, the affective ties begin to break down and their family connections weaken. Or if those ties are weak to begin with, the children just move from one institution to another. After spending a number of years in this lifestyle many of the adolescents begin to lose hope in the possibility of significant change.

Rai, a 15-year-old boy from Rio de Janeiro, is among many who have experienced such turmoil since birth. He speaks of the time he spent living in institutions: "Oh, my life was . . . terrible." He stayed temporarily in 14 different places and never felt welcomed. Among these are Guardianship Councils, temporary shelters (*abrigos*), reception centers (*centros de triagem*), group homes (*casas de acolhida*), and clinics for treatment of drug addiction. By the end of the two long interviews about his life, he concluded: "I can only rely on myself, and . . . I got to have courage."

Among the pertinent characteristics of shelters, they tend to serve a particular age group and are segregated by gender. Typically they have a capacity of 20 to 30 children but are often overcrowded. The staff includes social workers, psychologists, educators, and volunteers, among other professionals. Whatever the professed mission of these facilities, children consider them way stations between periods of life on the streets.

Ruth, 16-years-old, affirms that view: "I stayed on the streets for some time, and afterward I went to a shelter that closed. . . . I stayed there for a month. I woke up, had breakfast, stayed sitting. After lunch, I stayed sitting. I took a bath and stayed sitting. I did not have anything to do but watch television. I think that the kids did not like it there." Nara, 14 years old, said: "I asked a boy on the street where I could find a shelter since I did not want to stay on the streets, because things would keep getting worse for me. I would suffer more because I didn't have a way of working, and a way to eat."

Staff members describe the problems of these facilities as overcrowding, high staff turnover, the consequent lack of continuity of care for children, and the lack of a developmental and educational perspective. As one educator who works in a shelter puts it: "The problem of shelters has turned into a vicious cycle; the adolescents enter one day and are out the next, creating a "false" service. The work that should be done ends up never occurring."

INSTITUTIONS THAT HOUSE CHILDREN FOR LONG PERIODS OF TIME   Some institutions are focused on providing longer term care for children at risk. In these institutions children are cared for by workers named "social educators" or "social parents." The institutions provide appropriate courses and enroll the children in schools. Examples of these types of institutions are *casas de acolhida* (group homes) and *casas lar* (substitute homes). The *casas lar* are supposed to reproduce a nuclear family with a couple called "social parents" caring for up to 12 children. These people are trained to offer children guidance, education, and a healthy environment.

The adolescents we interviewed helped us to distinguish between shelters (*abrigos*) and group homes (*casas de acolhida*). The shelters can be characterized as a "passport" to the group homes. According to their reports there seems to be a "worthiness" criteria for moving to a group home. In their words: "The difference is that at the group home there is a school, and different types of courses. They provided everything and the shelters don't and you ought to behave because otherwise you won't be taken to the group home." "The group home is better because they have school and they are obliged to give better attention to the children and adolescents" (Ruth, 16 years old). "The difference from the shelter is because the group home is more caring" (Nara, 14 years old).

The main characteristics of group homes are as follows: *(1)* they target children and adolescents in situations of risk or abandonment. In some cases family ties have begun to fall apart or the young people find it impossible to return to their families; *(2)* the child/adolescent gains a degree of stability; *(3)* group homes provide an open system of care inside small residential units of 15–30 children; *(4)* all children attend school and some are enrolled in different courses in the group home; *(5)* other cultural and pedagogical activities are provided by social educators and/or psychologists and social workers; *(6)* children and adolescents are allowed to stay in the group homes until they are 18.

The reality is that in group homes the children still face instability, residential problems, and turnover among other children and adolescents, which makes it harder for family and community reinsertion. A variety of sources about group homes in Rio de Janeiro suggest these institutions function in general as shelters. Contributing to their lack of stability are the enormous demand for taking more children and the lack of other types of care for children and adolescents.

Challenges and Future Directions

A review of the literature on the institutionalization of children and adolescents, together with our experience of being involved in research, policy development,

technical assistance and training in this area, brought us to the following conclusions about the principal challenges in current philosophy and practices and about
avenues for change.

An increase in the number of institutions is not good for children. Numerous
studies that were released during the twentieth century clearly reveal the disastrous
consequences of institutionalization for human development. Professionals from
Rio de Janeiro who work in these institutions report that in the last few years the
problems in the children's lives have worsened—for example, the cases of violence
in the family, the community, the streets, and the institutions. They also insist it is
getting harder to achieve positive outcomes for the children. They emphasize that
what occurs is "false service," since generally they are not able to maintain a stable
program that responds to the needs of the children in shelters. They also mention
conditions of overcrowding of the institutions, a high turnover in the shelters, and
a mixture of highly compromised adolescents with those who have a better chance
of returning to their families. Yet we start the third millennium with the knowledge
that a significant number of children still live in institutions.[14]

In many countries, the principal causes of institutionalization are similar to
those we experience in Brazil; institutions are an alternative for low-income families who see them as providing the opportunity for their children to be fed, to be
secure, and to have access to education. And so the condition of poverty continues
to cause the placement of children who do not need to be removed from their families or communities. In addition, civil and other wars, family and community violence, the HIV/AIDS epidemic, and the organizational pride of staff and donors
contribute to the large number of children who remain in institutions.

The practice persists despite the globally recognized fact that institutional care
is, in general, ineffective and expensive, costing up to six times more than initiatives
that support families to take care of their children themselves (Ministry of Foreign
Affairs, 2001).

Developing Alternatives for Institutional Care

Children should not be institutionalized for being poor, but they still are. Alternatives
need to be created that respect both the needs of children and their rights.

In the cases where institutional care is considered unavoidable as a temporary
measure, an institution should not deprive a child of a broader social life or try to
occupy all the space of the family. Alternatives to institutional care have a sufficient
track record both here and abroad to be preferable to institutions. They include a
variety of familial and communal supports and the use of substitute families and
adoption. Most important, the responsible public bodies cannot be allowed to abdi-
cate their responsibilities to the police as has been the case throughout the nineteenth
and twentieth centuries. Unfortunately, this is still the current practice, at least in large
Brazilian cities as the police continue sweeps to remove children from the streets.

Some progress has occurred in Brazil in the past two year, however. Several
states, including the State of Rio de Janeiro, have established, with the help of feder-
ally mandated Children's Rights Councils, specific guidelines for the appropriate

care of children in residential placement. In addition, a presidential decree established a commission that recommended a national plan to guarantee and promote children's and adolescents' rights to live with their families and in their communities. These recommendations are now being considered by the appropriate national bodies.

In addition, in 2004, the government established a national policy for social welfare that emphasized the priority of supporting families and of preventing the placement of children outside their homes. The policy is based on the assumption that to sustain the family, the family must in the first place be guaranteed the means to sustain itself (Ministério do Desenvolvimento Social e Combate à Fome, 2004, pp. 34–36).

Placing children and adolescents in institutions for short periods of time should be seen as a part of a range of services available to them in very special circumstances. Institutional care should not be an end in itself but a resource to be utilized only when there are no alternatives. This recommendation is in accord with the principles established by the United Nation Convention of Rights of the Child and Adolescent as well as the Statute of the Child and Adolescent. In the spirit of the convention, when care outside of family is unavoidable, every effort should be taken to ensure that the placement best meets the needs of the child or adolescent after taking into consideration their opinions and wishes.[15]

Conclusion

We discussed in this chapter the development of a strong pro-institution culture in Brazil that in many ways has persisted until the present, and we noted important changes that have occurred beginning in the 1980s. We have shown how questions about institutional care developed and how these questions brought pressure for reforms in legislation and practice. Currently there is a resurgence of interest in the problem and a new drive to rethink the issue and combat the practice of unnecessary institutional placements. It is critically important to place reform on the active national political agenda.

It is important to establish participatory processes so that interested groups and communities can be involved in the identification and clarification of the issues. For example, how should different family and community actors be involved in the search for solutions to problems related to the education and nurturing of their children? This is not an easy challenge. The task requires a change in attitudes and service practices that have flourished in this country for centuries.

Among the fundamental questions in thinking about reducing the incidence of institutional care are these: Are institutions necessary? In what cases? For whom? When institutional care is unavoidable, how can we ensure an environment that respects the child's humanity and encourages the full development of the child? What alternatives now exist or should be created? The alternatives to institutional care should be acceptable to the children themselves and to parents who have run out of resources to cope with the challenges of child rearing.

However, the problem will not be resolved just by focusing on the question of institutional care. The problem and its solutions are intimately connected to the macroeconomic conditions and policies that produce persistent poverty. The continued existence of that poverty is the major reason for the conditions for which institutional care is the unacceptable response.

NOTES

1. The use of boarding schools by upper middle-class parents seems to have disappeared in Brazil, unlike other countries. We were not able to find any substantive research on the ending of this tradition.

2. The study, funded by the Swiss NGO *Terre des homes,* was commissioned by the newly founded *Rede Rio Criança—Rio Child Network*—an initiative aimed at integrating the ideas, experiences, and actions of 17 organizations that work with children's rights in Rio de Janeiro. In this study, 67 youngsters were interviewed both on the streets and in institutions. We found various cases of boys and girls who, by the age 15, had already passed through more than 10 different institutions. However, contrary to popular belief, only a comparatively small number of children in the urban centers of Brazil actually live on the streets. But large numbers of children spend their days on the street, returning to their homes or the homes of friends or relatives at night (Rizzini et al., 2003).

3. This information is based on the statements of children and adolescents interviewed in Rio de Janeiro, during the period from October 2001 to September 2002 (Rizzini, Soares, Caldeira, and Butler, 2002).

4. Though "minor" ("menor") is a legal category applied to children/youth 0 to 18, it became popularly used to label a child who was an object of the legal and welfare systems, thus becoming a target of the politics of institutionalization. In Portuguese, the word "menor" means diminished, smaller. The term "abandoned and delinquent minors" ("menores abandonados e delinqüentes") was commonly used from the 19th century up to the 1990s to refer to disadvantaged children.

5. Brazil gained its independence from Portugal in 1822 when the Portuguese Regent of Brazil, Dom Pedro, son of the Emperor John VI of the United Kingdom of Brazil and Portugal, declared Brazil's independent from Portugal and himself first emperor of Brazil. This monarchy survived until 1889 when, with very little struggle, the then emperor, Dom Pedro II, was sent back to Portugal and the country was declared a republic.

6. The Statute tries to go beyond the declaration of child rights and actually determines the means to facilitate the implementation of these rights. It mandates that every one of the approximately 5,700 Brazilian municipalities should have two Municipal Child Councils: a Child Rights Council (Constitution, Articles 204, 227; and ECA Article 88) and a Child Guardianship Council (Articles 131 – 140; 13, 98, 105, 101, 129, 96, 90, 191, The Guardianship Council is responsible to oversee the attainment of the rights of the child and adolescent. The obligation of the Guardianship Council is to intervene in cases which the rights of the child and the adolescent have been threatened and/or violated. Statute of the Child and Adolescent (1991, Articles 131 to 140). The Child Rights Council has the responsibility for addressing child and adolescent rights at the macro, collective level. It was instituted by federal law but has to be implemented by municipal ordinances. A mixed body, it includes appointed government members and

elected, unpaid community representatives See *The Evolution of Child Rights Councils in Brazil.* Duarte, C., Hoven, C. (Columbia University), Rizzini I. (Pontifical Catholic University of Rio de Janeiro), Earls, F., and Carlson, M. (Harvard University). *International Journal of Children's Rights* (2007).

7. Interviews carried out in Rio de Janeiro in 2002 (Rizzini, Soares, Caldeira, and Butler, 2002).

8. This section on the democratic movements to improve the condition of children in Brazil is taken from Irene Rizzini, Gary Barker, and Neide Cassaniga, *Children, Participation and Democracy: A Case Study of the Statute of the Child and Adolescent in Brazil,* 1998.

9. Also see: Almeida, 1982; Alves, 2000; Prada, 2002; Weber, 2000.

10. Interview with a worker in an institution for children in Rio de Janeiro in May 2002 (Rizzini, Soares, Caldeira, and Butler, 2002).

11. In this text we use the term "children at risk" simply because it is commonly used to refer to children who are in adverse or vulnerable circumstances. We would like to point out, though, that this term has been misused to label mostly poor and black children thus contributing to processes of segregation, marginalization, and discrimination that affect these children (Rizzini, Barker, and Cassaniga, 2002).

12. Interview conducted in November 2002 in one of the institutions for temporary shelter in Rio de Janeiro (Rizzini, Soares, Caldeira, and Butler, 2002).

13. The terms used to describe particular residential care facilities vary within the country and while we chose the most appropriate equivalent terms in use in North America and Western Europe, the reality of such care is likely to be quite different, in some respects, in Brazil than in these other countries.

14. There is no way of measuring the problem. We are limited to inadequate public reports. A report conducted by the Swedish government estimates that there are between 8 and 10 million children in institutions of some sort or another in the world (Ministry of Foreign Affairs, 2001).

15. Bullock, Little, Ryan, and Tunnard, 1999.

REFERENCES

Almeida, Fernanda M. B. G. (1982). A vida num educandário de meninas (Life in an institution for girls). In *Educação para a marginalidade: a problemática do sistema de assistência ao menor.* Dissertação (Mestrado em Educação). Salvador: Universidade Federal da Bahia.

Altoé, Sônia E. (1990). *Infâncias perdidas: o cotidiano dos internatos-prisão* (Lost childhoods: Everyday lives in a closed institution). Rio de Janeiro: Xenon.

Alves, Emeli S. (2000) *Abrigamento de crianças e realidade familiar: a desmistificação do abandono* (The institutionalization of children and family reality). Dissertação. Florianópolis: Universidade Federal de Santa Catarina/Departamento de Psicologia.

Bullock, R., Little, M., Ryan, M., and Tunnard, J. (1999). *Structure, culture and outcome: How to improve residential services for children.* Dartigton: Dartington Social Research Unit.

Campos, Angela V. D. (1984). *O menor institucionalizado: um desafio para a sociedade* (The institutionalized child: A challange for society). Petrópolis: Vozes.

Collen, Paulo. (1987). *Mais que a realidade* (More than reality). São Paulo: Cortez.

Duarte, C., Rizzini, I., Hoven, C., Earls, F., and Carlson, M. (2007). The evolution of Child Rights Councils in Brazil. *International Journal of Children's Rights, 15,* 269–282.

FUNABEM (National Foundation for the Well-being of Children). (1974). Brasil Jovem (Young Brazil). Rio de Janeiro: *FUNABEM*, n.28, p. 44.

Guirado, M. (1980). *A criança e a FEBEM* (The child and FEBEM). São Paulo: Perspectiva.

Herzer. (1982). *A queda para o alto* (Falling high above). Petrópolis: Vozes.

IPEA/CONANDA. (2004). *O direito à convivência familiar e comunitária: os abrigos para crianças e adolescentes no Brasil.* Brasília: IPEA/CONANDA.

Luppi, C. A. (1987). *Malditos frutos do nosso ventre.* São Paulo: Ícone.

Ministério do Desenvolvimento Social e Combate à Fome; Secretaria Nacional de Assistência Nacional. (novembro de 2004). *Política Nacional de Assistência Social.* Brasília: MDS/SAS.

Ministry of Foreign Affairs. (2001). *Children in institutions.* Stockholm: International Development Cooperation.

Prada, C. G. (2002). *A família, o abrigo e o futuro: análise de relatos de crianças que vivem em instituições* (The family, the shelter and the future: Analysis of testimonies of children who live in institutions). Curitiba: Universidade Federal do Paraná, Departamento de Psicologia. Dissertação de Mestrado; Departamento de Psicologia.

Rizzini, I., Barker, G., and Cassaniga, N. (1998). Children, participation and democracy: A case study of the Statute of the Child and Adolescent in Brazil. *Family Futures*, *2*(1), 35–42.

Rizzini, I., Barker, G., and Cassaniga, N. (2002). From street children to all children: Improving the opportunities of low income urban children and youth in Brazil. In Marta Tienda and William Julius Wilson (Eds.), *Youth in cities. A cross-national perspective.* Cambridge, UK: Cambridge University Press.

Rizzini, I., Soares, A., Caldeira, P., and Butler, U. M. (2002, October). *Crianças e adolescentes e as instituições de abrigamento* (Children and youth in institutional care in Rio de Janeiro). Rio de Janeiro: CIESPI. Report submitted to Chapin Hall Center for Children, University of Chicago.

Rizzini, I. (1985). A internação de crianças em estabelecimentos de menores: alternativa ou incentivo ao abandono? (The placement of children in institutions for "minors": Alternative or stimulus to the abandonment of children?). *Cadernos de Cultura*, *11*, 17–38.

Rizzini, I., and Altoé, S. (1985). Sobre as relações afetivas nos internatos para menores (On love relationships in closed institutions for children). *Cadernos de Cultura*, *11*, 111–128.

Rizzini, I., et al. (Eds.). (2003). *Vida nas ruas. Crianças e adolescentes nas ruas: trajetórias inevitáveis?* (Life on the streets. Children and adolescents on the streets: inevitable trajectories?). Rio de Janeiro: Loyola, Editora PUC-Rio, CIESPI.

Rizzini, I., and Rizzini, I. (2004). *A institucionalização de crianças no Brasil: perspectivas históricas e desafios do presente* (The institutionalization of children in Brazil: Historical perspectives and current challenges). Rio de Janeiro: UNICEF/Editora PUC-Rio/CIESPI, 2004.

Statute of the Child and Adolescent. (1991). Federal law number 8.069, July 13, 1990. Brasília: Imprensa Nacional, Governo do Brasil.

Stockholm Declaration. (2003, May 12–15.). *Child and residential care. New strategies for a new millennium.* 2nd International Conference. Stockholm: Stockholm University, the Swedish National Committee of ICSW, International Council on Social Welfare, Swedish National Committee for UNICEF.

Weber, L. N. D. (2000). *Os filhos de ninguém: abandono e institucionalização de crianças no Brasil* (Children of no one: Abandonment and institutionalization of children in Brazil). São Paulo: Conjuntura Social.

11

Residential Care in the United States of America

Past, Present, and Future

MARK E. COURTNEY and DARCY HUGHES-HEURING

> Practice abhors a vacuum. In the absence of knowledge, belief abounds. Lacking criticism, belief becomes dogma. "Institutions are good." "Foster homes are good." "Institutions and foster homes are part of a program." What is true or false in these views depends on the framework, the time, the service patterns, the child. As slogans they may be useful. They are not, however, "facts." (Wolins and Piliavin, 1964, p. 32)

These comments by Martin Wolins and Irving Piliavin, published in 1964 in *Institution or Foster Family: A Century of Debate*, are no less relevant today. The debate in the United States over the relative merits of residential care versus family-based care for abused and neglected children has become somewhat less strident than it was for much of the past 150 years. Nevertheless, champions of family-based, out-of-home care still argue that few if any children ever need placement in residential care (Foster Family-Based Treatment Association, 2003). Moreover, if anyone doubts that advocates for residential care are alive and well, they need only pick up a copy of *Rethinking Orphanages for the 21st Century*, a volume that argues for a significant expansion of the use of residential care for maltreated children (McKenzie, 1999). Unfortunately, advocates for and against residential care still have relatively few facts on which to base their claims.

We are not optimistic that the debate over the appropriateness of residential care for children in need of protective placement will end any time soon, at least in the United States. The debate will continue because it relies heavily on ideological positions that are not easily disturbed by empirical evidence, and, unfortunately, recent history does not suggest that much empirical evidence pertinent to the debate will be forthcoming anyway. Our sense is that the niches currently filled by residential care are likely to remain in need of filling for some time to come and that alternatives will emerge only slowly. At the same time, we do not believe that there will be any rush to expand residential care in the United States in the near future.

In this chapter, we examine the history of U.S. residential care in an attempt to understand the factors that have influenced its development. We then describe recent trends in and the current state of residential care. Finally, we speculate about its future. We have focused our review on the use of residential care for children removed from their families due to abuse or neglect. Of course, other populations of children such as delinquents and children with disabilities also experience residential care. We make no claim that our review does justice to the history, development, and scope of these other forms of residential care, though their histories do overlap to a large extent. We also recognize that particular residential facilities have sometimes housed more than one population of children. Nevertheless, since at least the 1970s, federal and state policy has favored housing abused and neglected children separately from other populations of children in residential care. The term "residential care" is used in this chapter to describe settings ranging from small group homes that house no more than six children to large children's institutions. The primary distinguishing characteristic of this form of out-of-home care is not the size of the facility per se but that the settings do not provide a substitute "family," in contrast to family foster care and kinship foster care.

The Historical Roots of Residential Care in the United States

The American colonies were founded on deeply ingrained societal values of work and thrift. Prospects for success in the New World encouraged the notion that no person need be poor unless he or she was idle, deviant, or a moral failure. The poor were thus responsible for their own situation. This idea heavily influenced the foundation of the U.S. child welfare system and residential care.

To a great extent, America inherited the English system of dealing with the poor, one based on indenture, poorhouses, workhouses, and miserly distributions of home relief, overseen by local administrative units. Dependent children were dealt with much the same as impoverished and needy adults. In the seventeenth and eighteenth centuries, as LeRoy Ashby (1997) points out in *Endangered Children: Dependency, Neglect, and Abuse in American History*, "abuse" and "neglect" of children did not exist as legal concepts. Older children were often apprenticed, indentured, or boarded out to other families, and younger ones put in poorhouses until they were old enough to be apprenticed or boarded out. Local authorities had the power "to take poore children from indigent parents to place them to worke in those houses" (Ashby, 1997, p. 14). Children in poorhouses usually ended up in the care of older inmates, who were frequently in no condition to care for a child. As the population of dependent children grew, space in poorhouses ran out, and it became clear that a new solution was needed.

The first institution established solely for the care of dependent children was founded in 1727 in New Orleans by an Ursuline Convent for children orphaned through Native American massacres (Trotzkey, 1930). The founding of the Ebenezer orphanage by British Evangelicals and the Bethesda orphanage by German Lutherans soon followed in Georgia in 1738. The first public orphanage was established in Charleston, South Carolina, in 1790 (Ashby, 1997).

Care of needy children in colonial America was seen as a matter for the private sector. Religious organizations were the primary founders of most institutions, created primarily to educate and provide religious training for their charges. Prior to the nineteenth century, most were Protestant institutions, although Catholics and Jewish institutions were soon founded in several American cities. Each religious organization, as Andrew Billingsley and Jeanne Giovannoni point out in *Children of the Storm: Black Children and American Child Welfare* (1972, pp. 22–23), "saw its continuance and vitality in the early indoctrination of the young. Quite logically, then, each religious group had an enormous stake in seeing to it that children not adequately cared for by their parents were placed under its dominion." Religious competition among private institutions thus became a deeply rooted part of the U.S. child welfare system.

The founding of institutions solely for the care of dependent children demonstrated a change in the way children were perceived. In the last decades of the eighteenth century, with the coming of the Industrial Revolution, a view of children as different and more vulnerable than adults began to emerge. Children were singled out for services, most likely as a measure of social protection for the future (Wolins and Piliavin, 1964). One of the first public reactions to this new thinking was against poorhouses, and after the Revolutionary War a movement began to place as many children as possible in orphanages, "houses of refuge" (reformatories), and other institutions specifically for children. The word "orphanage," however, was a misnomer. Many of the children in these institutions were not orphans but rather children whose parents could not care for them, usually temporarily.

Orphan asylums became the primary method of caring for dependent children in the 1830s, and they continued to be founded at a rapid pace throughout the 1840s and 1850s, particularly after epidemics. From 1830 to 1860, the number of orphan asylums in the nation rose from about 33 to nearly 200, increasing at more than three times the rate of the population (Hacsi, 1997). Nearly all of the asylums established during this time were tied to specific religious groups, as society's desire to care for needy children without raising taxes kept the burden largely on private institutions (Ashby, 1997). Asylums also multiplied as home relief systems were cut in the early nineteenth century owing to the perception that they encouraged depravity and intemperance.

Orphanages, while primary, were not the only type of residential care for needy children that boomed during the nineteenth century. The label "juvenile delinquent" appeared during the mid nineteenth century, and youths designated as such were moved out of orphanages, poorhouses, even adult jails, and were placed in reformatories. As precise as this division between dependent and deviant children may have been in rhetoric, it was not so clean in reality. Reformatories commonly housed children who were not juvenile delinquents. An 1858 study of the New York City House of Refuge found that only 38 percent of the children had broken the law; 61 percent were simply "bad" or "unfortunate" (Ashby, 1997, p. 26).

Foster Care and the Beginnings of Controversy

Until the mid nineteenth century, residential care and substitute care (in the form of apprenticeship or indenture) existed simultaneously in the United States with little apparent conflict (Wolins and Piliavin, 1964). This changed when Charles Loring Brace founded the New York Children's Aid Society (NYCAS) in 1855 and began placing New York's destitute children with midwestern farm families. For the first time, an organized and large-scale alternative to residential care existed. Through his work with the NYCAS, Brace became increasingly critical of residential care, accusing institutions of encouraging dependency and pauperism, thereby contributing to the dangers of unemployment, overcrowding, and violence in the cities (Ashby, 1997). Increasingly the public agreed with Brace's views. A large-scale attack on residential care ensued and proponents of institutions fought back.

The arguments for which type of care was preferable for needy children involved religion, environment, labor, economics, community image, education, and the long-term effects of care (Wolins and Piliavin, 1964). Extremists on both sides called for the abolition of the other entirely. Critics of residential care held that asylums were overcrowded, militant bodies that compromised childhoods and allowed indolent parents free child care. Although other child welfare proponents and members of the public agreed, many parents who were forced to give up their children preferred institutions, as their children might then be somewhat accessible. "A nearby asylum," Ashby states, "whatever its deficiencies, would be far more accessible and accountable than some distant Midwest farm" (Ashby, 1997, p. 51).

Between 1860 and 1890, the population of the United States almost doubled, mainly due to a steady flow of immigrants. Despite opposition to residential care and availability of the more recent option of adoption, orphan asylums continued to be the nation's foremost method of caring for dependent children. The number of orphanages expanded from 170 before the Civil War to approximately 600 by 1890. In 1910, the census showed that 111,514 children lived in 1,151 institutions—at least 836 of which were orphanages. The same census showed an estimated 61,000 children in foster care (Ashby, 1997). A sparse few institutions in the late nineteenth and early twentieth centuries were racially integrated, and even fewer took only minorities. Destitute and dependent African American children had very few available resources beyond traditional kinship circles (Ashby, 1997; Billingsley and Giovannoni, 1972).

The Civil War was a major factor in the rise of institutions in the late nineteenth century. The large number of children orphaned or half-orphaned through the war prompted many states to open publicly managed Soldier's Orphan's Homes in the 1860s and 1870s. At the forefront of this institutional expansion was the Catholic Church. Nearly one-half of the approximately 50,000 children in orphan asylums at the end of 1890 were in Catholic institutions. Thousands more lived in Protestant institutions, and Jewish and fraternal institutions also began to appear (Hacsi, 1997).

Another factor contributing to the explosion of institutions in the late nineteenth and early twentieth centuries was the anticruelty movement (Hacsi, 1997). Historical accounts generally trace the origin of widespread media attention and public concern over the plight of maltreated children to the case of Mary Ellen Wilson, a young girl living in New York City who was removed from the home of her abusive out-of-home caregivers in 1874 by the intervention of the leader of the American Society for the Prevention of Cruelty to Animals, Henry Bergh (Costin, 1991). After intervening for Mary Ellen, Bergh and others established the New York Society for the Prevention of Cruelty to Children (NYSPCC). The NYSPCC and other anticruelty organizations quickly raised awareness of child neglect and abuse, and they subsequently gained authority to remove afflicted children from their homes, contributing to the population of children needing care.

Toward the end of the nineteenth century, state involvement in residential care began to increase. Several state governments subsidized private institutions. By the turn of the century, the four different types of dependent children's institutions— publicly subsidized private institutions, county-based institutions, state institutions, and private intuitions—were operating in full force (Hacsi, 1997). As residential care increased, however, so did opposition toward it.

In 1909, President Theodore Roosevelt, at the urging of prominent child welfare reformers (none of whom were advocates of institutional care), called a White House Conference on the Care of Dependent Children (Hacsi, 1997). At the closing of the conference, participants resolved, "Home life is the highest and finest product of civilization" (Ashby, 1997, p. 79). This conclusion quickly became the basis for Progressive-era child welfare reform, which held that "children should be kept in homes, either their own or foster homes, and not in institutions" (Hacsi, 1997, p. 38). These resolutions contributed to the widespread implementation by the 1920s of mothers' pensions meant to allow "deserving" mothers to care for their children at home (Ashby, 1997).

These Progressive-era ideals instigated a movement to improve institutions, and soon "anti-institutional institutions" began to appear, such as family-style cottages and institutions with self-governing formats. "Houses of refuge" and "reformatories" almost everywhere changed their titles to "training school," "industrial school," or "boys' school" (Rothman, 1980). Institutional managers chose these new titles with intended impressions in mind. "A reformatory . . . was old-fashioned, crude and primitive. A training school was modern, sophisticated, in accord with the latest developments" (Rothman, 1980, p. 264). However, Ashby notes, "Despite more flexibility and improved conditions within a number of institutions, changes were perhaps more often rhetorical than substantive" (Ashby, 1997, p. 93). Lack of money prohibited many well-intentioned institutions from restructuring.

Despite mounting criticism, in most states institutions continued to care for more children than foster care or mothers' pensions until at least the 1920s (Hacsi,

1997). Progressive though the ideal was of keeping children in their own homes or foster homes, the reality was that the foster care system could not cope with the escalation of children who needed care. Institutions, for all their shortcomings, could at the least, as Ashby puts it, offer "minimal subsistence and shelter to tens of thousands of children in desperate need" (Ashby, 1997, p. 63).

An additional Progressive-era innovation was the formation of the juvenile court in 1899. Cook County, Illinois, created the first juvenile court, and by 1920 these courts existed in all but three states. They became a major factor in the growth in the population of children's institutions in the first decades of the twentieth century, from almost 61,000 in 1890 to 205,000 in 1923 (Ashby, 1997).

From 1910 to 1933, the population of the United States rose from 92 million to 125 million, and the number of orphanages alone rose from 972 to 1,321 (Hacsi, 1997). By 1919, 39 states had some type of mothers' pension law, which undoubtedly allowed many children who would have otherwise been institutionalized or placed in foster care to stay with their families. Nevertheless, mothers' pensions were limited, leaving many families still struggling "to feed their children and themselves. Those who could not manage to do so . . . often turned to orphan asylums, as they always had" (Hacsi, 1997, p. 50).

An Overview of the "Orphanage" Era

What was life like for the institutionalized child in the United States? And what was it *meant* to be like? What did superintendents see as the function of their institutions, and how do we perceive it, with the benefit of hindsight? From the establishment of the first orphan asylum in the United States, superintendents and other proponents of residential care saw their primary function as providers of shelter, food, and clothing for dependent children. Their secondary function, as they saw it, was to raise decent, educated, and God-fearing citizens.

Unfortunately, statistics on institutions are scattered and inconsistent. Collection of statewide statistics did not seriously begin until after Civil War when given impetus by the creation of the U.S. Department of Education (Marks, 1973). Even these later data only describe the number of children in care, not the quality of their experience. Yet we do know, mostly through accounts of those who lived and worked in them, that institutions varied widely but shared many common features and problems, such as insufficient funding, overcrowding, and, writes Ashby, "a regard for poor families that was at best ambivalent and sometimes even hostile" (Ashby, 1997, p. 18).

As some institutions were better funded than others, the quality of care children received varied (Ashby, 1997). Large institutions might have been better off financially but less able to provide a home-like atmosphere for the children than smaller institutions. Chores, playtime, education, and religious training all served a similar purpose—to teach the children obedience, respect for authority, and morality. Children were largely blocked off from the outside world for much of the nineteenth century, kept in by bars on the windows and spiked fences.

The larger the institution, the more austere, severely disciplined, and impersonal it tended to be. The more financially stressed the institution was, the harder it tended to be on the lives of the children. Kenneth Cmiel (1995) notes an example in his study *A Home of Another Kind: One Chicago Orphanage and the Tangle of Child Welfare*, when in 1880 the Chicago Nursery and Half-Orphan Asylum "expanded" the children's diet to include fruit once a week, and in 1881 chose to save money by giving the children coffee instead of milk at breakfast. Such decisions undoubtedly contributed to the high mortality rates in institutions, as epidemics commonly swept through and inflicted the youngest and weakest of the children. As harsh as asylum life could be, however, Ashby reminds us that "living conditions, and discipline in the asylums were in many respects no worse, and in some respects perhaps even better, than children expected in the tenements" (Ashby, 1997, p. 87).

As conditions began to improve during the Progressive era, the outside world became more available to institutionalized children as many entered public schools and joined church organizations. But even if the children were better off materially than they had been before, they seldom received the kind of affection that children require. "'Love is the thing I think they missed the most,' said one former orphanage resident. . . . 'Some of those kids couldn't cope with not having somebody to hug them and kiss them.'" (Ashby, 1997, p. 87).

Institutions also functioned in ways their proponents and superintendents may or may not have realized. They helped impoverished families survive by temporarily caring for children when their parents could not. In this way, they served as early welfare agencies by assisting poor families (Ashby, 1997). For example, in her study of a nineteenth-century orphanage, Judith Dulberger (1996) argues that impoverished families, instead of being manipulated by the system, used institutions to advance their own interests. She posits that rather than functioning as a mechanism to separate children from their families to end lines of poverty, institutions functioned as instruments to keep families together.

Institutions also functioned as a means of social control. Hacsi (1997), referring specifically to orphan asylums, identifies three ideal types: protective, isolating, and integrative asylums. Although protective asylums aimed only to temporarily replace a child's parents, isolating asylums "wanted to permanently replace poor children's parents with what they considered superior parenting and socialization tactics" (Hacsi, 1997, p. 6). Isolating asylums, he notes, maintained tight control of their children, keeping them "completely inside the institution, educating them there and blocking off contact with whatever family remained in the hopes of breaking children away from their parents' world and making them into 'Americans'" (7).[1] What Hacsi refers to as "protective" institutions also functioned to "protect" certain community values. "Many of the groups that founded orphan asylums did so to protect themselves and their community's future" (Hacsi, 1997, p. 6, Efforts of private Catholic and Jewish children's institutions to control placement of the children of ethnic immigrants during the nineteenth and twentieth centuries exemplify this aspect of residential care. The "integrative" asylums in many ways approximated the typical residential care settings of today in that they "helped children interact with the world outside asylum walls" (Hacsi, 1997, p. 7). Indeed, Hacsi observes that many asylums that operated in an isolating or protective way in the nineteenth century had shifted to an integrative approach by the 1910s. Integrative asylums encouraged children to interact with children in local schools and churches even though they slept and ate in the institution. Children in these residential care settings also had regular contact with their own families and returned to them once parents were able to resume their caregiving responsibilities.

The Rise of the American Welfare State and the End of Orphanages

In the mid twentieth century, residential care began to decline in the United States. In the 1930s, the number of children under age 16 in institutions fell by one-third (Ashby, 1997). Public interest in issues of child dependency and welfare faded in the face of two world wars and an economic depression, although the Great Depression would temporarily push the numbers of institutionalized children to an all-time high. These political, economic, and social crises brought serious trouble for institutions. Aging institutions ran out of funds, fell into disrepair, and simply ran out of space for children. Visitors to children's institutions in the 1930s and 1940s often found children in abhorrent conditions. A 1926 survey found that of Pennsylvania's 240 institutions, "84 had no toothbrushes, 93 lacked adequate bathing facilities, 99 were without individual combs, and 91 were without individual towels. . . . Fifty-four of the asylums had only cold water in the washrooms " (Ashby, 1997, p. 104).

In 1935, the federal government created Aid to Dependent Children (ADC) as Title IV of the Social Security Act. The successor to mothers' pensions, ADC greatly hastened the decline of institutions (Ashby, 1997). It meant that the federal government gave aid directly to needy families instead of institutions. ADC served the same purposes as institutions in many ways but did so without tearing families apart (Hacsi, 1997). By the 1940s, ADC had supplanted institutional care as the main method of caring for dependent children in the United States.

With aid going directly to the clientele they once served, institutions for dependent children, some observers believed, no longer had a "meaningful role to play in American society" (Hacsi, 1997, p. 50). The era of the institution as the primary means for care of needy children had ended. Other factors, such as the growing prominence of social work, with its focus on preserving the integrity of families, and the growing popularity of foster care, also had roles to play.

With no choice but to adapt or close their doors, institutions were forced to alter their missions. Many surviving institutions became foster care agencies. Many more began to limit their focus to the care of specialized groups, becoming residential treatment centers for children and youth with emotional, behavioral, or psychological disorders. In 1958, for the first time, more dependent children were in foster care than in institutions (Ashby, 1997).

Interest in institutions for dependent children had severely diminished and would continue to do so for some time. As child welfare scholar Alfred Kadushin points out, the scholarly literature being published in the 1960s was "almost devoid of references to the experiences, activities and problems of such institutions. It was as if," he wrote, they had been "written off" (quoted in Ashby, 1997, p. 138). This decline reflected not only the shifts in social policy toward poor families described above but also the growth in the 1960s and 1970s of a movement against the institutionalization of a wide variety of populations (e.g., mentally ill adults, persons with physical disabilities, and the developmentally disabled). This movement provided support for critics of residential care of children (Dore, Young, and Pappenfort, 1984). It also helped spur the development of perceived alternatives to residential treatment, such as treatment foster care (Chamberlain and Reid, 1991; Meadowcroft, Thomlison, and Chamberlain, 1994).

Federal Policy and the Evolution of Residential Care in the United States

Until the latter half of the twentieth century, the U.S. federal government provided little funding for foster or residential care. As a result, it played a limited role in state and local decisions on the use of these placement resources. In 1961, as a result of a regulatory decision (the Flemming Rule), the federal government began to reimburse states, using ADC funding, for the cost of out-of-home care for abused and neglected children removed by court order from families that were receiving, or eligible for, ADC (that is, poor children). In 1980, the Adoption Assistance and Child Welfare Act of 1980 (Public Law 96-272) separated foster care funding from public assistance by creating Title IV-E of the Social Security Act, which provided states with reimbursement for foster care (that is, foster family home and residential care) and adoption assistance payments for children removed from the care of poor families. The federal foster care program therefore remains essentially an aspect of U.S. poverty policy in that federal funding for out-of-home care of abused and neglected children provided through Title IV-E of the Social Security Act only supports the care of children from poor families. In practice, however, states generally create uniform rules for administering out-of-home care for abused and neglected children, regardless of their Title IV-E eligibility.

   Enactment of Public Law 96-272 reflected concern over the perception that families that came to the attention of public child welfare authorities often received little in the way of services that might help them retain or regain custody of their children. It also reflected concern that once in out-of-home care, children often drifted for long periods without going home or being adopted. This concern had coalesced into a "permanency planning movement" during the 1970s, an effort by child advocates to ensure that child welfare agencies made every effort to assist families before placing children in out-of-home care and to actively plan to find children permanent homes as quickly as possible when they were removed from home. Public Law 96-272 embodies the values of permanency planning by requiring states to provide "reasonable efforts" to prevent placement and to reunify children with their families whenever safely possible. Children were to be placed in the "least restrictive" and most "family-like" out-of-home care settings. The law also provided funds to reimburse states for adoption payments made on behalf of children with special needs.[2]

Public Law 96-272 embodied the attitudes that most child advocates and policy makers held at the time toward residential care—attitudes that still prevail today. The premium on placement in the least restrictive environment was consistent with the ongoing deinstitutionalization movement and clearly preferred family foster care over residential care. The law made no mention of long-term residential care given that the very idea was anathema to the principles of permanency planning. Residential care was to be a short-term intervention for troubled children and youth who were on the way to more permanent family-based settings. Public Law 96-272 also restricted federal reimbursement of state expenditures on public residential care facilities to those with 25 beds or fewer, a sign of the common suspicion of larger institutions. Subsequent changes in federal child welfare policy, such as the Adoption and Safe Families Act of 1997, continued to reflect the philosophy of permanency planning and have been largely silent on the issue of residential care.[3]

Interestingly, by the end of the 1970s, residential care for abused and neglected children had already taken on many of the characteristics that it exhibits today, even though federal child welfare policy was only beginning to gain steam by that point. This no doubt reflects the permanency planning movement's already considerable impact on state and local child welfare practice. The results of the comparison of the 1966 and 1982 national surveys of residential group care facilities by Dore and colleagues (1984) illustrate this point. They note that although the number of residential care facilities serving neglected or abused children and youth grew, from 1,424 in 1965 to 1,770 in 1981, the total capacity of these facilities remained essentially unchanged due to the rapid increase in small facilities such as group homes and a decline in the number of large institutions. For example, while 24 percent of residential facilities in 1961 served 20 or fewer children, by 1981 57 percent were serving such numbers. It seems reasonable that the move toward smaller institutions reflected the deinstitutionalization movement rather than the 1980 change in federal policy, since it is unlikely that public and private child welfare agencies had time to change their practices in a mere year (Dore et al., 1984).[4] In both surveys, Dore and colleagues (1984) found that slightly more than one-half of the national residential care bed capacity was accounted for by private agencies, with the remainder operated directly by state and local governments.

Recent History and Current Situation

Today, as in the past, residential care is provided under governmental, voluntary not-for-profit, and proprietary auspices. Recent attempts in the social work practice literature to describe the essential features of U.S. residential care focus on the more dominant forms of care— community-based group homes and residential treatment centers—with all such settings considered therapeutic milieus. Modern residential care is seen as a form of *treatment*, not simply a substitute living arrangement for dependent children. Moreover, the residential care provider community increasingly sees itself as providing a range of services to children and families in the context of residential care. This shift is reflected in the title change to the Child Welfare League of America's (CWLA) manual. The 1991 version is *Standards for Excellence in Residential Group Care Settings* whereas the 2004 version is *Standards of Excellence for Residential Services*. In the most recent edition, the CWLA (2004) asserts, "The primary purpose of residential services is to provide specialized therapeutic services in a structured environment for children with special developmental, therapeutic, physical, or emotional needs" (p. 20).

According to the CWLA standards, residential care settings should include an appropriate mix of services for children and families, including mental health services, health and nutritional care, recreation, education, independent living skills training, family reunification services, and after care. The current standards emphasize the importance of involving children's families in the treatment process, coordinating efforts with other service providers, and grounding residential care practice in the communities from which children come. These standards, and those provided by the Council on Accreditation, do not necessarily bear any relation to what actually goes on in the typical residential care setting, given that the vast majority of state and local governments do not require that providers be accredited or belong to the CWLA or other provider associations.

Although the last national study of the characteristics of residential care was in 1981, available data suggest that residential care accounts for roughly the same percentage of total out-of-home care of abused or neglected children in the United States today as it did in the late 1970s. Two national random-sample studies of the characteristics of children in out-of-home care conducted approximately 17 years apart illustrate this point. The *National Study of Social Services to Children and Their Families* (Shyne and Schroeder, 1978), conducted in 1977, found that 20 percent of the 543,000 children and youth in out-of-home care lived in residential or group care, the same percentage as found in the 1994 *National Study of Protective, Preventive, and Reunification Services Delivered to Children and Their Families* (U.S. Department of Health and Human Services, 1997), although slightly fewer children (502,000) were living in out-of-home care in 1994. The most notable change during this period was the growth of kinship foster care, which was not common enough to even be considered a separate category of care in 1977 but accounted for 24 percent of all placements in 1994 (U.S. Department of Health and Human Services, 1997). Although the methods used in these studies are similar, the earlier study apparently went beyond just the child welfare population to include a significant number of children placed for reasons other than abuse or neglect. For example, whereas abuse or neglect was the reason for opening 80 percent of the cases in the 1994 study, this was true for only 45 percent of the cases in the 1977 study (U.S. Department of Health and Human Services, 1997).

Other data suggest that residential care has accounted for about one-fifth of all out-of-home care for abused and neglected children in the United States in recent years. For example, a point-in-time estimate based on data reported by states to the federal Adoption and Foster Care Analysis and Reporting System (2006) finds approximately 20 percent (94,650) of U.S. children and youth in out-of-home care on September 30, 2005, lived in either a group home or institution.[5] The Multistate Foster Care Data Archive at the Chapin Hall Center for Children allows for selected analysis of out-of-home care histories for children in Alabama, California, Illinois, Maryland, Michigan, Missouri, New Jersey, New York, and Ohio, or nearly one-half of all children in out-of-home care.[6] Analysis of these archive data shows that the percentage of children first placed in residential care varied little between 1991 and 2001 (at between 19 and 23 percent).[7]

Archive data also help describe selected characteristics of children entering residential care in recent years and the relation between residential care placement and case status outcomes. For example, the data from 1991 to 2001 show that 10 to 12 percent of children under age 1, 11 to 16 percent of those age 1–5, 18 to 22 percent of those aged 6–12, and 45 to 47 percent of those aged 13 and older were initially placed in residential care. Not surprisingly, older children and youth are much more likely to enter residential care, given that these placements are now generally reserved for children with significant behavioral or emotional problems. Still, a nontrivial number of young children and even infants are in residential care. Although many of these children no doubt have special needs requiring intensive supervision and care, such as medical problems, the appropriateness of residential care for young children under any circumstances has been questioned (Berrick, Barth, Needell, and Jonson-Reid, 1997).

The relation between care type and race-ethnicity is also noteworthy. Among states in the archive with comparable data, 22 percent of white children who entered care between 1990 and 1995 and whose care histories are known through 2001 but only 13 percent of African Americans had residential care as their primary care type.[8] In contrast, African Americans were much more likely to live in kinship foster care (33 percent) than were whites (11 percent). Although some of this difference in care may be because white children in out-of-home care in these states tend to be younger than African American children, this does not explain all of the difference. It appears that greater use of kinship foster care for African American children is associated with a decrease, compared with whites, in residential care placement. This finding is consistent with earlier analysis of the correlates of residential care placement in California (Barth, Courtney, Berrick, and Albert, 1994).

Unfortunately, little knowledge exists about residential care in the United States beyond these basic demographic statistics on the children served. The lack of interest in residential care among scholars and policy makers during the last three decades has resulted in a sparse knowledge base on the nature of residential care (for example, organizational characteristics of residential care providers; the nature of common treatment modalities; characteristics of the residential care workforce). Perhaps even less is known about the outcomes of residential care, particularly its effectiveness in achieving its new, treatment-oriented goals.

It would be unfair to claim that nothing has been learned in recent years. Reports occasionally describe the characteristics of children served by a particular agency or within a state and may even provide some evidence regarding the correlates of certain child-level outcomes (see, e.g., Budde et al., 2004; Dale, Baker, Anastasio, and Purcell, 2007; Daly et al., 1998). The recent studies from the Odyssey Project, a multi-agency longitudinal study of residential care and treatment foster care sponsored by CWLA, provide some sense of the characteristics of the children and youth entering care in the participating agencies (Baker, Archer, and Curtis, 2005; Baker, Archer, and Curtis, 2006; Drais-Parrillo et al., 2005) and describe changes in some aspects of child functioning over time (Drais-Parrillo et al., 2005).[9] Taken as a whole, however, these studies provide no clear picture of either the children served by residential care in the United States or the programs serving them. Practitioners and scholars continue to develop and occasionally write about new treatment models (see, e.g., Daly et al., 1998; Krueger and Drees, 1995; Leichtman, Leichtman, Barber, and Neese, 2001; Ponce, 1995). However, none of these new models has been rigorously compared with any other.

We believe that the assessment of the U.S. General Accounting Office, which reviewed the research literature on residential care and conducted site visits to "notable" programs in 1992 and 1993, is still true today:

> Not enough is known about residential care programs to provide a clear picture of which kinds of treatment approaches work best or about the effectiveness of the treatment over the long term. Further, no consensus exists on which youth are best served by residential care rather than community-based care or how residential care should be combined with community-based care to best serve at-risk youth over time. Many program officials and other experts we spoke with said that further research is needed into the effectiveness of residential care and other treatment approaches. (U.S. General Accounting Office, 1994, p. 6)

Our reading of prior reviews on residential care (Barth, 2005; Bates, English, and Kouidou-Giles,1997; Curry, 1991, 1995; Whittaker and Pfeiffer, 1994)— keeping in mind the considerable conceptual and methodological limitations of the research to date—suggests the following conclusions:

- Residential care can stabilize the problematic behavior of at least some youth while they are in care
- The quality of supports in the postdischarge environment is the best predictor of community adjustment
- Positive involvement of children with their families during and after treatment and positive family functioning in general are associated with favorable postdischarge adjustment
- Although most child characteristics (e.g., age, gender, IQ, length of time in care) appear weakly or not at all related to outcomes, children with organic disorders and psychoses exhibit poorer outcomes

- Concentrating youth with externalizing behavior problems in group settings can produce iatrogenic effects

Unfortunately, these conclusions, while reasonable, do not provide a very comprehensive basis for deciding which children and youth are best served by residential care as opposed to other interventions, nor do they provide guidance on the most promising models of residential care. Although we strongly agree with Whittaker (2000) and others that the long-standing use of residential care as a mode of treatment for troubled children and youth calls for a concerted program of research on its effectiveness, sadly no such effort appears forthcoming.

The Future of Residential Care in the United States

We believe that the future of residential care in the United States will look much like the present, at least for the foreseeable future. This is because residential care is no longer seen as a reasonable option for children who simply cannot remain at home for some period. The orphanage is no longer a serious topic of discussion. Residential care is now reserved almost exclusively for children and youth with emotional and behavioral problems. It is likely to remain an important resource for public authorities that must provide out-of-home care for children who seem too troubled for available family-based alternatives.

Although we believe them to be unlikely, certain developments could change this picture. For example, the "technology" of caring for troubled children could change enough to either increase or decrease demand for residential care. In particular, convincing evidence that wrap-around, in-home services or treatment foster care are effective alternatives to residential care could decrease demand for residential care. The practice community in the United States has shown great interest in developing such alternatives, but the evidence of their effectiveness has yet to equal the level of excitement. Nevertheless, the theoretical justifications are sound for trying family-based treatment modalities with troubled children and youth, and it may only be a matter of time before particular approaches pan out and gain favor among practitioners and policy makers (Barth, 2005). It is also possible that new approaches to residential care will prove highly effective, although we are unaware of any significant innovation of this kind.

Perhaps the "return to orphanages" envisioned by some neoconservative social policy scholars in the United States will take place, significantly increasing the use of residential care (McKenzie, 1999). During the debates that took place in the 1990s over the reform of U.S. public assistance programs, some observers suggested that orphanages would be a reasonable way to cope with any increase in the number of neglected or abandoned children resulting from parents' loss of cash assistance. Advocates of this position often shared the view of nineteenth-century managers of "isolating" asylums that permanently removing children from such "dysfunctional" families and communities would be doing the children a great favor (Wilson, 1995).

Although it is difficult to forecast how the political winds would blow during a serious economic crisis, the way the orphanage debate played out in the United States provides little comfort to orphanage advocates. A few conservative politicians jumped on the orphanage bandwagon, most notably Newt Gingrich, then Republican Speaker of the House of Representatives. Yet public opinion turned against the idea so quickly that nearly all policy makers, regardless of their political affiliation, eventually dismissed the idea (Weaver, 2000).

Conclusion

There is no disputing that residential care in the United States was, and remains, imperfect. Orphanages, no matter how hard they tried, could not create environments that were realistically homelike, nor could they give each child the individual attention and affection that he or she might need, and deserve. Yet residential care was an essential part of the U.S. child welfare system for a large part of the nation's history, largely because it gave tens of thousands of children—destitute, neglected, abused, and orphaned—a chance they might not otherwise have had. Similarly, although no empirical evidence as yet provides conclusive evidence of the necessity of residential care for specific groups of children, neither is evidence available to clearly identify the alternatives. So long as public authorities find themselves at their wit's end on what to do with troubled children, residential care will remain alive, if not well.

NOTES

1. An important example of the isolating institution is the Indian boarding school (Holt, 2001). Starting in the late nineteenth century and continuing into the latter half of the twentieth century, the U.S. Bureau of Indian affairs systematically removed thousands of children from their homes and tribal communities and placed them in boarding schools. In these institutions, Indian children were forbidden from speaking their native languages or wearing their native dress. The explicit purpose of these schools was to eliminate the children's connection to their community of origin.
2. Although originally "special needs" status applied primarily to children with disabilities, the category evolved to include children considered "hard to adopt," such as older children and racial minorities.
3. The Adoption and Safe Families Act did allow states to claim federal funds for board and care payments for residential care provided by private for-profit institutions, whereas previously states could claim reimbursement only for care provided by private agencies when the agencies were not-for-profit entities.
4. The evolution in terminology over this period also shows the impact of the deinstitutionalization movement. The report of the 1966 survey refers to a census of "children's residential institutions" whereas the latter report uses the term "residential group care facilities" (Dore et al., 1984).
5. This percentage is derived by dividing the number of children in group homes or institutions by the total number in some kind of out-of-home care placement and

excludes from the denominator those categorized as runaways or on trial home visits with their families.

6. The foster care archive integrates state administrative data on children's care histories into a database that allows for comparison across states on a variety of child welfare services outcomes. Owing to limitations of the state data, some analyses are possible only for selected states in the archive or for limited time periods. Analyses reported in this chapter pertain to all nine of the archive states (Alabama, California, Illinois, Maryland, Michigan, Missouri, New Jersey, New York, and Ohio) unless otherwise noted. The authors wish to thank Fred Wulczyn, director of the archive, for providing the data analyses reported here.

7. The archive uses the term "congregate care" to describe residential care placements identified in state records as group homes, residential treatment centers, and emergency shelters. This comparison relies on data from seven states: Alabama, California, Illinois, Maryland, Michigan, Missouri, and New York.

8. States used for this analysis were Alabama, Illinois, Maryland, Michigan, Missouri, and New York.

9. The Odyssey Project involved a highly selective group of residential care providers who paid to participate in the study, calling into serious question how representative the programs are of residential care generally. In addition, the study suffered from serious sample attrition.

REFERENCES

Adoption and Foster Care Analysis and Reporting System. (2006). *The AFCARS report: Preliminary FY 2005 estimates as of September 2006.* U.S. Children's Bureau Web site: www.acf.hhs.gov/programs/cb/stats_research/afcars/tar/report13.htm.

Ashby, L. (1997). *Endangered children: Dependency, neglect, and abuse in American history.* New York: Twayne.

Baker, A. J. L., Archer, M., and Curtis, P. A. (2005). Age and gender differences in emotional and behavioral problems during the transition to residential treatment: The Odyssey Project. *International Journal of Social Welfare, 14,* 184–194.

Baker, A. J. L., Archer, M., and Curtis, P. A. (2006, February). Prior placements of youth admitted to therapeutic foster care and residential treatment centers: The Odyssey Project. *Child and Adolescent Social Work Journal, 23,* 38–60.

Barth, R. P. (2005). Residential care: From here to eternity. *International Journal of Social Welfare, 14,* 158–162.

Barth, R. P., Courtney, M. E., Berrick, J. D., and Albert V. (1994). *From child abuse to permanency planning: Child welfare services pathways and placements.* New York: Aldine de Gruyter.

Bates, B. C., English, D. J., and Kouidou-Giles, S. (1997). Residential treatment and its alternatives: A review of the literature. *Child and Youth Care Forum, 26,* 7–51.

Berrick, J. D., Barth, R. P., Needell, B., and Jonson-Reid, M. (1997). Group care and young children. *Social Service Review, 71,* 257–273.

Billingsley, A., and Giovannoni, J. M. (1972). *Children of the storm: Black children and American child welfare.* New York: Harcourt Brace.

Budde, S., Mayer, S., Zinn, A., Lippold, M., Avrushin, A., Bromberg, A., Goerge, R. M., and Courtney, M. E. (2004). *Residential care in Illinois: Trends and alternatives.* Chicago: Chapin Hall Center for Children at the University of Chicago.

Chamberlain, P., and Reid, J. B. (1991). Using a specialized foster care community treatment model for children and adolescents leaving the state mental hospital. *Journal of Community Psychology 3*, 266–276.

Child Welfare League of America (CWLA). (1991). *Standards for excellence in residential group care settings*. Washington, DC: Author.

Child Welfare League of America (CWLA). (2004). *CWLA standards of excellence for residential services*. Washington, DC: Author.

Cmiel, K. (1995). *A home of another kind: One Chicago orphanage and the tangle of child welfare*. Chicago: University of Chicago Press.

Costin, L. B. (1991). Unraveling the Mary Ellen legend: Origins of the "cruelty" movement. *Social Service Review 65*, 203–223.

Curry, J. F. (1991). Outcome research on residential treatment: Implications and suggested directions. *American Journal of Orthopsychiatry, 61*, 348–357.

Curry, J. F. (1995). The current status of research in residential treatment. *Residential treatment for children and youth, 12*, 1–17.

Dale, N., Baker, A. J. L., Anastasio, E., and Purcell, J. (2007). Characteristics of children in residential treatment in New York state. *Child Welfare, 86*, 5–27.

Daly, D. L., Schmidt, M. D., Spellman, D. F., Criste, T. R., Dinges, K., and Teare, J. F. (1998). The Boys Town residential treatment center: Treatment implementation and preliminary outcomes. *Child and Youth Care Forum, 27*, 267–279.

Dore, M. M., Young, T. M., and Pappenfort, D. M. (1984). Comparison of basic data for the national survey of residential group facilities: 1966–1982. *Child Welfare*, 485–495.

Drais-Parrillo, A. A., Baker, A., Fojas, S., Gunn, S., Kurland, D., and Schnur, E. (2005). *The Odyssey Project: A descriptive and prospective study of children and youth in residential group care and therapeutic foster care. Final report*. Washington, DC: Child Welfare League of America.

Dulberger, J. (1996). *Mother donit fore the best: Correspondence of a nineteenth-century orphan asylum*. Syracuse, NY: Syracuse University Press.

Foster Family-Based Treatment Association. (2003). *What is treatment foster care?* Available at www.ffta.org/what_is_tft.html.

Hacsi, T. (1997). *Second home: Orphan asylums and poor families in America*. Cambridge: Harvard University Press.

Holt, M. I. (2001). *Indian orphanages*. Lawrence: University of Kansas Press.

Krueger, M., and Drees, M. (1995). Generic teamwork: An alternative approach to residential treatment. *Residential Treatment for Children and Youth, 12*, 57–69.

Leichtman, M., Leichtman, M., Barber, C., and Neese, T. (2001). Effectiveness of intensive short-term residential treatment with severely disturbed adolescents. *American Journal of Orthopsychiatry, 71*, 227–235.

Marks, R. B. (1973). Institutions for dependent and delinquent children: Histories, nineteenth-century statistics, and recurrent goals. In D. M. Pappenfort, D. M. Kilpatrick, and R. W. Roberts (Eds.), *Child caring: Social policy and the institution* (pp. 9–67). Chicago: Aldine.

McKenzie, R. B. (Ed.). (1999). *Rethinking orphanages for the 21st century*. Thousand Oaks, CA: Sage.

Meadowcroft, P., Thomlison, B., and Chamberlain, P. (1994). Treatment foster care services: A research agenda for child welfare. *Child Welfare, 93*, 565–581.

Ponce, D. E. (1995). Value orientation: Clinical applications in a multi-cultural residential treatment center for children and youth. *Residential Treatment for Children and Youth, 12*, 29–42.

Rothman, D. (1980). *Conscience and convenience: The asylum and its alternatives in Progressive America*. Boston: Little, Brown.

Shyne, A., and Schroeder, A. (1978). *National study of social services to children and their families* (DHEW Publication No. 78-30150). Washington, DC: U.S. Department of Health and Human Services, Children's Bureau.

Trotzkey, E. (1930). *Institutional care and placing out: The place of each in the care of the dependent child*. Chicago: Marks Nathan Jewish Orphan Home.

U.S. Department of Health and Human Services, Children's Bureau. (1997). *National study of protective, preventive and reunification services delivered to children and their families*. Washington, DC: U.S. Government Printing Office.

U.S. General Accounting Office. (1994). *Residential care: Some high-risk youth benefit but more study needed* (Publication No. GAO/HEHS-94-56). Washington, DC: Author.

Weaver, R. K. (2000). *Ending welfare as we know it*. Washington, D.C.: Brookings Institution Press.

Whittaker, J. K. (2000). The future of residential group care. *Child Welfare, 79*, 59–74.

Whittaker, J. K., and Pfeiffer, S. I. (1994). Research priorities for residential group child care. *Child Welfare, 93*, 583– 601.

Wilson, J. Q. (1995). Welfare reform and character development. *City Journal* (Winter 1995): downloaded at http://www.city-journal.org/html/5_1_welfare_reform.html.

Wolins, M., and Piliavin, I. (1964). *Institution or foster family: A century of debate*. New York: Child Welfare League of America.

Looking Backward to See Forward Clearly

A Cross-National Perspective on Residential Care

MARK E. COURTNEY, TALAL DOLEV, AND
ROBBIE GILLIGAN

A casual reader of the *Stockholm Declaration on Children and Residential Care* might easily conclude that the nations of the world had declared as a goal a definitive end to a centuries-long period in which dependent children had lived in group settings away from family and that a clear road map existed to a future that would be free of residential care. Our case studies of the evolution of residential care around the world call this viewpoint into question. Although it is certainly true that some parts of the world use residential care to a far lesser degree than others, we are unaware of any country with an industrial or postindustrial economy that does not place at least some of its children in residential care. A review of the English-language research and writing about residential care might lead one to believe that postindustrial democracies have come to a consensus that residential care should be used rarely if at all for children and then only for children with mental health problems or other special needs (Barth, 2005; Bates, English, and Kouidou-Giles, 1997; Curry, 1995). However, the case studies in this volume from Brazil, Israel, and South Korea, where residential care continues to be widely used for less-troubled children and youth, raise questions about even this seemingly safe conclusion. Moreover, the rethinking going on in Australia about the unintended consequences of that nation's "success" in reducing residential care should give pause to those who assert that alternatives to residential care always exist. Residential care is alive, if not always well, all over the world and seems to us to be likely to remain a part of child welfare service provision for the foreseeable future.

In this chapter we take on three related tasks. First, we identify themes that emerge in synthesizing the information from our case studies regarding the historical development of residential care around the world. Second, based on these historical trends and other information provided in the case studies, we describe likely future developments in residential care. Last, we make some recommendations regarding the future of residential care.

Lessons from History

Why dwell on the history of residential care? We have chosen to do so for two reasons. First, we believe that our volume provides an unusual scholarly opportunity to provide a cross-national historical examination of the development of this important social institution. We are unaware of any other source of historical material on residential care that includes information from such a widely varying group of countries. Second, we believe that an understanding of why nations came to rely on residential care in the past and how it has evolved over time can put into proper perspective current and future uses of residential care. This seems particularly important given the strong and competing opinions voiced these days by the proponents and opponents of residential care.

We employ a historical perspective to gain a better understanding of the growth, and sometimes decline, of residential care around the world, relying on the material in each of the case studies to compare and contrast its development. Our purpose in this chapter is not to draw conclusions about the overall appropriateness of residential care; rather, we seek to understand the distinct factors that have conditioned its development over time and how these factors interact with each other within a particular national context. Our case study chapters suggest that economic, political, ideological, and cultural factors have all played roles in the development of residential care. In addition, in some countries it is clear that precipitating events (e.g., the abuse scandals associated with Catholic residential schools in Ireland) led to rapid change in residential care. The forces we describe seldom operate in isolation from each other. Indeed, the interaction between these forces has led the characteristics and scope of residential care to change over time in distinct ways across nations.

Economic Development, the Welfare State, and Economic Upheavals

Economic development influences the evolution of social welfare institutions generally and the institution of residential care is no exception. Economic development can create *demand* for residential and other forms of out-of-home care by disrupting family and community structures that had previously provided for the care of children. Indeed, this is arguably the most consistent story that emerges from a reading of our case studies. Our case studies indicate that large-scale use of residential care for children often occurred in the wake of industrialization as families moved into cities, leaving behind the support of extended families and communities. To be sure, economic development occurred at different points in history for the countries represented in our case studies, which partially explains why residential care arose earlier in places like the UK, Ireland, Sweden and the United States than in most of the other countries (Bullock and McSherry, Ch. 2 this volume; Courtney and Hughes-Heuring, Ch. 11 this volume; Gilligan, Ch. 1 this volume; Sallnäs, Ch. 3 this volume).

At the same time, economic development also generates the economic surplus necessary to provide government funding for out-of-home care, thereby potentially affecting the *supply* of residential care. Countries with less developed economies tend not to have the resources to provide government funding for out-of-home care of any kind. The philanthropic sectors in these countries are also generally less developed. At first glance this might suggest that more economically developed countries will make relatively greater use than less economically developed countries of residential care, since they can afford to do so. The fact that countries such as Botswana and South Africa have relatively few residential care settings compared to the size of their populations, and that many of these settings are supported by religious charities or international nongovernmental organizations (NGOs), seems consistent with this point of view (Maundeni, Ch. 6 this volume; Stout, Ch. 7 this volume).

However, our case studies also provide evidence that the relationship between national prosperity and the use of residential care is complicated by the fact that nations can invest their wealth in very dissimilar ways; overall, welfare state policies do affect the utilization of residential care. For example, all of the wealthier countries represented in this volume provide government funding for family-based out-of-home care settings, creating an alternative to residential care. All else being equal, a wealthy country that provides financial support to foster parents will make less use of residential care than a country that does not fund this alternative. These countries do not, however, invest equally in the kinds of support for families (e.g., cash assistance, housing, child care) that can reduce the likelihood that children will be removed from their homes in the first place. In the chapter on Sweden, for example, the observation is made that the expansion of the Swedish welfare state in the twentieth century led to "improvement in the lives of single mothers and their children; a group that has historically populated residential care units" (Sallnäs, Ch. 3 this volume). In contrast, while mothers' pension programs in the United States evolved into public assistance for single-parent families and federal funding of foster care, the basic safety net for families has not been as generous as it has been in Sweden, arguably contributing to a greater demand for out-of-home care (Courtney and Hughes-Heuring, Ch. 11 this volume).

Significant discontinuities in economic development, particularly economic upheavals, have also affected the utilization of residential care. The Great Depression represented the last high point for residential care in the United States, as thousands of children were voluntarily placed in orphanages by their parents who could no longer provide for their basic needs (Courtney and Hughes-Heuring, Ch. 11 this volume). Similarly, the economic failure and dislocation of the populace associated with communism contributed to thousands of parents choosing to give up the care of their children to Romanian orphanages (Gavrilovici, Ch. 4 this volume).

Religion, Culture, and Political Ideology

Every case study in this volume speaks in some way to the importance of religious institutions in the emergence and evolution of residential care for children. In nearly all of the countries represented here, the earliest examples of children's homes were founded by religious leaders or organizations. In Europe and the United States, the growth of children's institutions partly reflected the changing nature of religious charity, away from "outdoor relief" toward a variety of institutions for various categories of the "worthy" and "unworthy" poor (i.e., institutions for the mentally ill and orphaned children; workhouses for employable adults). These institutions served the function of hiding populations that were considered undesirable from public view while offering the possibility that religious values could be imparted to the residents. In some cases, where distinct religious traditions (e.g., Protestant, Catholic, Jewish) competed for the hearts and minds of the population, the care of dependent children took on added importance as it represented an arena in which religious institutions could lay claim to the souls of children born into other religious traditions, or at least "save" the souls of children from the same tradition. This was particularly true in the United States, where early debates over the benefits or harm of residential care for children reflected ongoing conflicts between charities organized by the long-established Protestant economic and political elites, on the one hand, and Catholic and Jewish charities serving primarily recent immigrants on the other (Courtney and Hughes-Heuring, Ch. 11 this volume).

In countries that experienced urbanization and industrialization later, particularly former European colonies, religious institutions still established many of the early children's homes, but in a very different context. In these countries (e.g., Brazil, Botswana, and South Africa), it was usually either the colonial power or foreign religious orders that established orphanages and other residential care programs for children, often with an explicit missionary purpose (Maundeni, Ch. 6 this volume; Rizinni and Rizzini, Ch. 10 this volume; Stout, Ch. 7 this volume). This is not to say that indigenous religious and cultural institutions that cared for children did not exist. Nevertheless, the nature of residential care provision in countries that experienced European colonization reflects the fact that the imposition of political rule by European powers usually coincided with state sanction of Christian missionary work, including the establishment of children's homes.

We include culture and political ideology along with religion in this part of our discussion because they are closely related. This is more obvious in some of the nations represented in this volume than others. For example, it is easy to see the historical influence of the Catholic Church on political debates in Ireland that have enormous consequences for child welfare (e.g., divorce and abortion) (Gilligan, Ch. 1 this volume). Still, the interplay of religion, culture, and politics is present in all of our case studies, with each factor looming larger in some countries than in others.

Not surprisingly, culture appears to exert its greatest influence on the evolution of residential care through attitudes toward the relationship between children, families, and communities. For example, the Confucian tradition's emphasis on the primacy and privacy of the family has affected the demand for out-of-home care in Korea by making Korean adults less likely than adults in many other countries to report child maltreatment to government authorities. Likewise, Confucianism's "strong emphasis on the importance of blood-relatedness in keeping the family's continuity and cohesion" (Lee, Ch. 8 this volume) makes it more difficult for Korean child welfare authorities to develop foster care and adoption, even after governmental policy has shifted away from residential care to these alternatives.

Romania provides an excellent example of a country where political ideology loomed large as a contributor to the growth of residential care (Gavrilovici, Ch. 4 this volume). Like its European counterparts, Romania had seen the establishment of homes for abandoned children and orphans going back as far at the sixteenth century. However, unlike the Western European countries represented in our volume, Romania saw its national government much more directly involved during the latter half of the twentieth century in promoting policies that rapidly increased the use of residential care of children—policies that were a direct outgrowth of the government's attempt to create a Communist utopia. Some of the policies (e.g., banning abortion and family planning) indirectly affected demand for residential care by rapidly increasing the number of children in the context of a struggling economy. Ultimately, the state engaged in a deliberate policy of institutionalizing the children of the very poor, justifying this with the contention that children were better off being raised by the state than by their families.

The emergence of residential care in Israel provides an excellent example of the ways in which religion, culture, and ideology can interact to influence the use of residential care (Dolev et al., Ch. 5 this volume). Prior to the creation of the State of Israel, some Jewish families had relied on yeshiva, Jewish religious schools, for the care and supervision of their children, meaning that the concept of residential care would have seemed more normative to many Jewish families than it would have been for members of other ethnic and religious groups that did not have religious schools. Zionist ideology contributed to further normalization of the use of residential care by supporting the creation of kibbutzim, where children and youth from the vast Jewish diaspora could be brought together and resocialized and reeducated as members of a new nation. Although neither yeshiva nor kibbutzim were settings intended primarily for dependent or maltreated children, it is not surprising that Israel turned to residential care when confronted with the need to provide out-of-home care for such populations. After all, if group residence was good enough for the best of Israel's children, why would it not be good enough for the less fortunate?

Of course, cultural norms regarding middle- and upper-class children going to live in group educational settings were not unique to Jews. Indeed, our volume provides several examples of the ways in which practices of the well-to-do influenced the care of dependent children. In Brazil, for example, through the first half of the twentieth century children of the wealthy often went to boarding schools (Rizzini and Rizzini, Ch. 10 this volume). In the UK this was common until much later, though it has become less so in recent years (Bullock and McSherry, Ch. 2 this volume).

Colonialism, Race, and Ethnicity

The efforts of dominant elites to socialize and control ethnic or racial minorities and indigenous populations, and the responses of those populations to assimilation efforts, have played a role in the development of residential care in many of the countries represented in this volume. We have already noted how religious orders that sought to establish children's homes in European colonies generally did so with the acquiescence and often the active support of the colonial government (Maundeni, Ch. 6 this volume; Rizinni and Rizzini, Ch. 10 this volume; Stout, Ch. 7 this volume). They were not only saving souls in these institutions but they also generally attempted to educate the indigenous children in the language of, and to socialize them according to the cultural norms of, the colonizer. In contrast, the nineteenth-century Catholic and Jewish children's institutions in the United States were founded in part to help preserve the religious identity of children who were orphaned, abandoned, or otherwise could not remain in the care of their parents (Courtney and Hughes-Heuring, Ch. 11 this volume). Still, these institutions were created in response to efforts of Protestant elites to resocialize the children of ethnic populations they considered inferior (e.g., Irish and Italian immigrants) by placing the children in Protestant foster homes.

Some of the most troubling examples of residential care found in our case studies involve efforts to resocialize indigenous populations. In the United States, the Indian boarding schools were a deliberate effort of organized charities and the U.S. government to break the connection between Native American children and their communities and cultures of origin (Courtney and Hughes-Heuring, Ch. 11 this volume). Similarly, on an even larger scale, the Australian government created the so-called stolen generation of Aboriginal people by systematically rounding up Aboriginal children and placing them in boarding schools (Ainsworth and Hansen, Ch. 9 this volume). Though the two programs of forced assimilation differ from each other in some ways and they were both discontinued decades ago, they have in common the active deprivation of native children of their language and culture. Moreover, both the United States and Australia have had to confront overwhelming evidence of physical and sexual abuse of native children in their boarding schools.

Race and ethnicity have also played a role in the evolution of residential care as a result of the segregation of child welfare services generally within some countries. South Africa provides the most extreme example of this (Stout, Ch. 7 this volume). Prior to the development of segregation via apartheid, poor relief was provided only to poor whites whereas blacks had to rely exclusively on the organization of self-help. Even after the profession of social work evolved over the course of the twentieth century, ultimately in the context of apartheid, government social welfare expenditures were overwhelmingly distributed to the minority white population. In this context residential care, like other types of social services, was virtually nonexistent in black South African communities. The situation in the United States, though not as extreme, was nevertheless similar (Courtney and Hughes-Heuring, Ch. 11 this volume). Even into the latter half of the twentieth century, charities in the United States provided child welfare services almost exclusively to whites even though government was increasingly providing funding for such services. Blacks needed to rely on the support of kin and their own, much less well-endowed, charitable resources.

Notions of Childhood and Child Development

Evolving notions of childhood have been obvious contributors to the development of residential care. The clearest example of this is in the emergence of concern about child maltreatment. To be sure, the need to provide housing for orphans and abandoned or otherwise dependent children existed long before any large-scale concern about or policy response to child maltreatment. Still, there can be little doubt that the social construction of child maltreatment over the past two centuries as a problem worthy of public response has created much greater demand for out-of-home care, including residential care, than existed prior to this development. As our case studies demonstrate, attention to child maltreatment emerged at very different points in history depending on the country in question. For example, "child saving" became a focus of organized charity in Europe and the United States in the late nineteenth century and government began to intervene in families in response to child maltreatment in the early twentieth century (Bullock and McSherry, Ch. 2 this volume; Courtney and Hughes-Heuring, Ch. 11 this volume). Since the 1970s, the United States has had laws that require professionals who work with children to report suspected child maltreatment to child welfare authorities, whereas South Korea started implementing such legislation in 2000, and in Botswana the public still appears to remain ambivalent about whether government should interfere in family life to prevent child abuse (Courtney and Hughes-Heuring, Ch. 11 this volume; Lee, Ch. 8 this volume; Maundeni, Ch. 6 this volume). Again, public concern about child maltreatment and resulting governmental interventions have affected residential care in an indirect manner through increasing demand for out-of-home care more generally.

Prevailing attitudes of child development professionals regarding ideal child rearing have had a more direct effect on residential care. Since at least the nineteenth century there has been a debate about when, if ever, a group setting can be as appropriate an environment for child development as a family or a "family-like" setting. The closing resolution of the U.S. participants in the 1909 White House Conference on the Care of Dependent Children—"home life is the highest and finest product of civilization"—sounds in essence very similar to the sentiments expressed by the authors of the 2003 Stockholm Declaration (Courtney and Hughes-Heuring, Ch. 11 this volume). Legislation reflecting the family-is-best philosophy has emerged at different points over the last century in different contexts, but this view is clearly in ascendance around the world. The philosophy is implicit in child welfare services practice that privileges "permanency planning" (i.e., finding a permanent family home for children in out-of-home care through family reunification or adoption) and placement of children in the "least restrictive environment" (i.e., preferably not in residential care).

Our case study chapters provide ample evidence regarding the impact of the philosophical preference for family placement on residential care. In much of Europe, the United States, and industrialized former colonies of the UK, residential care has been relegated to a last option; children are generally placed in residential care only when all other family-like options have been exhausted (Ainsworth and Hansen, Ch. 9 this volume; Bullock and McSherry, Ch. 2 this volume; Courtney and Hughes-Heuring, Ch. 11 this volume; Gilligan, Ch. 1 this volume; Sallnäs, Ch. 3 this volume). In these countries residential care has evolved into an intensive treatment setting for children and youth with serious emotional and behavioral disorders. Even the forms of residential care that remain are being rethought in some cases in light of the new focus. For example, in Sweden the "new therapeutic" context that emerged in the 1960s and 1970s saw the development of smaller group care settings located in neighborhoods and involving the child's entire family in treatment (Sallnäs, Ch. 3 this volume). The net result of these changing attitudes is that the percentage of children in out-of-home care placed in residential care declined dramatically over the past 50 years in Australia, Ireland, the UK, and the United States, and also declined until recently in Sweden (Ainsworth and Hansen, Ch. 9 this volume; Bullock and McSherry, Ch. 2 this volume; Courtney and Hughes-Heuring, Ch. 11 this volume; Gilligan, Ch. 1 this volume; Sallnäs, Ch. 3 this volume). Although all of these countries but the United States ratified the United Nations Convention on the Rights of the Child (UNCRC), they were all long on the road to minimizing the use of residential care before the UNCRC became a factor in nations' consideration of child welfare policy.

In contrast, change has come more slowly in the other countries represented in this volume and appears to be driven in many cases by norms being imported from abroad, or even by international pressure. For example, Brazil's Statute of the Child (1990) was inspired by the UNCRC (Rizzini and Rizzini, Ch. 10 this volume). While attitudes toward residential care had already begun to change in Israel due to changes in professional norms, the authors of our case study note that scrutiny of residential care increased in the wake of Israel's ratification of the UNCRC (Dolev et al., Ch. 5 this volume). The impact of changing international norms regarding the use of residential care is most apparent in Romania, where that country's membership in the European Union was made contingent on reducing the number of children in residential care and improving the conditions of children remaining in Romania's children's institutions (Gavrilovici, Ch. 4 this volume).

Precipitating Events

Our historical overview would not be complete without mention of the events that appear to have played pivotal roles in altering the direction of residential care in the countries represented in this volume. In some cases these events merely sped up or delayed the inevitable, but in other cases it is impossible to make any sense of a country's use of residential care without taking them into account. A consideration of the importance of these contributors to the development of residential care helps put into proper perspective the broader social forces discussed above.

Disease has from time to time contributed to the use of residential care around the world. Most significantly, the worldwide HIV/AIDS epidemic has been one of a number of contributors to the demand for residential care in some places and may prove to be a decisive factor in others (Maundeni, Ch. 6 this volume; Stout, Ch. 7 this volume). In one of the countries hit hardest by this calamity, South Africa, there are still relatively few children in residential care, but the international NGO community appears to be falling back on historical precedent and investing in residential care for HIV/AIDS orphans (Stout, Ch. 7 this volume).

Abuse scandals have also affected the use of residential care in multiple countries. In Australia, for example, publicity surrounding the historical abuse of children in residential care, including the public outcry of former residents, contributed to negative public impressions of residential care and the rapid reduction in its use (Ainsworth and Hansen, Ch. 9 this volume). In Ireland, revelations regarding the extent of physical and sexual abuse of children in Catholic children's institutions and the government investigation of such abuse contributed to increased scrutiny of group care in general and the withdrawal of the Catholic Church from the provision of residential care (Gilligan, Ch. 1 this volume).

Other contributors to the residential care landscape are clearly related to particular national or world historical contexts. For example, forced child migration to Australia of the so-called lost innocents from Britain and Ireland created both demand for residential care and a later backlash against its abuses (Ainsworth and Hansen, Ch. 9 this volume). The need for residential care of dependent Jewish children as a result of massacres in Eastern Europe became apparent prior to 1948, in what would later become Israel (Dolev et al., Ch. 5 this volume). Last, the Korean Civil War clearly played a foundational role in the development of residential care in South Korea (Lee, Ch. 8 this volume).

Current Developments in Residential Care

Our discussion of the historical contributors to the development of residential care around the world should make clear that differences between countries in the characteristics of residential care will often loom larger than similarities. Nevertheless, a few issues emerge repeatedly across multiple case studies as being important to the ongoing evolution of residential care. Some of these are long-standing issues whereas others are relatively recent in origin. Consideration of these issues along with the historical forces that have shaped residential care provides some ground for speculation about the future.

Changes in the Needs of Children Served Leads to Specialization

In several countries it seems clear that the decline in the utilization of residential care was accompanied by a considerable change in the children whose needs are addressed in these settings. In Australia, Ireland, Israel, Sweden, the United Kingdom, and the United States, over time care came to be increasingly provided as a result of family dysfunction related to abuse or neglect, or as a result of children's own serious behavioral or emotional problems, rather than as a response to the need to house dependent children (Ainsworth and Hansen, Ch. 9 this volume; Bullock and McSherry, Ch. 2 this volume; Courtney and Hughes-Heuring, Ch. 11 this volume; Dolev et al., Ch. 5 this volume; Gilligan, Ch. 1 this volume; Sallnäs, Ch. 3 this volume). These changes in the needs and characteristics of the children cared for by residential facilities and changes in beliefs about the relationship between institutional characteristics and child development have influenced the nature of residential care provision. For example, facilities in these countries are generally (though not always) smaller than they were in the days of "orphanages." While sometimes this decline in facility size may be largely attributable to overall reductions in the number of children in care (e.g., Korea and Romania), in most cases it reflects the belief, often supported by research in these countries, that smaller, more family-like facilities offer a more normalizing experience for children and youth (Ainsworth and Hansen, Ch. 9 this volume; Bullock and McSherry, Ch. 2 this volume; Courtney and Hughes-Heuring, Ch. 11 this volume; Gavrilovici, Ch. 4 this volume; Gilligan, Ch. 1 this volume; Lee, Ch. 8 this volume; Sallnäs, Ch. 3 this volume). Also, as the number of children entering the child welfare system with behavioral and family-related problems has increased, so has the necessity of providing therapeutic care in residential settings rather than providing primarily for only basic needs. Consistent with the more treatment-oriented view of residential care, efforts have been made in some places to shorten lengths of stay in residential care.

Greater Attempts to Involve Family

Influenced by societal values and reinforced by both research and the approaches to children and their families reflected in the UNCRC, residential care facilities in some countries have emphasized improving connections between child residents and their families. For example, some Israeli group homes are introducing living quarters for parental overnight visits and special intervention programs for parents and children (Dolev et al., Ch. 5 this volume). Most facilities intended for young children in Sweden accept parents as well and offer assessments not only of the status of the child but also of how parents are coping with their parental roles (Sallnäs, Ch. 3 this volume). And recent developments in child welfare policy in South Africa encourage the creation of small residential care units, close to children's families and communities (Stout, Ch. 7 this volume).

This is not to say that these efforts are always successful; our case studies suggest that numerous barriers remain to improving links between child and family.

For example, while parental visits are encouraged in the UK, parental involvement in care plans is not significant (Bullock and McSherry, Ch. 2 this volume). Research on residential care in Israel finds that residential care staff often do not have the professional skills to involve parents in the therapeutic process and have ambivalent feelings toward parents (Dolev et al., Ch. 5 this volume).

Integrating Educational Supports in Residential Care Settings

Poor educational achievement is a problem experienced widely by children in residential care, both in settings devoted to caring for orphaned or abandoned children and in more therapeutically oriented settings. For example, many children in UK institutional settings do not attend school because they have been suspended or excluded from school or have difficulty gaining admission (Bullock and McSherry, Ch. 2 this volume). Many children's shelters in Brazil are theoretically meant to provide only temporary care and consequently do not focus on educational and social activities; however, in practice, shelter care is often not temporary and, in any case, children typically wander between the streets, their homes, and multiple institutions, compromising educational quality (Rizzini and Rizzini, Ch. 10 this volume). Half of the children in Israeli residential facilities have below-average education achievement levels and studies of Swedish children who have been in residential facilities in childhood document low levels of education (Dolev et al., Ch. 5 this volume; Sallnäs, Ch. 3 this volume).

This challenge is at least partly a function of out-of-home care itself; even under the best of circumstances, removing children from their home can lead to disruption of their education. Moreover, children entering out-of-home care, particularly those being placed for reasons of abuse or neglect, often enter care with significant educational deficits. However, some of the educational difficulties faced by children in residential care seem to be at least partly a function of the characteristics of the residential facilities themselves. Improving educational outcomes for children and youth in residential care requires efforts to ensure the continuity of education, clear communication and planning between schools and residential care providers, and more emphasis in the residential settings on the importance of education to children's well-being.

Providing Care After Children and Youth Leave Residential Care

At some point, children and youth placed in residential care must make the transition back to their communities and often the families whom they originally left. In some cases, particularly when residential care is used as a means of caring for dependent children and youth, this happens when youth in care reach adulthood and are expected to become independent. Of course, many youth in treatment-oriented residential care also make the transition to adulthood from care. In many cases, however, children and youth exit residential care long before the transition to adulthood, either to return to the care of their parent(s) or to another nonresidential care setting such as family foster care or relative foster care. Some of our case studies note the poor outcomes often experienced by children and youth after they leave residential care and some authors note the importance of the postdischarge environment for the quality of these outcomes (Bullock and McSherry, Ch. 2 this volume; Courtney and Hughes-Heuring, Ch. 11 this volume). Some authors note concern about the lack of after-care planning and services in their countries (Dolev et al., Ch. 5 this volume; Maundeni, Ch. 6 this volume) and no case study described a country in which the transition of children from residential care back into the community appears to be handled well. Clearly much work needs to be done to better integrate residential care into the communities from which children are removed and with the other public institutions charged with supporting children and families.

Staffing Issues

Our case studies also provide ample evidence that staffing problems, including high turnover, identifying and maintaining appropriate child/staff ratios, and providing suitable training, are problems facing residential care providers in many places around the world. The complexity of the therapeutic needs characteristic of children with severe emotional, behavioral and family problems have raised the profile of this issue. Staff-to-child ratios in institutions that provide therapeutic services have reportedly improved in some countries in recent years, but high staff turnover and adequate training appear to be significant issues wherever staff conditions are examined. Moreover, there is a general lack of clarity about what kind of staffing and training is most appropriate. For example, even in the UK where social work training is seen as the primary requirement for residential care staff there is concern that this training may not be sufficient (Bullock and McSherry, Ch. 2 this volume). In Korea, there is a perceived need to reexamine education and facility licensing policy as they pertain to staff qualifications (Lee, Ch. 8 this volume). There are major differences across Swedish institutions in staff training, particularly between public and privately operated homes (Sallnäs, Ch. 3 this volume). And in the United States there are no governmentally recognized national standards concerning staff ratios or qualifications for residential care staff (Courtney and Hughes, Ch. 11 this volume).

Across a wide range of countries there is a sense that training standards are insufficient and that the necessary qualifications are unclear. These difficulties may be expected, as Bullock and McSherry (Ch. 2 this volume) note, given the scant available evidence regarding the kinds of training necessary to achieve good outcomes for children with emotional or behavioral problems. The available evidence cannot sort out the relative importance of levels or kinds of training, staff characteristics (e.g., confidence, morale, culture or leadership), and organizational factors that permit training to be put into practice.

Monitoring Quality

The authors in this volume document a clear need to develop the infrastructure necessary to carry out quality assurance processes. At the institutional level, some report that quality standards for residential care facilities have been established but that it is often difficult to provide the oversight necessary to enforce them. For example, a study of residential care homes in England found that most had no written statement of purpose, even several years after this was required by legislation (Bullock and McSherry, Ch. 2 this volume). A national monitoring system has been in place in Israel, but only since 1995 (Dolev et al., Ch. 5 this volume). In many countries there are no national standards (e.g., the United States) and decentralization makes it unlikely that standards could be enforced in any case. In Romania, where there has been a marked trend toward decentralization of care to the county level, the local authorities do not have the capacity to monitor the quality of the residential care programs under their auspices (Gavrilovici, Ch. 4 this volume). Decentralization had led to a similar situation in Sweden (Sallnäs, Ch. 3 this volume). In countries without a long history of public welfare provision, effective monitoring is a more recent challenge. For example, in Botswana, although residential care is provided only by NGOs, the government passed regulations in 2005 to guide the establishment of facilities and to monitor the kind of care provided (Maundeni, Ch. 6 this volume).

Other issues revolve around the capacity to regularly monitor the quality of children's care at the individual level. Recent reforms in Romania require an assessment of all children in placement centers every three months, but two years after the reform most children had not been reassessed in the prior year (Gavrilovici, Ch. 4 this volume). Gaps in assessment of children's mental and physical health are reported in the UK (Bullock and McSherry, Ch. 2 this volume) and care review processes are inadequate in Israel, particularly for youth over age 14 (Dolev et al., Ch. 5 this volume). The U.S. government does not require states to track the kinds of child well-being outcomes for which residential care providers should be held accountable (e.g., school attendance, changes in problematic child behavior) (Courtney and Hughes-Heuring, Ch. 11 this volume).

Development of Alternatives to Residential Care

In several of the countries represented in our volume, alternatives to residential care have evolved in recent years. These developments sometimes reflect the fact that countries that have relied heavily on residential care in the past have chosen to develop family foster care. For example, between 1997 and 2002, foster care in Romania grew more than 300 percent (Gavrilovici, Ch. 4 this volume). In addition to foster care, community-based programs that are alternatives to residential care have also begun to emerge in some countries. Day care facilities are becoming more available in Brazil and efforts have been made to develop forms of care that help children remain with their families and communities (Rizzini and Rizzini, Ch. 10 this volume). In Romania, as a result of reforms, the number of public service alternatives to residential institutions increased nearly fivefold between 2000 and 2003 and include family reintegration services, day care centers, services for youth, "family" residential models, and support centers for youth exiting residential centers (Gavrilovici, Ch. 4 this volume). In the United States, models of therapeutic foster care have been touted as cost-effective alternatives to residential care that in some studies have been shown to lead to better outcomes for troubled youth (Courtney and Hughes-Heuring, Ch. 11 this volume).

Need for Caution in Attempting to Reduce the Use of Residential Care

While deliberate efforts have been made to develop alternatives to residential care, in some countries observers have noted that the limits of family foster care may have been reached and that, increasingly, there is a need for specialized residential facilities for the growing number of children with serious emotional and behavioral problems that are not being well accommodated by foster care. For example, there is concern that Irish foster and kinship care may not be able to meet current demands and that the small public residential care system will not be able to fill the unmet need (Gilligan, Ch. 1 this volume). Increases in the 1990s in residential care in Sweden are attributed, at least in part, to concern about the instability of foster home placements, particularly for troubled teens (Sallnäs, Ch. 3 this volume). Australia has almost completely eliminated its residential care sector in recent years, but in the process the foster care system may have reached the limits of its capacity to serve youth with multiple behavior and social problems (Ainsworth and Hansen, Ch. 9 this volume).

The Likely Future(s) of Residential Care

Based on an understanding of the history of residential care, the needs of the current and emerging populations of at-risk children, the current characteristics of their residential care systems, and the availability of alternatives to residential care, each of the authors of our case studies provides an assessment of the likely future role of residential care in their countries. While it is not possible to discern some neat universal linear movement in any single direction in regard to the future of residential care, it does seem that its future is constrained by a number of largely common factors across a range of countries. Although ideological and economic forces may combine to threaten or constrain its future, the pragmatic reality is that every society, and every state, has to find socially and politically feasible solutions that address the needs of dependent and hard-to-serve children and youth; every one of our case studies provides evidence that there is indeed a future for residential care around the world.

In most of the countries with a relatively well-developed public sector (e.g., Australia, Ireland, Israel, Sweden, the UK, and the United States), children most likely to be placed in residential care in the future would appear to be those who suffer from serious emotional and behavior problems (Ainsworth and Hansen, Ch. 9 this volume; Bullock and McSherry, Ch. 2 this volume; Courtney and Hughes-Heuring, Ch. 11 this volume; Dolev et al., Ch. 5 this volume; Gilligan, Ch. 1 this volume;

Sallnäs, Ch. 3 this volume). Future out-of-home care in these countries will be aimed at determining best practices for addressing the needs of this population and finding the best mix between residential and other out-of-home and in-home care options. To the extent that family- and community-based alternatives to residential care are developed and are seen as cost-effective in comparison to residential care, they may account for an increasing proportion of all out-of-home care for dependent and maltreated children and youth. However, the experience of countries like Sweden, where the growing population of adolescents in care contributed in recent years to growth in residential care, and Australia, where the push to eliminate residential care has had unwanted consequences, draws attention to the need for caution in arbitrarily reducing the availability of any child welfare service, including residential care (Ainsworth and Hansen, Ch. 9 this volume; Sallnäs, Ch. 3 this volume).

By contrast, in countries with a less developed public sector, much of the future role of residential care within the context of out-of-home care more generally will depend on the ongoing willingness and capacity of governments to respond to some of the factors underlying parental poverty and early death, as well as to become involved in developing, guiding, and monitoring out-of-home care options, including those provided by NGOs. For example, in Brazil, a national focus on drug trafficking and related violence might significantly reduce the overall need for out-of-home care (Rizzini and Rizzini, Ch. 10 this volume). Romania, in confronting the demands of more difficult populations of children and youth, is attempting to adjust to these changing demands with appropriate services—both residential and other out-of-home options, as well as community-based alternatives (Gavrilovici, Ch. 4 this volume). In both countries, however, the future of residential care will depend in large measure on the effectiveness of national welfare policies aimed at reducing poverty and providing economic, educational, and social supports to families.

As in the past, the expectations of residential care are also likely to be closely tied to population-level developments that seriously disrupt family ties and functioning. Wars and the current AIDS crisis in Africa are examples. For example, since the collapse of apartheid, South African social welfare policy has undergone enormous changes, and systems for addressing child welfare needs are in transition (Stout, Ch. 7 this volume). These systems are, on the one hand, attempting to integrate current thinking about best practices in out-of-home care including the preference for family-like settings, but on the other hand are still largely addressing the needs of a population of children abandoned or orphaned as a result of poverty or parental death due to AIDS. Largely in response to its own struggles with AIDS, Botswana has developed a small sector of residential care virtually without public support; there was no coherent child welfare policy until regulations for children in care were passed in early 2005 (Maundeni, Ch. 6 this volume). A small number of NGO-supported residential facilities exist to handle out-of-home care needs and there is currently no foster care system in the country. The extent to which countries like South Africa and Botswana rely on residential care to address the growing problem of AIDS orphans will depend on the number of such children, government success in implementing health policies to stem the spread of HIV, and support for community- and family-based alternatives to residential care through government provision and government influence on international NGOs.

Cultural norms will also continue to play a major role in the development of residential care regardless of countries' level of economic development. For example, the nature of out-of-home care in Korea is significantly influenced by the strong cultural preference for residential care as opposed to foster care or adoption (Lee, Ch. 8 this volume). It is unlikely that residential care in Korea will be rapidly reduced relative to its current role despite recent policies aimed at strengthening foster care. It is quite likely that such cultural norms influence, and will continue to influence, the development of residential care in other countries around the world.

Looking to the future, globalization is likely to have wide-ranging impacts on the development of residential care. The influence that the UNCRC has already had in some countries provides evidence of the potential influence of international norms. To the extent that national governments and international NGOs take seriously the policies of the United Nations and other transnational policy-making bodies, this could have significant influence on the evolution of residential care, particularly in the developing world. For example, the growing international consensus that family-like settings are preferable to institutional settings when it comes to raising children will likely lead residential care in the future to increasingly be tied to other child welfare provision and to take on more of an integrating rather than isolating role in the lives of the children and young people it serves.

Globalization and the liberalizing of trade rules may increase the role that the private sector will play, over time, in provision of residential care in countries where the public sector has long dominated child welfare services provision. As central and local governments withdraw from direct provision of personal social services in many countries, there is the likelihood that the private sector will grow as a provider of residential care, though it should be remembered that in some countries private charity provided residential care long before government did so. In any case, residential care will continue to evolve in the context of ongoing debates about the role of the state, market, and civil society in the delivery of child and youth care.

Limitations of Our Approach

We point out here the most obvious limitations of our examination of residential care around the world, both to remind the reader to exercise caution in interpreting the information provided in this volume and to encourage further comparative scholarship on residential care. First, the breadth of countries included in the volume is by no means exhaustive. We have taken pains to include countries that vary on a number of important dimensions (e.g., economic development; population heterogeneity; religious traditions; political systems and ideology). Six nations (Australia, Ireland, South Korea, Sweden, the UK, and the United States) represented in this volume are members of the Organization for Economic Cooperation and Development (OECD), one has been invited to consider membership (Israel), and four are not members (Botswana, Brazil, Romania, and South Africa), reflecting their varying levels of economic development. Nevertheless, there is good reason to believe that our case studies do not do justice to the variability that exists in nations' use of residential care. For example, it would be helpful to consider the use of residential care by an Islamic country or a country with a communist government, such as the People's Republic of China. Second, our case study chapters provide varying levels of detail regarding the history, current condition, and future of residential care. This reflects cross-national variability in the availability of historical information about residential care as well as variation in our colleagues' interests and expertise. Third, we have not tried to be exhaustive in our analysis of each of the contributing factors we identified, preferring instead to simply describe ways in which a given factor might influence residential care and then provide a relevant example or two. For instance, we did not describe in this chapter all of the ways that race and ethnicity come up in the case studies as influencing the development of residential care and its potential future. A more exhaustive examination of how each of the factors we describe has played out in each country might lead to a more nuanced appreciation of the effect of one or more of the factors. Last, as we noted at the outset, we have not examined how these factors interact over time to result in the country-specific trajectories that residential care has taken, preferring instead to focus on what might be called "main effects." We leave further exploration of these issues to others.

Conclusion

While it may be true that the situation in many countries reflects a broad decline in the standing and importance of residential care for children and young people, it would seem highly premature to write its obituary. We believe that our overview of the forces that have helped shaped the history of residential care around the world should provide food for thought for those who see residential care as either an evil to be avoided at all costs or as a panacea. Residential care has certainly been associated with some of the more troubling aspects of the history of the treatment of children in some of the countries we studied. In some cases it has also met the basic needs of children who otherwise would have suffered even worse fates than those they experienced in residential care. Wealthy countries continue to find residential care invaluable for some populations, particularly young people with serious emotional problems, and some of them appear to have begun to reap the unintended consequences of going too far in restricting access to residential care. Less-wealthy countries may find that they have little choice but to place children in residential care, at least in the short term, when they find themselves with large numbers of desperate children and no family- or community-based alternative.

Residential care, for all its limitations, can seem very attractive to key stakeholders when faced with no alternative for high-profile categories of hard-to-serve young people for whom other kinds of provision are not available or culturally appropriate. At the end of this book, we are not writing a resounding declaration proclaiming a bright and expanding future for residential care. But we are writing with a more modest but certain confidence that residential care will survive and that it will be a field in which people will work, in which children will be served, and about which people will be researching a hundred years from now. Even where attempts have been made to eliminate residential provision, as in Australia for specific reasons of history and culture, it is nevertheless notable how remarkably resistant residential care is to such elimination. It reappears in a new guise, weakened perhaps, but not obliterated.

Regardless of the extent and focus of its future roles, residential care needs to rise to the challenges facing adequate provision. In addition to long-standing dilemmas (such as ensuring educational quality and continuity), the complexity of problems faced by the new populations of children in residential care has served to emphasize the importance of hiring appropriately qualified staff, of finding ways to strengthen a child's family relationships, and of integrating residential care more firmly within an overall system of care, with services that range from prevention to treatment, and from home- and community-based to residential care.

Against this backdrop, the authors of this volume also make it clear that further evidence is needed to define what constitutes quality care for children. As the role of residential care within the child welfare systems in each country continues to evolve, the authors raise a number of questions about the efficacy both of residential care and its alternatives. Research is scarce or inconsistent regarding the characteristics of residential care that produce the best outcomes, under what circumstances, and for what kinds of children (Ainsworth, 2005; Whitaker, 2000).

As we search internationally for models of care appropriate to meeting the needs of at-risk children, this volume tells us that many of the dilemmas we confront and the solutions we imagine are shared across cultural and geographic boundaries, and across time. It highlights the importance of developing a body of evidence to support our care choices and asks us to pay more attention to identifying and preventing the conditions underlying the growth of populations of impoverished children and of children experiencing serious behavioral problems.

REFERENCES

Ainsworth, F. (2005). A research agenda for group care. *Child and Youth Care Forum, 24,* 215–230.

Barth, R. P. (2005). Residential care: From here to eternity. *International Journal of Social Welfare, 14,* 158–162.

Bates, B. C., English, D. J., and Kouidou-Giles, S. (1997). Residential treatment and its alternatives: A review of the literature. *Child and Youth Care Forum, 26,* 7–51.

Curry J. F. (1995). The current status of research in residential treatment. *Residential Treatment for Children Youth, 12(3),* 1–17.

Whittaker, J. K. (2000). The future of residential group care. *Child Welfare, 79,* 59–74.

INDEX